TRAGEDIES—OLD AND NEW

"To be, or not to be, —"
*Laurence Olivier as Hamlet in
the Screen Production*

Noble's Comparative Classics

HAMLET

AND OTHER TRAGEDIES

OLD AND NEW

Edited by

HELEN E. HARDING, M.A.

NOBLE AND NOBLE, *Publishers, Inc.*

67 IRVING PLACE   NEW YORK

THE COMPARATIVE CLASSICS SERIES

In recognition of the demand for more modern literature and in the belief that a study of the classics is greatly enhanced by comparison, the publishers have launched this new series, *The Comparative Classics,* based upon a new idea: that of presenting an older classic side by side with a modern one of the same type. This plan has several advantages. There has been a strong demand for more modern literature in secondary school courses; there is at the same time a feeling that no education is complete without some knowledge of the great classics. The present plan meets both demands. To place side by side plays, poems, or essays in which the same theme is treated by different writers, makes clear at once the characteristics of the authors. It also affords a means of studying the larger aspects of the different works, of comparing them in theme and treatment, rather than concentrating upon the text of one. It is the practice of many teachers, after studying a classic, to assign as supplementary reading a modern book of the same type. Here two classics and a modern play are conveniently placed within a single cover.

iii

Noble's Comparative Classics

CONTENTS

Contents

INTRODUCTION

TRAGEDY—OLD AND NEW

REASON FOR POPULARITY

WHY should anyone wish to see a tragedy? One goes to a comedy to be amused, to watch for a while the struggle between the hero and his antagonist, secure in the knowledge that victory must at last fall on the right side. But in a tragedy, the certainty is quite different. The hero is doomed to failure, perhaps to death, no matter how bravely he fights. Whether his opponent is Fate, his own nature, or another man, however he may seem for a while to prosper, he must eventually fail. We know this from the start. Why then should we wish to witness the losing struggle?

The answer is probably to be found in that quirk of human nature which makes some people enjoy a "good cry." We all like to suffer a little—through the woes of an imaginary hero—and to be frightened a little—as by tales of ghosts and goblins. Besides, the Greek philosopher Aristotle discovered long ago that tragedy acts as a sort of harmless, necessary medicine, "cleansing our hearts by filling them with pity and awe." Identifying ourselves momentarily with the characters in the play, we both feel and pity their sufferings; we see in their experience a likeness to our own; we note what results follow certain causes and we are awed by fear for ourselves in a like situation. Thus we learn at the cost of slight discomfort the lessons that reality would teach us with greater pain. In other words, we both enjoy and profit by a little vicarious sorrow, if it is not made too terrible or too real.

COMPARISON OF THE TRAGEDIES

The tragedies represented in this book have all won popular acclaim. *Hamlet* is a standard box office attraction and the other two plays are frequently performed. Moreover, they have certain points of similarity which make a comparative study worth while. The stories of *Electra* and *Hamlet* are closely related. There is the murder of a king, the remarriage of the queen with the murderer, and the vengeance of the children. Of course in *Electra* it is the daughter who remains as a thorn in the flesh to the guilty pair and who meditates vengeance though she does not perform it. Orestes is a much slighter Hamlet. Or we might say Hamlet is a combination of Electra and Orestes.

With *Beyond the Horizon, Hamlet* is linked by a psychological likeness. Each of the two main characters, Hamlet and Robert, finds his tragedy through a fatal flaw of weakness in his character. Each is called upon to perform a task unsuited to his temperament and beyond his powers. Hamlet, the philosopher and scholar, must transform himself into a resolute man of action and demand payment for his father's murder. Robert Mayo, caught in a net of circumstances, struggles vainly with a task for which he has neither ability nor physical strength. In his case alone, death comes not as a crowning tragedy but rather as a release and a promise of fulfillment.

THE DEVELOPMENT OF TRAGIC DRAMA

The three plays, moreover, represent three eras of great importance in the development of the tragic drama. With the Greeks, tragedy originated. When Æschylus added a second actor to the one which Thespis had introduced, he made it possible to present action dramatically before the eyes of the spectators instead of having it tamely reported by messengers. Shakespeare's contribution is so great that it can hardly be summed up in a brief survey. Perhaps we may call it chiefly an enrichment of character study. He found tragedy largely Senecan, that is, it followed the example of the Latin writer Seneca who filled his tragedies with blood and horror, apparently for the sole purpose of shocking and terrifying. Some of Shakespeare's own early work, notably *Titus Andronicus* is of this nature; and indeed *Hamlet* itself is sometimes called a Senecan tragedy. But, though there is bloodshed and horror in abundance, it is redeemed by the wisdom of its philosophy, the beauty of phrasing, and the emphasis on character development. Ophelia's madness, for instance, which in other hands might seem merely terrible, is here softened into pathos and sad loveliness. Hamlet's delayed vengeance is less important than the mental struggle that causes the delay. In other plays, also, this stress is laid on person rather than event so that the essential tragedy is not in the final, inevitable destruction but in Macbeth's vaulting ambition, in Lear's fatal folly, in Othello's mad jealousy, or in Romeo's ruinous haste.

Until well into the eighteenth century, tragedy had been concerned chiefly with high-born or royal personages. It literally dealt with "sad stories of the death of kings." But the discovery was finally made that common men could suffer also, and domestic tragedy was introduced.

The tragedy of today is too near at hand for a dispassionate appraisal. It is safe to say, however, that it shows every prospect of adding a significant chapter to the history of tragic drama. The modern playwright has freed himself from most of the entangling conventions, such as the three unities, stage asides, restricted themes; he may experiment as he likes; he has at command almost unlimited resources in the way of lighting, costuming, and other stage effects; he has a vastly enlarged audience. However, he must still set before us real men and women struggling as we ourselves might struggle against adversity in some form or other. Eugene O'Neill has again and again shown his ability to do this. We look forward with assurance to his holding his place in the front rank of the modern writers of tragedy.

PLOT STRUCTURE

Drama implies struggle. The uneventful life, pursuing the even tenor of its way without serious ups or downs, may be happy but it is not dramatic. Such a life might be graphically represented by a straight line. Nothing happens and we leave the hero just where we found him, older perhaps, but otherwise unchanged.

But suppose something does happen. An inciting force of some kind drives this complacent person to action. He tries to gain an end and is met with opposition. He fights against a rival, or against his own nature, or against fate. Drama is present at once, and his line of life shows a steady rise in interest.

Presently affairs reach a crisis. A decisive step settles his future fortunes. Its importance may not be immediately apparent, but it is a turning point in his fate and his success or failure is now inevitable. The action falls.

Finally the end of the adventure is reached. He has succeeded and the ending is happy, or he has failed and we have tragedy, perhaps death. At any rate, his life has been dramatic.

In recognition of this principle, Shakespearean drama was divided always into five acts. The first explained the situation of the hero and introduced the complication that was to stir him from his even path. The second act increased difficulties, tying the action securely into a knot. Act III rose to a turning point and began the falling action. The fourth act resolved the difficulties, and the fifth provided the catastrophe or the happy outcome. Often, just before the end, there was a moment of suspense when the hero's fate hung in the balance. But the turning point was always a sure guide. As it pointed toward success or failure, so must the ending be.

This division is often graphically represented thus:

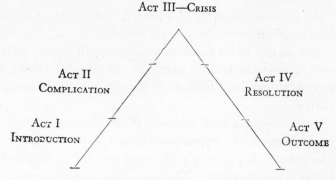

For this reason, one who wishes to understand a Shakespearean play, must discover first what is the task to be attempted and what are the clashing interests. Next he must watch each act to learn what definite step in the progress of the play is made; he must decide what is the turning point and where it occurs; he must trace the falling action and note the outcome. Only so may he appreciate the full dramatic import.

One convention, generally ignored by Shakespeare, but carefully observed by many of his contemporaries, is known as *the three unities*. *Unity of time* provided that the action of the play should cover no more than twenty-four hours. *Unity of place* made all action occur in one spot. Whatever could not so occur must be related by messengers. *Unity of action* forbade the introduction of more than one main plot or focus of interest. As the first two greatly limited the playwright's scope, we are grateful to Shakespeare for disregarding them.

The third, evidently, is still in force, although sub-plots are allowed if they are distinctly secondary to the main action.

Modern drama has changed principally in the matter of simplification and shortening. It still recognizes the necessity of contending interests. Without struggle, there is no play. The old outline of introduction, complication, crisis, resolution, outcome is still followed. But it is a bit more casual; the edges are not quite so clean-cut. Sometimes it is difficult to follow. Moreover, the action has been condensed. Acts I and II have been combined, as have Acts IV and V. A modern play of more than three acts is rare, and often there are but two, or even one.

Many of the old stage conventions have disappeared. The first two of the unities are entirely outmoded. Long speeches, so dear to the Elizabethans, do not suit the modern taste. The soliloquy and the aside, which were such convenient ways of showing the actor's inmost thought, are seldom used. Yet O'Neill, in *The Great God Brown* and *Strange Interlude,* experimented with a new form of the old stage aside. The success of this venture is still in doubt. However, the essential element of conflict remains in modern plays.

HISTORICAL BACKGROUND

THE ATHENS OF SOPHOCLES

SOPHOCLES lived in Athens at the time of its greatest glory. It was one of those happy eras, occurring at intervals in the life of a nation, when so many men of genius are alive and at work, that the period is rightly known as the "Golden Age." The contemporaries of Sophocles were not only his great rivals, Æschylus and Euripides, but such men as Aristophanes, the writer of comedies; Pericles, the great statesman; Phidias, the sculptor; Themistocles, the general; Herodotus and Thucydides, the historians; and Socrates, the philosopher. Such a galaxy of stars of the first magnitude would have made any age or nation famous; but, in addition, the beauty of the city was such as the world has seldom seen.

The Persian Wars were over, and Athens had emerged from the conflict rich and powerful—able, as head of the Delian League, to dominate neighboring communities and to exact tribute from them. The city, which Xerxes had burned, had risen from its ashes. Splendidly rebuilt with magnificent buildings of Pentelic marble, it was then the most beautiful city in the world. Under the guidance of Themistocles, new walls about seven and a half miles in circumference encircled the city and extended in a double line to Piræus, the principal seaport.

8

A stranger arriving at Piræus, perhaps coming to attend the spring festival of Dionysus, could catch even from the sea his first glimpse of the city. His eyes would be awed by the great statue of Athena towering over the Acropolis, the gilded head of her spear flashing in the sun. Ashore in the spacious harbor town, he could look up a broad, straight highway and see the marble city gleaming white in the clear air. The splendid temples of the Acropolis stand out against the hazy purple of Mt. Lycabettus. Low, olive-clad hills break the monotony of the plain, while over all shines the intense, vivid blue of the Athenian sky.

When he approached the city, our traveller would see the Areopagus or Mars' Hill, a rocky height where the city council met and from which Paul preached to the Athenians of a later day. Lower down he would see the Pynx, the place of public assembly. Nearby in the low Attic plain clustered, in ancient days, the homes of the citizens. These houses were modest structures of one or two stories, flat-roofed, with few windows and no chimneys, but each had its inner court open to the sky. Loving the outdoors as did every Athenian, it was the city, rather than his own home, that he chose to adorn. So in every open place he set up monuments and public buildings that were marvels of architecture. But the glory of Athens was the Acropolis.

The Acropolis was a rocky plateau, about one hundred fifty feet high, with a flat summit, perhaps a thousand feet long and half as wide. Here were the most beautiful buildings ever seen in so small a space. The entire western side was occupied by the Propylæa, or entrance gate, which was approached by a marble stairway, seventy feet broad. The Propylæa was also built of marble. It was a series of pillared porticoes, flanked by wings, one of which served as an art gallery. Beyond the Propylæa stood the gigantic bronze statue of Athena, which archeologists think may have been done by Phidias. The statue represented the goddess armed for war; and her spear and helmet, towering seventy feet above the ground, were easily visible to ships entering Piræus. The chief building on the Acropolis was the Parthenon, a temple of Athena of pure Doric architecture, not large, but of such perfect proportions and exquisite detail, that it has been the wonder and admiration of succeeding ages. Within the temple was another colossal statue of the goddess wrought by Phidias, this time in ivory and gold. The Erechtheum, a temple probably built in honor of Poseidon, was a perfect example of Ionic architecture and especially noted for its southern portico, or porch of the Maidens. These Caryatides, as we call them, were exquisitely carved female figures that supported upon their heads the roof of the southern portico. Besides the Parthenon and the Erechtheum, smaller temples and statues added to the beauty of the Acropolis.*

Not far from the Propylæa, but on the the southeastern slope of the Acropolis, stood the famous Theater of Dionysus. Here audiences of fifteen to twenty thousand often gathered to see

* Models of most of these buildings are in the Metropolitan Museum, New York City. Students would undoubtedly find a visit there of interest.

The Acropolis in the time of Sophocles

The Acropolis today

plays presented and to quarrel over the prizes that were awarded to the successful dramatist.

In this beautiful city lived a populace of perhaps one hundred thousand—a gay, laughter-loving people, socially inclined, fond of meeting friends and of talking, devoted to outdoor life, worshipping their city and the beauty they had helped to create. Naturally the citizens of such a city would be interested in its government. Theoretically, each citizen had a hand in city affairs. The government was headed by ten elected men known as generals, because they were expected to take control of the army in time of war. These men were assisted by the Upper Council. Another body, the Council of Five Hundred, was chosen by lot to direct a general assembly which met four times a month. Actually, Athens was not at this time a perfect democracy, since four out of every five men were either aliens or slaves. The assembly still existed, but it had delegated most of its power to Pericles, who was the real ruler of Athens.

To the average Athenian, festivals, even though held in honor of the gods, were occasions of great revelry. Greatest of all was the festival in honor of Athena, held every fourth year in July. This was the grand national holiday, when light-hearted and gaily-clad people thronged the city to attend the competitions in music and oratory. Many of them took part in the athletic contests, each trying to rival his companion in running, jumping, wrestling, and throwing the spear and the discus.

Of the two yearly festivals held in honor of Dionysus, the

spring festival was the more popular; it attracted not only the entire Athenian population, but also strangers from a distance. There was first a spectacular parade, a sort of Mardi Gras, and then the statue of the god was placed with ceremony in the theater. For five or six days following, there were daily presentations of plays until the judges finally announced the proud victor. The city, meanwhile, was in holiday humor and attire. Disorder or crime was regarded as a sacrilege and was severely punished. Happiness was the order of the day.

Thus more than two thousand years ago, there lived in old Athens a beauty-loving, keenly intellectual race; and, not seeing the handwriting on the wall, they doubtless thought— even as you and I—that with them civilization had reached its peak and that the wonders they had wrought would endure forever. In such an atmosphere and before such audiences, the great Greek dramatists presented their work. Fortunate Sophocles, to have lived in a city so beautiful and an age so golden!

GREEK TRAGEDY

Greek tragedy is supposed to have arisen from the worship of Dionysus, god of wine and revelry. At the yearly festivals held in his honor as guardian of the vineyards, a chorus of men dressed as satyrs, mythical creatures who were half-men, half-goats, danced about his altar chanting songs in his praise. Because *tragos*, the Greek word for goat, was probably a common term for satyr, this song and dance was called *tragœdia* (tragedy) or goat-song.

The chorus of satyrs was gradually limited to fifty, and conversation about the god was introduced. Soon an actor, who was not dressed as a satyr, was added to carry on the conversation with the chorus or its leader, and the seed of drama was sown. It germinated fully when Æschylus, the greatest of the three writers of tragedy, added a second actor. The story could now be acted instead of being always told. The acted parts were called *episodes* because they followed the choral *odes*. Actors often had to play several roles, but this could be easily done since more than two actors were seldom on the stage at the same time. Later Sophocles added a third actor. Meantime the range of stories had been widened; the chorus, cut down to fifteen, were no longer dressed as satyrs, and a tale that included suffering came to be preferred to the fantastic adventures of Dionysus. So what we call *tragedy* came into existence. The old satyr-play, however, was still retained and in it the adventures of Dionysus were sometimes set forth.

In structure Greek tragedy never quite forgot its origin. The chorus became secondary, but it never entirely disappeared. It often served as the voice of public opinion; through its leader, it gave sympathetic advice to the main characters, and it relieved the tension of the play by dancing and singing at the end of each dramatic episode. At times the chorus was composed of old men, as in *Œdipus at Colonus*; or of the immortal daughters of Oceanus, as in *Prometheus Bound*; or again it represented a gathering of Argive women, as in

An ancient Greek theater as it appears today

The modern Greek theater at the University of California

Electra. Since it was the root from which tragedy grew, it always remained an essential part of the play.

The Greek playwright generally drew his plot from the great store of old myths. Like the Elizabethan dramatist, he saw no reason for originating plots. He showed skill by taking a well-known story and presenting it either in a new light or with unexpectedly happy phrasing. The attitude of the Athenian playgoer must have been much the same as ours when a new actor plays Hamlet. Enjoyment grows with repetition. Perhaps Milton meant this when he wrote of the Greeks as

> *"Presenting Thebes or Pelops' line*
> *Or the tale of Troy divine."*

From Thebes came the sad story of Œdipus, as we find it in *Œdipus The King*, *Œdipus At Colonus*, *Antigone*, and *Seven Against Thebes*. Pelops was the ancestor of Agamemnon; some of the stories about him are reproduced in such plays as *Agamemnon*, *Iphigenia In Aulis*, *Iphigenia In Tauris*, *Electra*, *Orestes*, *The Furies*. The tale of Troy gives us *The Trojan Women*, *Hecuba*, *Philoctetes*, and many others.

Greek drama presents a story through action. The playwright must show how the successive incidents arise naturally from the circumstances and the feelings of men and women, and how these men and women are affected by the circumstances. This often takes the form of a struggle in which the hero or heroine seems foredoomed by Destiny. But the

Greeks were very much like ourselves; they believed that at times even the noblest nature made mistakes. They drew inspiration from seeing such a nature, purged by suffering, rise above the net of circumstances to a true nobility of character.

The plays were produced at yearly festivals which lasted three days. Rival dramatists contested with one another. Each presented four plays. Æschylus usually connected three tragedies in a *trilogy,* telling in each one a part of the story. Such an arrangement was like three long acts in a great trilogy, the third of which brings the story to a close in peace and reconciliation. Sophocles and Euripides, as far as we know, did not connect their plays. The fourth play in the series was the traditional satyr-play, which might or might not deal, in a lighter way, with some part of a preceding tragedy.

The flourishing age of Greek tragedy was from about 500 B.C. to 400 B.C. Of the three great writers, Æschylus (525-456 B.C.), called the Father of Tragedy, excels in the majesty of his conceptions and the seriousness of his moral purpose; Sophocles (496-406 B.C.), in the construction of his plots and the development of character; while Euripides (480-407 B.C.), known today as a realist, reflects the newer philosophy and the advanced thought of his time. He excels in pathos and tragic fantasy.

PRESENTATION OF A GREEK PLAY

If we could step backward through the centuries, we might find ourselves among the throng going up to the Theater of Dionysus on the southeast slope of the Acropolis, in Athens. Perhaps it would be that memorable day when young Sophocles defeated his older rival Æschylus, and thus drove him into exile. Or it might be a later day when *Electra* itself was to be presented.

At any rate, climbing up through the beautiful Athenian city we presently emerge into a vast, almost circular, unroofed stadium. Seats rise in tiers around the sides of the huge bowl, and aisles ascending from the orchestra cut them into monstrous wedges. Most of the 17,000 places are already taken, for practically the entire male population of Athens is here. If anyone is too poor to pay the nominal price of admission, the state will give him a free ticket. But we shall find a seat here, under the blue sky, looking out across the marble buildings of the city toward the sea.

Down there in the front row are the dignitaries of the state. In the seat of honor in the very center, sits the priest of Dionysus. In the level space below is the altar of the god, around which the action will take place. Behind it rises the scene building with doors and columns in front. The chorus and actors will enter the orchestra through open passages at either end of this building. The chorus, once it has entered, will remain until the end of the play; but actors will come

The Theater of Dionysus
In the center of the front row is the seat reserved for the priest of Dionysus

and go, and messengers will appear to tell us what is happening within doors or in some more distant place.

We need not be afraid of not hearing, for the actors will wear masks fitted with small mouthpieces to magnify the sound. Since the play is a tragedy, the actors will wear buskins or high shoes, to make them seem taller.

The audience is growing quiet. The play is about to begin. The actor who is to speak the prologue appears. With him are Orestes and Pylades; for Orestes, Electra's brother, has come at last to avenge his father's death. Presently Electra herself appears and after her the chorus files in, chanting its entrance song. Soon it will divide into two parts, to sing and dance around the altar in solemn strophe and antistrophe.* Now Electra begins her tale of woe. The chorus leader is filled with sympathy. Swiftly the play unfolds. After each dramatic episode the chorus, moving back and forth in stately dance, chants its lovely lyric song. And now Electra holds aloft the urn. She thinks that it contains her brother's ashes. A whisper flies through the audience; the actor who is playing Electra—a man, of course—has just lost a dearly-beloved son, and the urn he holds enshrines a sacred relic. The audience is deeply moved by his voice. But joy follows sorrow. Orestes discloses himself, and Electra sees her hopes fulfilled. Punishment will fall upon Ægisthus and Clytemnestra. With the punishment of the guilty pair, the play comes to an end.

* (In the Greek choral dance, the movement to one side of the stage was called the *strophe;* the reverse movement, the *antistrophe.*)

The chorus, saddened by the terrible deed, chants its closing song as it files slowly out and away.

We step back once more through the centuries to our own day. The "glory that was Greece" is no more. The great Theater of Dionysus is a ruin and the magnificent Acropolis a shadow of itself. But human nature still responds to the touch of pathos, and Electra's woes are not forgotten.

ELIZABETHAN ENGLAND

MANY factors besides her own dynamic personality combined to make Elizabeth's reign a vivid, adventurous, and intensely interesting age. In the breathing space of peace that her reign afforded, England had an opportunity to realize the force of several previous influences. The Renaissance, or revival of interest in classic learning, which had been active for some time in Europe, now opened to the people of Elizabethan times the marvelous stories of Greek and Latin literature. The printing press made these more widely available. The discovery of America was being exploited, and tales of adventure fired the imagination. Drake circumnavigated the globe. The successful challenge to the might of Spain in the defeat of the Invincible Armada gave a satisfying impression of power. Life was full of glamor; excitement was in the air.

Then, too, comforts and even luxuries were multiplying rapidly. Feudal castles, dark and gloomy, gave way to Tudor palaces with many-paned glass windows and huge chimneys. To be sure, the floors were spread only with rushes which in time became unspeakably filthy, but rich hangings covered the walls and there was much fine furniture and silver plate. As a crowning refinement, forks came into use, and it was no longer necessary to hold the meat firmly with one hand while cutting it with a huge knife grasped in the other hand. Dress was elaborate and costly. The ladies wore widely billowing skirts, narrow jeweled stomachers, huge sleeves and great ruffs, stiffly starched. The men, too, wore ruffs and the slashed and padded doublet and hose with which pictures have made us familiar.

London was a city of a hundred thousand, already overflowing its walls and spreading out into the suburbs. It was a city of contrasts. The dissolution of the monasteries had brought wealth to some great families, but it had fastened abject poverty on many of the lower class so that richly dressed gentlemen and swarming beggars alike filled the highways. Magnificence and squalor were side by side. Fine coaches rumbled through streets that were narrow, crowded, and dirty. The river, thronged and picturesque, was the principal means of transportation.

Education was eagerly sought. Young men of fashion attended the universities and completed their course by a grand tour of Europe. Shakespeare often pokes gentle fun at these traveled Englishmen. "How oddly he is suited," Portia remarks of her English wooer. "I think he bought his doublet in Italy, his round hose in France, his bonnet in Germany, and his behavior everywhere."

But in spite of education and travel, superstition was rife. Ghosts, witches, and all sorts of portents were accepted as possible. To an Elizabethan, it would seem quite natural that the ghost of Hamlet's father should "bode some strange eruption to our state." Astrology was considered seriously, and chemists spent their time searching for the elixir of youth and the wondrous stone that would change base metal to gold.

Yet at this time Bacon, "taking all knowledge for his province," was making an approach toward pure science.

The Elizabethan loved sports. Hunting, by means of trained hawks or falcons, was a favorite. Shakespeare has many allusions to this custom. Dancing, dicing games, and card playing were common, and bear-baiting was as incomprehensibly popular as the bull fights of modern Spain. But most of all, Elizabeth's England reveled in the theater. To the playhouses across the Thames, flocked all classes, and there, no mere passive spectators, they entered with enthusiasm into the mimic life presented, shouting approval or disgust, picturing with quick imagination the scene so meagerly displayed. They did not mind a few slips in accuracy of custom or dress, but they resented poor acting or slipshod characterization.

It was an ideal audience for a great playwright. Never was a more perfect combination of the time, the place, and the man. One cannot help speculating a bit as to what would have happened had Shakespeare been born in another time. Without this keen, quick appraisal, constantly demanding more of the very best, would even this myriad-minded one have been able to pour forth such floods of treasure as he lavished on the men of Elizabeth's England?

THE ELIZABETHAN THEATER

In that mid-period when drama had left the shelter of the church and had not yet attained the haven of the theater,

Only masked ladies attended the performance at an
Elizabethan theater

strolling bands of actors offered their wares in the courtyard of inns. It was natural, therefore, that when in 1574 James Burbage decided to build a permanent playhouse, he should follow the model he knew best. In the same way all the early theaters, The Curtain, The Globe, The Fortune, The Swan, The Rose, were built like an inn courtyard. Even the interior of the theater was open to the sky, except for the roofed galleries which extended around three sides. The stage projected out into the center, so that the audience practically surrounded the actors. To add to this difficulty, those who were willing to pay the price, had seats upon the stage itself, and often hindered the course of the performance. The unfloored space in front, unprovided with seats, was occupied by the "groundlings," London apprentices and men of the poorer class who paid only a small admission fee. People of the middle class sat in the galleries.

The stage was equipped with no front curtain and no footlights. At the back, two doors led to the dressing rooms and served for exit and entrance. A small inner stage, separated from the larger one by a curtain, occupied a recess between these doors. This inner stage could be used in various ways; such as the casket scene in *The Merchant of Venice*, for the witches' cavern in *Macbeth,* for the tent of Brutus in *Julius Cæsar*, and for the presentation of the play in Act III in *Hamlet*. It gave an opportunity to "set the stage" when action was still going on. Above this recess was a balcony, used for the musicians, for Juliet's balcony, for the hill in *Julius Cæsar*, for the wall of a town, the upper room in a house, or for any other place where the action needed to be a little removed. Still higher than the balcony was the "hut" or small tower from which the flag was flown to announce the performance. A trap door, a canopy called the heavens, and various bits of stage machinery completed the resources of the Elizabethan stage.

Of scenery, there was very little. A desk, a bed, a throne or chair served to suggest the proper setting to the quick-witted audience. If that were not enough, the author's careful description made all clear. Note how often Shakespeare's words announce the change of scene. Costumes were as elaborate as the resources of the company allowed, but there was no attempt at historical accuracy. Undoubtedly Hamlet wore the doublet and hose of an Elizabethan gentleman rather than the garb of a Dane of a much earlier period.

Because of the lack of lighting facilities, plays were given in the afternoon. The flag flying from the hut would announce

The Globe and the Swan Theaters

the performance, and the audience would gather, coming on horseback by way of London Bridge or by boat across the river. The trumpet would sound and the prologue, dressed in black, would give a general idea of the play. In the absence of programs, this was necessary.

Then the play would begin. While the groundlings swayed and jostled in the pit, the gallants swaggered on the stage, and food venders plied their trade, the actors played their parts. They needed to be good to hold such an audience. Perhaps Richard Burbage, the best of them all, would please the groundlings with his Falstaff, or Shakespeare himself might take a part. No actresses would appear; boys took the women's parts; and no ladies attended the performance except occasionally and then well masked.

THE MODERN THEATER

WHAT changes the years have brought! The stage no longer thrusts out into the audience, but has retired behind the proscenium arch. We sit, securely housed, in our comfortable seats in the orchestra, once the groundlings' pit, and we see the action as if we looked through a picture frame into a three-walled room. We are not now one with the actors; we are on-lookers, slightly aloof. Does this, perhaps, color our reactions?

Programs make the prologue unnecessary and long descriptions superfluous. The curtain rises to reveal new settings or falls to conceal awkward situations. Polonius' dead body need not now be borne from the stage in the sight of all.

The two doors that were the sole means of exit and entrance have disappeared. Our actors come in from the wings, or the garden, or the next room. It is not necessary to mark their movements by rhyme tags, or sennets, or the announcement, "Look where Publius is sent to fetch me."

Costumes are meticulously accurate. Stage machinery has infinitely multiplied; all the magic resources of color and light are at hand. Only in one respect are we reverting to something like Elizabethan practice. Our scenery is becoming increasingly simple. This trend is illustrated in the Mercury Theater's recent production of *Julius Cæsar*, in which a very dramatic setting was gained by the effective use of lights on a bare stage.

There was a time when realism was demanded. We must have authentic palaces for Macbeth, real graveyards for Ophelia, actual Roman Forums for Cæsar. But the reaction has set in. Suggestion rather than realism is the ideal. It was discovered that sometimes the scenery got in the way of the action, and that greater flexibility as well as more imaginative reaction could be gained by simpler means. Setting aside the rather bald performances of such troops as the *Ben Greet Players*, we may yet find many a more pretentious and artistic production using a single stage setting. The very beautiful presentation of *Hamlet* by Norman Bel Geddes was a case in point. With the lavish use of lights and a few trifling changes in properties, the same background represented the Danish battlements, the king's palace, Ophelia's grave, and Gertrude's boudoir. Another play simply staged, without scenery, was a recent Pulitzer Prize play, *Our Town,* by Thornton Wilder.

The modern stage has both gained and lost. It has gained infinitely in historical accuracy, in variety of effects, in picturesqueness; but it has lost something of the close association between actor and audience, and something of robust, whole-hearted appraisal. It would be interesting if we could, for a moment, be transported back to a Shakespearean playhouse. Perhaps then we might decide where the advantage lies.

THE TRAGEDY OF HAMLET

By

William Shakespeare

THE CHARACTERS IN THE PLAY

CLAUDIUS, *King of Denmark*
HAMLET, *son to the late, and nephew to the present King*
POLONIUS, *lord chamberlain*
HORATIO, *friend to Hamlet*
LAERTES, *son to Polonius*
VOLTIMAND,
CORNELIUS,
ROSENCRANTZ,
GUILDENSTERN, } *courtiers*
OSRIC,
A Gentleman,
A Priest
MARCELLUS,
BERNARDO, } *officers*
FRANCISCO, *a soldier*
REYNALDO, *servant to Polonius*
Players
Two Clowns, *grave-diggers*
FORTINBRAS, *prince of Norway*
A Captain
English Ambassadors

GERTRUDE, *Queen of Denmark, and mother to Hamlet*
OPHELIA, *daughter to Polonius*
Lords, Ladies, Officers, Soldiers, Sailors, Messengers, and other
Attendants

Ghost of Hamlet's father

SCENE: Elsinore, Denmark

The Tragedy of Hamlet

ACT ONE

Scene I

Elsinore. A platform before the castle. Francisco *at his post.*

   Enter Bernardo.

Bernardo. Who 's there?

Francisco. Nay, answer me; stand, and unfold yourself.

Bernardo. Long live the king!

Francisco. Bernardo?

Bernardo. He.   5

Francisco. You come most carefully upon your hour.

Bernardo. 'T is now struck twelve; get thee to bed, Fran-
    cisco.

Francisco. For this relief much thanks; 't is bitter cold,
    And I am sick at heart.

Bernardo. Have you had quiet guard?

Francisco.   Not a mouse stirring.   10

Bernardo. Well, good night.
    If you do meet Horatio and Marcellus,
    The rivals of my watch, bid them make haste.

Francisco. I think I hear them. Stand, ho! Who is there?

---

2. **Answer *me*—**Francisco as sentinel should be the one to challenge
6. **You come most carefully upon your hour—**Promptly.
13. **Rivals—**Associates, companions.

Enter Horatio *and* Marcellus.

Horatio. Friends to this ground.

Marcellus.   And liegemen to the Dane.   15

Francisco. Give you good night.

Marcellus.   O, farewell, honest soldier;
   Who hath reliev'd you?

Francisco.   Bernardo has my place.
   Give you good night.   [*Exit.*

Marcellus.   Holla! Bernardo!

Bernardo.   Say,
   What, is Horatio there?

Horatio.   A piece of him.

Bernardo. Welcome, Horatio; welcome, good Mar-
      cellus.
                                          20

Horatio. What, has this thing appear'd again to-night?

Bernardo. I have seen nothing.

Marcellus. Horatio says 't is but our fantasy,
   And will not let belief take hold of him
   Touching this dreaded sight, twice seen of us;   25
   Therefore I have entreated him along
   With us to watch the minutes of this night,
   That if again this apparition come,
   He may approve our eyes, and speak to it.

Horatio. Tush, tush, 't will not appear.

Bernardo.   Sit down awhile;   30
   And let us once again assail your ears,

15. **Liegemen**—Vassals or loyal followers.
29. **Approve our eyes**—Confirm what we have seen.

That are so fortified against our story,
What we two nights have seen.

Horatio.   Well, sit we down,
And let us hear Bernardo speak of this.

Bernardo. Last night of all,   35
When yond same star that's westward from the pole
Had made his course t' illume that part of heaven
Where now it burns, Marcellus and myself,
The bell then beating one,—

Enter GHOST.

Marcellus. Peace, break thee off; look, where it comes
     again!   40

Bernardo. In the same figure, like the king that's dead.

Marcellus. Thou art a scholar; speak to it, Horatio.

Bernardo. Looks it not like the king? mark it, Horatio.

Horatio. Most like; it harrows me with fear and wonder.

Bernardo. It would be spoke to.

Marcellus.   Question it, Horatio. 45

Horatio. What art thou that usurp'st this time of night,
Together with that fair and warlike form
In which the majesty of buried Denmark
Did sometimes march? by heaven I charge thee,
     speak!

Marcellus. It is offended.

42. **Speak to it, Horatio**—There was a common belief that a ghost could
     not speak until it had been spoken to.   44. **Harrows**—Torments.
46. **Usurp'st . . . march**—To appear without right in the form of the
     late king.

Bernardo.   See, it stalks away!   50

Horatio.   Stay! speak, speak!   I charge thee, speak!

[*Exit* GHOST.

Marcellus.   'T is gone, and will not answer.

Bernardo.   How now, Horatio! you tremble and look
        pale;
    Is not this something more than fantasy?
    What think you on 't?   55

Horatio.   Before my God, I might not this believe
    Without the sensible and true avouch
    Of mine own eyes.

Marcellus.   Is it not like the king?

Horatio.   As thou art to thyself:
    Such was the very armour he had on   60
    When he th' ambitious Norway combated;
    So frown'd he once, when, in an angry parle,
    He smote the sledded Polacks on the ice.
    'T is strange.

Marcellus.   Thus twice before, and jump at this dead
        hour,   65
    With martial stalk hath he gone by our watch.

Horatio.   In what particular thought to work I know not;
    But, in the gross and scope of my opinion,

---

57. **Sensible**—Seeing.
57. **Avouch**—Assurance, testimony.   62. **Parle**—Parley, speech.
63. **Smote the sledded Polacks**—He struck the Polanders fighting on
    sledges.   65. **Jump at this dead hour**—Exactly at this very hour.
66. **Martial stalk**—Military step.
67. **In what . . . opinion**—I don't know exactly what to think, but in gen-
    eral my opinion is.

This bodes some strange eruption to our state.

Marcellus. Good now, sit down, and tell me, he that
    knows,   70
Why this same strict and most observant watch
So nightly toils the subject of the land,
And why such daily cast of brazen cannon,
And foreign mart for implements of war;
Why such impress of shipwrights, whose sore task   75
Does not divide the Sunday from the week.
What might be toward, that this sweaty haste
Doth make the night joint-labourer with the day?
Who is 't that can inform me?

Horatio.   That can I;   80
At least, the whisper goes so. Our last king,
Whose image even but now appear'd to us,
Was, as you know, by Fortinbras of Norway,
Thereto prick'd on by a most emulate pride,
Dar'd to the combat; in which our valiant Hamlet—
For so this side of our known world esteem'd him—   85
Did slay this Fortinbras; who, by a seal'd compact,
Well ratified by law and heraldry,
Did forfeit, with his life, all those his lands
Which he stood seiz'd of, to the conqueror:
Against the which, a moiety competent   90
Was gaged by our king; which had return'd

69. **Bodes**—Foretells.
83. **A most emulate pride**—Rivalry.   89. **Stood seiz'd of**—Possessed.
90. **A moiety competent was gaged**—An equivalent portion was wa-
    gered.   91. **Had return'd**—Would have returned.

To the inheritance of Fortinbras,
Had he been vanquisher; as, by the same cov'nant
And carriage of the article design'd,
His fell to Hamlet. Now, sir, young Fortinbras,　　95
Of unimproved mettle hot and full,
Hath in the skirts of Norway here and there
Shark'd up a list of lawless resolutes,
For food and diet, to some enterprise
That hath a stomach in 't; which is no other—　　100
As it doth well appear unto our state—
But to recover of us, by strong hand
And terms compulsative, those foresaid lands
So by his father lost: and this, I take it,
Is the main motive of our preparations,　　105
The source of this our watch, and the chief head
Of this post-haste and romage in the land.

Bernardo. I think it be no other but e'en so.
Well may it sort that this portentous figure
Comes armed through our watch, so like the king　　110
That was and is the question of these wars.

Horatio. A mote it is to trouble the mind's eye.
In the most high and palmy state of Rome,
A little ere the mightiest Julius fell,

93. **By the same cov'nant . . . design'd**—By the same agreement and the gist of the articles drawn up.
96. **Unimproved mettle**—Headstrong spirit or courage, not yet tried.
98. **Shark'd up**—Hastily collected.
103. **Compulsative**—Compulsory, not voluntary.
107. **Romage**—Disturbance, excitement.
109. **This portentous figure**—See page 428.

The graves stood tenantless and the sheeted dead   115
Did squeak and gibber in the Roman streets:
As stars with trains of fire and dews of blood,
Disasters in the sun; and the moist star,
Upon whose influence Neptune's empire stands,
Was sick almost to doomsday with eclipse: 120
And even the like precurse of fierce events,
As harbingers preceding still the fates,
And prologue to the omen coming on,
Have heaven and earth together demonstrated
Unto our climatures and countrymen.   125

Re-enter Ghost.

But, soft, behold! lo, where it comes again!
I'll cross it, though it blast me.   Stay, illusion!
If thou hast any sound, or use of voice,
Speak to me;
If there be any good thing to be done,   130
That may to thee do ease and grace to me,
Speak to me;
If thou art privy to thy country's fate,
Which happily foreknowing may avoid,
O, speak!   135

118. **Moist star**—The watery moon.
120. **Almost to doomsday**—The eclipse of the moon was supposed to fore-
     tell the end of the world.   121. **Precurse**—Forerunner.
122. **Harbingers**—Messengers.   125. **Climatures**—Regions.
127. **I'll cross it**—The way to stop a ghost was to cross its path, but whoever
     did so risked coming under its evil spell.
133. **If thou art . . . avoid**—If you know a danger threatening your coun-
     try, which could be avoided if we were forewarned.

Or if thou hast uphoarded in thy life
Extorted treasure in the womb of earth,
For which, they say, you spirits oft walk in death,

[*The cock crows.*

Speak of it; stay, and speak! Stop it, Marcellus.

Marcellus. Shall I strike at it with my partisan?   140

Horatio. Do, if it will not stand.

Bernardo.   'T is here!

Horatio.   'T is here!

Marcellus. 'T is gone!   [*Exit* Ghost.
We do it wrong, being so majestical,
To offer it the show of violence;
For it is, as the air, invulnerable,   145
And our vain blows malicious mockery.

Bernardo. It was about to speak when the cock crew.

Horatio. And then it started like a guilty thing
Upon a fearful summons. I have heard,
The cock, that is the trumpet to the morn,
Doth with his lofty and shrill-sounding throat
Awake the god of day; and at his warning,
Whether in sea or fire, in earth or air,
Th' extravagant and erring spirit hies
To his confine: and of the truth herein   155
This present object made probation.

Marcellus. It faded on the crowing of the cock.

136. **Uphoarded**—Ghosts were supposed to return to tell of ill-gotten or hidden wealth. 137. **Extorted**—Taken by force.
140. **Partisan**—Halberd or pike, a medieval weapon.
154. **Extravagant**—Wandering beyond bounds. 156. **Probation**—Proof.

Some say, that ever 'gainst that season comes
Wherein our Saviour's birth is celebrated,
The bird of dawning singeth all night long;   160
And then, they say, no spirit can walk abroad;
The nights are wholesome; then no planets strike,
No fairy takes, nor witch hath power to charm;
So hallow'd and so gracious is the time.

Horatio. So have I heard, and do in part believe it.   165
But, look, the morn, in russet mantle clad,
Walks o'er the dew of yon high eastern hill.
Break we our watch up; and, by my advice,
Let us impart what we have seen to-night
Unto young Hamlet; for, upon my life,   170
This spirit, dumb to us, will speak to him.
Do you consent we shall acquaint him with it,
As needful in our loves, fitting our duty?

Marcellus. Let's do 't, I pray; and I this morning know 174
Where we shall find him most conveniently.   [*Exeunt.*

160. **Bird of dawning**—Cock. 162. **Strike**—Exert evil influence.
163. **Takes**—Bewitches.

SCENE II

A room of state in the castle. Flourish. Enter the KING,
   QUEEN, HAMLET, POLONIUS, LAERTES, VOLTIMAND, COR-
   NELIUS, LORDS, *and* Attendants.

King. Though yet of Hamlet our dear brother's death
   The memory be green, and that it us befitted
   To bear our hearts in grief, and our whole kingdom
   To be contracted in one brow of woe,
   Yet so far hath discretion fought with nature,   5
   That we with wisest sorrow think on him,
   Together with remembrance of ourselves.
   Therefore our sometime sister, now our queen,
   Th' imperial jointress of this warlike state,
   Have we, as 't were with a defeated joy,—   10
   With one auspicious and one dropping eye,
   With mirth in funeral and with dirge in marriage,
   In equal scale weighing delight and dole,—
   Taken to wife; nor have we herein barr'd
   Your better wisdoms, which have freely gone   15
   With this affair along. For all, our thanks.
   Now follows that you know: young Fortinbras,
   Holding a weak supposal of our worth,

   9. **Jointress**—Joint tenant of the kingdom with the king.
   11. **One auspicious and one dropping eye**—An old saying advised a
        person in distress to wink with one eye and weep with the other.
   13. **Dole**—Grief.
   18. **Weak supposal of our worth**—Poor opinion of our power.

Or thinking by our late dear brother's death
Our state to be disjoint and out of frame,   20
Colleagued with the dream of his advantage,
He hath not fail'd to pester us with message,
Importing the surrender of those lands
Lost by his father, with all bonds of law,
To our most valiant brother. So much for him.   25
Now for ourself and for this time of meeting.
Thus much the business is: we have here writ
To Norway, uncle of young Fortinbras,—
Who, impotent and bed-rid, scarcely hears
Of this his nephew's purpose,—to suppress   30
His further gait herein; in that the levies,
The lists, and full proportions, are all made
Out of his subject; and we here dispatch
You, good Cornelius, and you, Voltimand,
For bearers of this greeting to old Norway;   35
Giving to you no further personal power
To business with the king, more than the scope
Of these dilated articles allow.
Farewell, and let your haste commend your duty.

Cornelius.
Voltimand. } In that and all things will we show our duty.

King. We doubt it nothing: heartily farewell.   41

                    [*Exeunt* VOLTIMAND *and* CORNELIUS.

---

21. **Colleagued . . . advantage**—He has no ally but his dream, and that
     is an imaginary advantage only. 29. **Impotent**—Helpless.
38. **Dilated**—Detailed.

"What wouldst thou beg, Laertes?"
John Gielgud, as Hamlet, is shown at the left

And now, Laertes, what's the news with you?
You told us of some suit; what is 't, Laertes?
You cannot speak of reason to the Dane,
And lose your voice; what wouldst thou beg, Laertes,   45
That shall not be my offer, not thy asking?
The head is not more native to the heart,
The hand more instrumental to the mouth,
Than is the throne of Denmark to thy father.
What wouldst thou have, Laertes?

Laertes.   Dread my lord,   50
Your leave and favour to return to France;
From whence though willingly I came to Denmark,
To show my duty in your coronation,
Yet now, I must confess, that duty done,
My thoughts and wishes bend again toward France,   55
And bow them to your gracious leave and pardon.

King.   Have you your father's leave?   What says
    Polonius?

Polonius.   He hath, my lord, wrung from me my slow
    leave
By laboursome petition, and at last
Upon his will I seal'd my hard consent;   60
I do beseech you, give him leave to go.

King.   Take thy fair hour, Laertes; time be thine,
And thy best graces spend it at thy will!
But now, my cousin Hamlet, and my son,—

45. **Lose your voice**—Not gain what you ask for.

Hamlet. [*Aside*] A little more than kin, and less than
    kind.   65

King. How is it that the clouds still hang on you?

Hamlet. Not so, my lord; I am too much i' th' sun.

Queen. Good Hamlet, cast thy nighted colour off,
    And let thine eye look like a friend on Denmark.
    Do not for ever with thy vailed lids   70
    Seek for thy noble father in the dust.
    Thou know'st 't is common; all that lives must die,
    Passing through nature to eternity.

Hamlet. Ay, madam, it is common.

Queen.   If it be,
    Why seems it so particular with thee?

Hamlet. Seems, madam! nay, it is; I know not 'seems.'
    'T is not alone my inky cloak, good mother,
    Nor customary suits of solemn black,
    Nor windy suspiration of forc'd breath,
    No, nor the fruitful river in the eye,   80
    Nor the dejected haviour of the visage,
    Together with all forms, moods, shows of grief,
    That can denote me truly; these indeed seem,
    For they are actions that a man might play:
    But I have that within which passeth show;   85

65. **More than kin . . . kind**—Possibly, too closely related (both uncle
    and stepfather), but my feelings are less than the natural affections
    due a kinsman.
66. **Clouds**—His mourning garments. (A prince should wear the royal
    scarlet.)
68. **Nighted colour**—Refers also to his mourning garments.
70. **Vailed lids**—Lowered lids, cast-down eyes.
81. **Dejected . . . visage**—Sorrowful expression on his face.

These but the trappings and the suits of woe.

King. 'T is sweet and commendable in your nature,
  Hamlet,
To give these mourning duties to your father:
But, you must know, your father lost a father;
That father lost, lost his; and the survivor bound,   90
In filial obligation, for some term
To do obsequious sorrow: but to persever
In obstinate condolement is a course
Of impious stubbornness; 't is unmanly grief;
It shows a will most incorrect to heaven,   95
A heart unfortified, a mind impatient,
An understanding simple and unschool'd:
For what we know must be and is as common
As any the most vulgar thing to sense,
Why should we in our peevish opposition   100
Take it to heart? Fie! 't is a fault to heaven,
A fault against the dead, a fault to nature,
To reason most absurd; whose common theme
Is death of fathers, and who still hath cried,
From the first corse till he that died to-day,   105
'This must be so.' We pray you, throw to earth
This unprevailing woe, and think of us
As of a father; for let the world take note,
You are the most immediate to our throne,

92. **Obsequious**—Funereal. 92. **Persever**—Persevere, continue.
93. **Obstinate condolement**—Stubborn grief.
99. **Most vulgar thing to sense**—The most ordinary experience.
105. **Corse**—Corpse, dead body.

And with no less nobility of love   110
Than that which dearest father bears his son
Do I impart toward you. For your intent
In going back to school in Wittenberg,
It is most retrograde to our desire;
And we beseech you, bend you to remain   115
Here in the cheer and comfort of our eye,
Our chiefest courtier, cousin, and our son.

Queen. Let not thy mother lose her prayers, Hamlet:
I pray thee, stay with us; go not to Wittenberg.

Hamlet. I shall in all my best obey you, madam.   120

King. Why, 't is a loving and a fair reply;
Be as ourself in Denmark. Madam, come;
This gentle and unforc'd accord of Hamlet
Sits smiling to my heart: in grace whereof,
No jocund health that Denmark drinks to-day,   125
But the great cannon to the clouds shall tell,
And the king's rouse the heavens shall bruit again,
Re-speaking earthly thunder. Come away.

> [*Flourish. Exeunt all but* Hamlet.

Hamlet. O, that this too, too solid flesh would melt,
Thaw and resolve itself into a dew!   130
Or that the Everlasting had not fix'd
His canon 'gainst self-slaughter! O God! O God!

114. **Retrograde**—Contrary.
125. **Jocund**—Joyful.
126. **Great cannon . . . bruit again**—The sky, re-echoing the sound of
    the cannon, shall proclaim the king's toast to Hamlet.
132. **Canon**—Law.

How weary, stale, flat, and unprofitable
Seem to me all the uses of this world!
Fie on 't! O fie! 't is an unweeded garden,   135
That grows to seed; things rank and gross in nature
Possess it merely. That it should come to this!
But two months dead! nay, not so much, not two:
So excellent a king; that was, to this,
Hyperion to a satyr; so loving to my mother   140
That he might not beteem the winds of heaven
Visit her face too roughly. Heaven and earth!
Must I remember? why, she would hang on him,
As if increase of appetite had grown
By what it fed on; and yet, within a month—   145
Let me not think on 't—Frailty, thy name is
     woman!—
A little month, or ere those shoes were old
With which she follow'd my poor father's body,
Like Niobe, all tears,—why, she, even she—
O God! a beast, that wants discourse of reason,   150
Would have mourn'd longer—married with my uncle,
My father's brother; but no more like my father
Than I to Hercules. Within a month;
Ere yet the salt of most unrighteous tears

140. **Hyperion to a satyr**—The contrast between my father and my uncle
     is like that between Apollo and Pan.
141. **Beteem**—Allow.
149. **Niobe**—Niobe mourned so excessively when her twelve children were
     killed by Apollo and Artemis that she has become a symbol of in-
     tense grief.
154. **Ere yet the salt . . . galled eyes**—Before her tears had ceased to
     redden her smarting eyes.

Had left the flushing in her galled eyes,   155
She married. O, most wicked speed, to post
With such dexterity to incestuous sheets!
It is not nor it cannot come to good:
But break my heart, for I must hold my tongue!

Enter Horatio, Marcellus, *and* Bernardo.

Horatio. Hail to your lordship!
Hamlet.   I am glad to see you well: 160
    Horatio,—or I do forget myself.
Horatio. The same, my lord, and your poor servant ever.
Hamlet. Sir, my good friend; I'll change that name with
    you:
    And what make you from Wittenberg, Horatio?—
    Marcellus?   165
Marcellus. My good lord—
Hamlet. I am very glad to see you. [*To* Bernardo]
    Good even, sir.
    But what, in faith, make you from Wittenberg?
Horatio. A truant disposition, good my lord.
Hamlet. I would not hear your enemy say so;   170
    Nor shall you do mine ear that violence,
    To make it truster of your own report
    Against yourself; I know you are no truant.
    But what is your affair in Elsinore?
    We'll teach you to drink deep ere you depart.   175

164. **What make you from Wittenberg**—What are you doing away
    from Wittenberg?

Horatio. My lord, I came to see your father's funeral.

Hamlet. I pray thee, do not mock me, fellow-student;
I think it was to see my mother's wedding.

Horatio. Indeed, my lord, it follow'd hard upon.

Hamlet. Thrift, thrift, Horatio! the funeral bak'd-meats
Did coldly furnish forth the marriage tables.   181
Would I had met my dearest foe in heaven
Or ever I had seen that day, Horatio!
My father,—methinks I see my father.

Horatio. O where, my lord?

Hamlet.   In my mind's eye, Horatio.   185

Horatio. I saw him once; he was a goodly king.

Hamlet. He was a man, take him for all in all,
I shall not look upon his like again.

Horatio. My lord, I think I saw him yesternight.

Hamlet. Saw? who?   190

Horatio. My lord, the king your father.

Hamlet.   The king my father!

Horatio. Season your admiration for a while
With an attent ear, till I may deliver,
Upon the witness of these gentlemen,
This marvel to you.

Hamlet..   For God's love, let me hear.   195

Horatio. Two nights together had these gentlemen,
Marcellus and Bernardo, on their watch,

---

182. **Dearest foe**—Shakespeare uses *dear* in the sense of closely concerned.
    It is equivalent here to "my bitterest enemy."
192. **Season your admiration**—Subdue your amazement.

In the dead vast and middle of the night,
Been thus encounter'd. A figure like your father,
Armed at point exactly, cap-a-pe,   200
Appears before them, and with solemn march
Goes slow and stately by them; thrice he walk'd
By their oppress'd and fear-surprised eyes,
Within his truncheon's length; whilst they, distill'd
Almost to jelly with the act of fear,   205
Stand dumb, and speak not to him. This to me
In dreadful secrecy impart they did;
And I with them the third night kept the watch:
Where, as they had deliver'd, both in time,
Form of the thing, each word made true and good,   210
The apparition comes. I knew your father;
These hands are not more like.

Hamlet.   But where was this?
Marcellus. My lord, upon the platform where we
    watch'd.
Hamlet. Did you not speak to it?
Horatio.   My lord, I did;
But answer made it none; yet once methought   215
It lifted up it head and did address
Itself to motion, like as it would speak;
But even then the morning cock crew loud,
And at the sound it shrunk in haste away,

200. **Cap-a-pe**—From the French expression meaning "head to foot."
204. **Truncheon**—Spear shaft or short staff.
216. **It head**—Its head. The possessive form did not come into general
    literary use until after Shakespeare's death.

And vanish'd from our sight.

Hamlet.   'T is very strange.   220

Horatio. As I do live, my honour'd lord, 't is true;
    And we did think it writ down in our duty
    To let you know of it.

Hamlet. Indeed, indeed, sirs, but this troubles me.
    Hold you the watch to-night?

Marcellus.}
Bernardo. }   We do, my lord.   225

Hamlet. Arm'd say you?

Marcellus.}
Bernardo. }   Arm'd, my lord.

Hamlet.   From top to toe?

Marcellus.}
Bernardo. } My lord, from head to foot.

Hamlet. Then saw you not his face?

Horatio. O, yes, my lord; he wore his beaver up.

Hamlet. What, look'd he frowningly?   230

Horatio. A countenance more in sorrow than in anger.

Hamlet. Pale, or red?

Horatio. Nay, very pale.

Hamlet.   And fix'd his eyes upon you?

Horatio. Most constantly.

Hamlet.   I would I had been there.

Horatio. It would have much amaz'd you.   235

Hamlet. Very like, very like. Stay'd it long?

229. **Beaver**—Part of the helmet that could be raised.

Horatio. While one with moderate haste might tell a
    hundred.

Marcellus.⎫
Bernardo.⎭ Longer, longer.

Horatio. Not when I saw 't.

Hamlet.   His beard was grizzled? no?

Horatio. It was, as I have seen it in his life,   240
    A sable silver'd.

Hamlet.   I will watch to-night;
    Perchance 't will walk again.

Horatio.   I warrant you it will.

Hamlet. If it assume my noble father's person,
    I'll speak to it, though hell itself should gape
    And bid me hold my peace. I pray you all,   245
    If you have hitherto conceal'd this sight,
    Let it be tenable in your silence still;
    And whatsoever else shall hap to-night,
    Give it an understanding, but no tongue:
    I will requite your loves. So, fare ye well;   250
    Upon the platform, 'twixt eleven and twelve,
    I'll visit you.

All.   Our duty to your honour.

Hamlet. Your love, as mine to you; farewell.

       [*Exeunt* HORATIO, MARCELLUS, *and* BERNARDO.
    My father's spirit in arms! all is not well;
    I doubt some foul play: would the night were come! 255

247. **Let it be tenable**—Let it be kept secret.   250. **Requite**—Repay.
255. **Doubt**—Suspect.

Till then sit still, my soul. Foul deeds will rise,
Though all the earth o'erwhelm them, to men's eyes.

[*Exit.*

Scene III

A room in Polonius' *house. Enter* Laertes *and* Ophelia.

Laertes. My necessaries are embark'd; farewell:
    And, sister, as the winds give benefit
    And convoy is assistant, do not sleep,
    But let me hear from you.
Ophelia.   Do you doubt that?
Laertes. For Hamlet, and the trifling of his favour,   5
    Hold it a fashion and a toy in blood,
    A violet in the youth of primy nature,
    Forward, not permanent, sweet, not lasting,
    The perfume and suppliance of a minute;
    No more.
Ophelia. No more but so?
Laertes.   Think it no more;   10
    For nature, crescent, does not grow alone
    In thews and bulk, but, as this temple waxes,
    The inward service of the mind and soul
    Grows wide withal. Perhaps he loves you now;

9. **Suppliance**—Trifling.
11. **For nature . . . wide withal**—Normal growth is not only in the
    muscles, but as the body (the temple) develops, the mind and soul
    develop, also.

And now no soil nor cautel doth besmirch   15
The virtue of his will; but you must fear,
His greatness weigh'd, his will is not his own;
For he himself is subject to his birth.
He may not, as unvalu'd persons do,
Carve for himself, for on his choice depends   20
The safety and health of this whole state;
And therefore must his choice be circumscrib'd
Unto the voice and yielding of that body
Whereof he is the head. Then, if he says he loves
        you,
It fits your wisdom so far to believe it   25
As he in his particular act and place
May give his saying deed; which is no further
Than the main voice of Denmark goes withal.
Then weigh what loss your honour may sustain,
If with too credent ear you list his songs,   30
Or lose your heart, or your chaste treasure open
To his unmaster'd importunity.
Fear it, Ophelia, fear it, my dear sister,
And keep you in the rear of your affection,
Out of the shot and danger of desire.   35
The chariest maid is prodigal enough,
If she unmask her beauty to the moon.

15. **Cautel**—Deception, trick.
17. **His greatness weigh'd**—Considering his high position. (Laertes
    fears that even if Hamlet loves Ophelia he may not be able to marry
    her, since royal marriages are matters of state, and a prince may not
    choose whom he will for his bride.)

Virtue itself scapes not calumnious strokes;
The canker galls the infants of the spring,
Too oft before their buttons be disclos'd;   40
And in the morn and liquid dew of youth
Contagious blastments are most imminent.
Be wary, then; best safety lies in fear:
Youth to itself rebels, though none else near.

Ophelia. I shall th' effect of this good lesson keep,   45
As watchman to my heart. But, good my brother,
Do not, as some ungracious pastors do,
Show me the steep and thorny way to heaven,
Whilst, like a puff'd and reckless libertine,
Himself the primrose path of dalliance treads,   50
And recks not his own rede.

Laertes.   O, fear me not.

Enter Polonius.

I stay too long; but here my father comes.
A double blessing is a double grace;
Occasion smiles upon a second leave.

Polonius. Yet here, Laertes? aboard, aboard, for shame!
The wind sits in the shoulder of your sail,
And you are stay'd for. There; my blessing with
     thee!

> [*Laying his hand on* Laertes' *head.*

---

39. **Canker galls . . . none else near**—Just as in the spring, half-open
     buds are sometimes killed by the canker worm, so youth is particu-
     larly subject to harm. Its own impulses are dangerous, even without
     outside suggestion.
51. **Recks not his own rede**—Does not follow his own advice.

And these few precepts in thy memory
See thou character. Give thy thoughts no tongue,
Nor any unproportion'd thought his act.   60
Be thou familiar, but by no means vulgar.
The friends thou hast, and their adoption tried,
Grapple them to thy soul with hoops of steel;
But do not dull thy palm with entertainment
Of each new-hatch'd, unfledg'd comrade. Beware 65
Of entrance to a quarrel; but being in,
Bear 't that th' opposed may beware of thee.
Give every man thine ear, but few thy voice;
Take each man's censure, but reserve thy judgment.
Costly thy habit as thy purse can buy,   70
But not express'd in fancy; rich, not gaudy;
For the apparel oft proclaims the man;
And they in France of the best rank and station
Are of a most select and generous chief in that.
Neither a borrower nor a lender be;   75
For loan oft loses both itself and friend,
And borrowing dulls the edge of husbandry.
This above all: to thine own self be true,
And it must follow, as the night the day,
Thou canst not then be false to any man.   80
Farewell; my blessing season this in thee!

58. **These few precepts . . . season this in thee**—See Notes, page 428.
59. **Character**—Write.
60. **Unproportion'd thought**—Unbalanced, rash thought.
70. **Habit**—Clothes.
74. **Chief in that**—Chiefly in that. The French are leaders in the matter of good taste in dress. 77. **Husbandry**—Thrift.

Laertes. Most humbly do I take my leave, my lord.

Polonius. The time invites you; go, your servants tend.

Laertes. Farewell, Ophelia; and remember well
     What I have said to you.

Ophelia.   'T is in my memory lock'd, 85
     And you yourself shall keep the key of it.

Laertes. Farewell.   [*Exit.*

Polonius. What is 't, Ophelia, he hath said to you?

Ophelia. So please you, something touching the Lord
          Hamlet.

Polonius. Marry, well bethought.   90
     'T is told me, he hath very oft of late
     Given private time to you, and you yourself
     Have of your audience been most free and bounteous.
     If it be so—as so 't is put on me,
     And that in way of caution—I must tell you,   95
     You do not understand yourself so clearly
     As it behoves my daughter and your honour.
     What is between you? give me up the truth.

Ophelia. He hath, my lord, of late made many tenders
     Of his affection to me.   100

Polonius. Affection! pooh! you speak like a green girl,
     Unsifted in such perilous circumstance.
     Do you believe his—tenders, as you call them?

Ophelia. I do not know, my lord, what I should think.

Polonius. Marry, I'll teach you; think yourself a baby,

---

103. **Tenders**—Polonius' play upon the word is an example of Elizabethan
     punning.

That you have ta'en these tenders for true pay,
Which are not sterling. Tender yourself more dearly;
Or—not to crack the wind of the poor phrase,
Running it thus—you'll tender me a fool.

Ophelia. My lord, he hath importun'd me with love 110
In honourable fashion.

Polonius. Ay, fashion you may call it; go to, go to.

Ophelia. And hath given countenance to his speech, my
  lord,
With almost all the holy vows of heaven.

Polonius. Ay, springes to catch woodcocks. I do know, 115
When the blood burns, how prodigal the soul
Lends the tongue vows; these blazes, daughter,
Giving more light than heat, extinct in both,
Even in their promise, as it is a-making,
You must not take for fire. From this time, daughter, 120
Be somewhat scanter of your maiden presence;
Set your entreatments at a higher rate
Than a command to parley. For Lord Hamlet,
Believe so much in him, that he is young,
And with a larger tether may he walk   125
Than may be given you. In few, Ophelia,
Do not believe his vows; for they are brokers,
Not of that dye which their investments show,
But mere implorators of unholy suits,

115. **Springes**—Traps for woodcocks (the silliest of birds).
121. **Be somewhat . . . parley**—Do not let him see you so often, nor
  stoop to answer his summons to a meeting.

Breathing like sanctified and pious bonds,   130
The better to beguile. This is for all;
I would not, in plain terms, from this time forth
Have you so slander any moment leisure
As to give words or talk with the Lord Hamlet.
Look to't, I charge you; come your ways.   135
Ophelia. I shall obey, my lord   [*Exeunt.*

SCENE IV

The platform. Enter HAMLET, HORATIO, *and* MARCELLUS.

Hamlet. The air bites shrewdly; it is very cold.
Horatio. It is a nipping and an eager air.
Hamlet. What hour now?
Horatio.   I think it lacks of twelve.
Marcellus. No, it is struck.
Horatio. Indeed? I heard it not; then it draws near the
      season   5
   Wherein the spirit held his wont to walk.
         [*A flourish of trumpets, and cannon fired, within.*
   What does this mean, my lord?
Hamlet. The king doth wake to-night, and takes his
      rouse,
   Keeps wassail, and the swaggering up-spring reels;

8. **The king . . . wassail**—The king is holding a revel to-night, and
   drinking. 9. **Up-spring reels**—The courtiers dance a wild dance.

And, as he drains his draughts of Rhenish down,   10
The kettle-drum and trumpet thus bray out
The triumph of his pledge.

Horatio.   Is it a custom?

Hamlet. Ay, marry, is 't;
But to my mind, though I am native here
And to the manner born, it is a custom   15
More honour'd in the breach than the observance.
This heavy-headed revel east and west
Makes us traduc'd and tax'd of other nations:
They clepe us drunkards, and with swinish phrase
Soil our addition; and indeed it takes   20
From our achievements, though perform'd at height,
The pith and marrow of our attribute.
So, oft it chances in particular men,
That for some vicious mole of nature in them,
As, in their birth—wherein they are not guilty,   25
Since nature cannot choose his origin—
By the o'ergrowth of some complexion,
Oft breaking down the pales and forts of reason;
Or by some habit that too much o'er-leavens
The form of plausive manners, that these men,   30

16. **A customed more honour'd . . . observance**—A custom better broken than observed.
18. **Traduc'd**—Exposed to shame.   19. **Clepe**—Call.
20. **Soil our addition**—By calling us drunkards and swine, they besmirch our reputation.
20. **And indeed . . . attribute**—It takes the real quality from praise due our most glorious deeds.   24. **Mole**—Blemish.
30. **Plausive**—Pleasing.

Carrying, I say, the stamp of one defect,
Being nature's livery, or fortune's star—
Their virtues else—be they as pure as grace,
As infinite as man may undergo—
Shall in the general censure take corruption   35
From that particular fault: the dram of eale
Doth all the noble substance of a doubt
To his own scandal.

Enter GHOST.

Horatio.   Look, my lord, it comes!
Hamlet.   Angels and ministers of grace defend us!
Be thou a spirit of health or goblin damn'd;   40
Bring with thee airs from heaven or blasts from hell;
Be thy intents wicked or charitable;
Thou com'st in such a questionable shape
That I will speak to thee: I'll call thee Hamlet,
King, father, royal Dane; O, answer me!   45
Let me not burst in ignorance; but tell
Why thy canoniz'd bones, hearsed in death,
Have burst their cerements; why the sepulchre,
Wherein we saw thee quietly inurn'd,
Hath op'd his ponderous and marble jaws,   50
To cast thee up again! What may this mean,
That thou, dead corse, again in complete steel,
Revisit'st thus the glimpses of the moon,

36. **Dram of eale . . . scandal**—Perhaps, the bit of evil casts doubt
    upon all his nobility. 48. **Cerements**—Shrouds, grave clothes.

Making night hideous; and we fools of nature
So horridly to shake our disposition   55
With thoughts beyond the reaches of our souls?
Say, why is this? wherefore? what should we do?

[GHOST *beckons* HAMLET.

Horatio. It beckons you to go away with it,
    As if it some impartment did desire
    To you alone.

Marcellus. Look, with what courteous action   60
    It waves you to a more removed ground;
    But do not go with it.

Horatio.   No, by no means.

Hamlet. It will not speak; then I will follow it.

Horatio. Do not, my lord.

Hamlet.   Why, what should be the fear?
    I do not set my life at a pin's fee;   65
    And, for my soul, what can it do to that,
    Being a thing immortal as itself?
    It waves me forth again; I'll follow it.

Horatio. What if it tempt you toward the flood, my lord,
    Or to the dreadful summit of the cliff   70
    That beetles o'er his base into the sea,
    And there assume some other horrible form,
    Which might deprive your sovereignty of reason
    And draw you into madness? think of it;
    The very place puts toys of desperation,   75

71. **Beetles**—Juts, projects over the base.
75. **The very place . . . beneath**—The high cliff itself tempts men to
    jump.

Without more motive, into every brain
That looks so many fathoms to the sea
And hears it roar beneath.

Hamlet.   It waves me still.
Go on; I'll follow thee.

Marcellus. You shall not go, my lord.

Hamlet.   Hold off your hands!

Horatio. Be rul'd; you shall not go.

Hamlet.   My fate cries out,
And makes each petty artery in this body   82
As hardy as the Nemean lion's nerve.   [Ghost *beckons.*
Still am I call'd. Unhand me, gentlemen;
                              [*Breaking from them.*
By heaven, I'll make a ghost of him that lets me!   85
I say, away! Go on; I'll follow thee.
                    [*Exeunt* Ghost *and* Hamlet.

Horatio. He waxes desperate with imagination.

Marcellus. Let's follow; 't is not fit thus to obey him.

Horatio. Have after. To what issue will this come?   89

Marcellus. Something is rotten in the state of Denmark.

Horatio. Heaven will direct it.

Marcellus.   Nay, let's follow him.
                              [*Exeunt.*

---

85. **Lets**—Hinders, prevents. (An example of a word that has completely
    reversed its meaning.)

SCENE V

Another part of the platform. Enter GHOST *and* HAMLET.

Hamlet. Where wilt thou lead me? speak; I'll go no
     further.
Ghost. Mark me.
Hamlet.   I will.
Ghost.   My hour is almost come,
    When I to sulphurous and tormenting flames
    Must render up myself.
Hamlet.   Alas, poor ghost!
Ghost. Pity me not, but lend thy serious hearing   5
    To what I shall unfold.
Hamlet.   Speak; I am bound to hear.
Ghost. So art thou to revenge, when thou shalt hear.
Hamlet. What?
Ghost. I am thy father's spirit,
    Doom'd for a certain term to walk the night,   10
    And for the day confin'd to fast in fires,
    Till the foul crimes done in my days of nature
    Are burnt and purg'd away. But that I am forbid
    To tell the secrets of my prison-house,
    I could a tale unfold whose lightest word   15
    Would harrow up thy soul, freeze thy young blood,
    Make thy two eyes, like stars, start from their spheres,
    Thy knotted and combined locks to part,
    And each particular hair to stand an end,

"I am thy father's spirit."

Hamlet as played by Leslie Howard

Like quills upon the fretful porpentine;   20
But this eternal blazon must not be
To ears of flesh and blood. List, list, O, list!
If thou didst ever thy dear father love—

Hamlet. O God!

Ghost. Revenge his foul and most unnatural murder.   25

Hamlet. Murder!

Ghost. Murder most foul, as in the best it is;
But this most foul, strange, and unnatural.

Hamlet. Haste me to know't, that I, with wings as swift
As meditation or the thoughts of love,   30
May sweep to my revenge.

Ghost.   I find thee apt;
And duller shouldst thou be than the fat weed
That roots itself in ease on Lethe wharf,
Wouldst thou not stir in this. Now, Hamlet, hear:
It's given out that, sleeping in mine orchard,   35
A serpent stung me; so the whole ear of Denmark
Is by a forged process of my death
Rankly abus'd; but know, thou noble youth,
The serpent that did sting thy father's life
Now wears his crown.

Hamlet.   O my prophetic soul!   40
Mine uncle!

Ghost. Ay, that incestuous, that adulterate beast,

20. **Porpentine**—Porcupine.
21. **Eternal blazon**—Announcement of mysteries of the other world.
33. **Lethe wharf**—Lethe was a river in Hades. Its water when drunk
    caused forgetfulness of the past.

With witchcraft of his wit, with traitorous gifts—
O wicked wit and gifts, that have the power
So to seduce!—won to his shameful lust   45
The will of my most seeming-virtuous queen.
O Hamlet, what a falling-off was there!
From me, whose love was of that dignity
That it went hand in hand even with the vow
I made to her in marriage; and to decline   50
Upon a wretch, whose natural gifts were poor
To those of mine!
But virtue, as it never will be mov'd,
Though lewdness court it in a shape of heaven,
So lust, though to a radiant angel link'd,   55
Will sate itself in a celestial bed,
And prey on garbage.
But, soft! methinks I scent the morning air;
Brief let me be. Sleeping within mine orchard,
My custom always in the afternoon,   60
Upon my secure hour thy uncle stole,
With juice of cursed hebenon in a vial,
And in the porches of mine ears did pour
The leperous distilment; whose effect
Holds such an enmity with blood of man   65
That swift as quicksilver it courses through
The natural gates and alleys of the body;
And with a sudden vigour it doth posset

61. **Secure**—Unsuspicious.
64. **Leperous distilment**—Liquid that would cause leprosy.

And curd, like eager droppings into milk,
The thin and wholesome blood: so did it mine;   70
And a most instant tetter bark'd about,
Most lazar-like, with vile and loathsome crust,
All my smooth body.
Thus was I, sleeping, by a brother's hand
Of life, of crown, of queen, at once dispatch'd;   75
Cut off even in the blossoms of my sin,
Unhousel'd, disappointed, unanel'd;
No reckoning made, but sent to my account
With all my imperfections on my head.
O, horrible! O, horrible! most horrible!   80
If thou hast nature in thee, bear it not;
Let not the royal bed of Denmark be
A couch for luxury and damned incest.
But, howsoever thou pursuest this act,
Taint not thy mind, nor let thy soul contrive   85
Against thy mother aught; leave her to heaven,
And to those thorns that in her bosom lodge
To prick and sting her. Fare thee well at once!
The glow-worm shows the matin to be near,
And gins to pale his uneffectual fire;   90
Adieu, adieu, adieu! remember me.   [*Exit.*

Hamlet. O all you host of heaven! O earth! what else?

69. **Eager**—Acid. (Acid dropped into milk will curdle it.)
71. **Tetter**—A skin disease. 72. **Lazar-like**—Leprous.
77. **Unhousel'd . . . head**—Killed without receiving the last rites of the
     church. 89. **Matin**—Morning. 90. **Gins**—Begins.

And shall I couple hell? O, fie! Hold, hold, my
   heart:
And you, my sinews, grow not instant old,
But bear me stiffly up. Remember thee!   95
Ay, thou poor ghost, while memory holds a seat
In this distracted globe. Remember thee!
Yea, from the table of my memory
I'll wipe away all trivial fond records,
All saws of books, all forms, all pressures past,   100
That youth and observation copied there;
And thy commandment all alone shall live
Within the book and volume of my brain,
Unmix'd with baser matter: yes, yes, by heaven!
O most pernicious woman!   105
O villain, villain, smiling, damned villain!
My tables, my tables,—meet it is I set it down,
That one may smile, and smile, and be a villain;
At least I'm sure it may be so in Denmark.
So, uncle, there you are. Now to my word;   110
It is, 'Adieu, adieu! remember me':
I have sworn 't.

Horatio.   ⎱
Marcellus. ⎰   [*Within*] My lord, my lord!

Marcellus.   [*Within*] Lord Hamlet!

Horatio.   [*Within*] Heaven secure him!

Hamlet. So be it!

98. **Table**—See Notes, page 428.   105. **Pernicious**—Wicked.
107. **Tables**—Tablets, a sort of notebook.

Marcellus. [*Within*] Hillo, ho, ho, my lord!   115
Hamlet. Hillo, ho, ho, boy!   Come, bird, come.

Enter HORATIO *and* MARCELLUS.

Marcellus. How is 't, my noble lord?

Horatio.   What news, my lord?

Hamlet. O, wonderful!

Horatio. Good my lord, tell it.

Hamlet.   No; you'll reveal it.

Horatio. Not I, my lord, by heaven.

Marcellus.   Nor I, my lord.

Hamlet. How say you, then, would heart of man once
    think it?

    But you'll be secret?

Horatio.   ⎫
          ⎬   Ay, by heaven, my lord.
Marcellus. ⎭

Hamlet. There's ne'er a villain dwelling in all Den-
    mark—

    But he's an arrant knave.

Horatio. There needs no ghost, my lord, come from the
    grave   125
    To tell us this.

Hamlet.   Why, right; you are i' th' right;
    And so, without more circumstance at all,
    I hold it fit that we shake hands and part:
    You, as your business and desire shall point you,

---

116. **Hillo, ho, ho**—This is the falconer's cry to his hawk.   So Hamlet
    carries out the idea by adding, "Come, bird, come."

For every man has business and desire,
Such as it is; and, for mine own poor part,
Look you, I'll go pray.

Horatio.   These are but wild and whirling words, my lord.

Hamlet.   I'm sorry they offend you, heartily;
Yes, faith, heartily.

Horatio.   There's no offence, my lord.   135

Hamlet.   Yes, by Saint Patrick, but there is, Horatio,
And much offence too. Touching this vision here,
It is an honest ghost, that let me tell you;
For your desire to know what is between us,
O'ermaster 't as you may. And now, good friends, 140
As you are friends, scholars, and soldiers,
Give me one poor request.

Horatio.   What is 't, my lord? We will.

Hamlet.   Never make known what you have seen to-night.

Horatio.   ⎫
Marcellus. ⎬ My lord, we will not.
                ⎭

Hamlet.   Nay, but swear 't.

Horatio.   In faith,
My lord, not I.

Marcellus.   Nor I, my lord, in faith.   146

Hamlet.   Upon my sword.

Marcellus.   We have sworn, my lord, already.

Hamlet.   Indeed, upon my sword, indeed.

Ghost.   [*Beneath*] Swear.

---

147. **Upon my sword**—As the hilt of the sword was in the form of a
cross, it could be used for a sacred object upon which to swear.

Hamlet. Ah, ha, boy! say'st thou so? Art thou there,
  truepenny?   150
 Come on; you hear this fellow in the cellarage.
 Consent to swear.
Horatio.   Propose the oath, my lord.
Hamlet. Never to speak of this that you have seen.
 Swear by my sword.
Ghost. [*Beneath*] Swear.   155
Hamlet. Hic et ubique? Then we'll shift our ground.
 Come hither, gentlemen,
 And lay your hands again upon my sword.
 Never to speak of this that you have heard,
 Swear by my sword.   160
Ghost. [*Beneath*] Swear.
Hamlet. Well said, old mole! canst work i' the earth
  so fast?
 A worthy pioner! Once more remove, good friends.
Horatio. O day and night! but this is wondrous strange.
Hamlet. And therefore as a stranger give it welcome.
 There are more things in heaven and earth, Horatio, 166
 Than are dreamt of in our philosophy.
 But come:
 Here, as before, never, so help you mercy,
 How strange or odd soe'er I bear myself—   170
 As I perchance hereafter shall think meet

151. **Cellarage**—Cellar, space below the level of the ground.
156. **Hic et ubique**—Here and everywhere. 163. **Pioner**—Trench-digger.
171. **As I perchance . . . antic disposition on**—As perhaps I shall
  think it best to act fantastically, crazily.

To put an antic disposition on—
That you, at such times seeing me, never shall,
With arms encumber'd thus, or this head-shake,
Or by pronouncing of some doubtful phrase,   175
As 'Well, well, we know,' or 'We could, and if we
    would,'
Or 'If we list to speak,' or 'There be, and if they
    might,'
Or such ambiguous giving out, to note
That you know aught of me;—this not to do,
So grace and mercy at your most need help you,   180
Swear.

Ghost. [*Beneath*] Swear.

Hamlet. Rest, rest, perturbed spirit! [*They swear.*] So,
    gentlemen,
With all my love I do commend me to you;
And what so poor a man as Hamlet is   185
May do, t' express his love and friending to you,
God willing, shall not lack. Let us go in together;
And still your fingers on your lips, I pray.
The time is out of joint: O cursed spite,
That ever I was born to set it right!   190
Nay, come; let's go together.   [*Exeunt.*

ACT TWO

Scene I

A room in Polonius' *house.   Enter* Polonius *and* Reynaldo.

Polonius.   Give him this money and these notes, Rey-
     naldo.

Reynaldo.   I will, my lord.

Polonius.   You shall do marvellous wisely, good Reynaldo,
     Before you visit him, to make inquire
     Of his behaviour.

Reynaldo.   My lord, I did intend it.   5

Polonius.   Marry, well said, very well said.   Look you sir,
     Inquire me first what Danskers are in Paris;
     And how, and who, what means, and where they keep;
     What company, at what expense; and finding
     By this encompassment and drift of question   10
     That they do know my son, come you more nearer
     Than your particular demands will touch it;
     Take you, as 't were, some distant knowledge of him;
     As thus, 'I know his father and his friends,
     And in part him.'   Do you mark this, Reynaldo?   15

Reynaldo.   Ay, very well, my lord.

Polonius. 'And in part him; but,' you may say, 'not well:

1. **Him**—Laertes. 7. **Danskers**—Danes.
10. **Encompassment and drift of question**—Indirect questioning.

But, if 't be he I mean, he 's very wild,
Addicted so and so'; and there put on him
What forgeries you please; marry, none so rank   20
As may dishonour him; take heed of that;
But, sir, such wanton, wild, and usual slips
As are companions noted and most known
To youth and liberty.

Reynaldo.   As gaming, my lord?

Polonius. Ay, or drinking, fencing, swearing, quarrelling,
Drabbing; you may go so far.   26

Reynaldo. My lord, that would dishonour him.

Polonius. Faith, no; as you may season it in the charge.
You must not put another scandal on him,
That he is open to incontinency;   30
That's not my meaning: but breathe his faults so
    quaintly
That they may seem the taints of liberty,
The flash and outbreak of a fiery mind,
A savageness in unreclaimed blood,
Of general assault.

Reynaldo.   But, my good lord,—   35

Polonius. Wherefore should you do this?

Reynaldo.   Ay, my lord,
I would know that.

Polonius.   Marry, sir, here 's my drift,
And I believe it is a fetch of warrant:
You laying these slight sullies on my son,

38. **Fetch of warrant**—A justified trap.

As 't were a thing a little soil'd i' the working,   40
Mark you,
Your party in converse, him you would sound,
Having ever seen in the prenominate crimes
The youth you breathe of guilty, be assur'd
He closes with you in this consequence;   45
'Good sir,' or so; or 'friend,' or 'gentleman,'
According to the phrase or the addition
Of man and country.

Reynaldo.   Very good, my lord.

Polonius. And then, sir, does he this—he does—what was
I about to say? By the mass, I was about to say
something; where did I leave?   51

Reynaldo. At 'closes in the consequence'; at 'friend or
so,' and 'gentleman.'

Polonius. At 'closes in the consequence,'—ay, marry;
He closes thus: 'I know the gentleman;   55
I saw him yesterday, or t' other day,
Or then, or then, with such, or such, and, as you say,
There was he gaming, there o'ertook in 's rouse,
There falling out at tennis'; or perchance,
'I saw him enter such a house of sale.'   60
See you now,
Your bait of falsehood takes this carp of truth;
And thus do we of wisdom and of reach,
With windlasses and with assays of bias,

43. **Prenominate**—Aforesaid.
62. **Carp**—A fish, also a jest.   (Note the play on words.)
64. **Assays of bias**—Indirect trials.

By indirections find directions out: 65
So, by my former lecture and advice,
Shall you my son. You have me, have you not?
Reynaldo. My lord, I have.
Polonius.   God b' wi' you! fare you well.
Reynaldo. Good my lord!
Polonius. Observe his inclination in yourself.   70
Reynaldo. I shall, my lord.
Polonius. And let him ply his music.
Reynaldo.   Well, my lord.
Polonius. Farewell!   [*Exit* Reynaldo.

Enter Ophelia.

                    How now, Ophelia! what's the matter?
Ophelia. O, my lord, my lord, I have been so affrighted!
Polonius. With what, i' the name o' God?   75
Ophelia. My lord, as I was sewing in my closet,
    Lord Hamlet, with his doublet all unbrac'd;
    No hat upon his head; his stockings foul'd,
    Ungarter'd, and down-gyved to his ankle;
    Pale as his shirt; his knees knocking each other;   80
    And with a look so piteous in purport
    As if he had been loosed out of hell
    To speak of horrors, he comes before me.
Polonius. Mad for thy love?

67. **You have me**—You understand me.
72. **Ply his music**—Attend to his music lessons. (In those days every-
    one was supposed to learn some sort of music.) 76. **Closet**—Room.
79. **Down-gyved**—Slipped down (like chains about the ankle).

Ophelia.   My lord, I do not know,
    But truly I do fear it.
Polonius.   What said he?   85
Ophelia. He took me by the wrist and held me hard;
    Then goes he to the length of all his arm,
    And, with his other hand thus o'er his brow,
    He falls to such perusal of my face
    As he would draw it. Long stay'd he so;   90
    At last, a little shaking of mine arm,
    And thrice his head thus waving up and down,
    He rais'd a sigh so piteous and profound
    That it did seem to shatter all his bulk
    And end his being: that done, he lets me go;   95
    And with his head over his shoulder turn'd
    He seem'd to find his way without his eyes;
    For out o' doors he went without their help,
    And to the last bended their light on me.
Polonius. Come, go with me; I will go seek the king.
    This is the very ecstasy of love,   101
    Whose violent property fordoes itself
    And leads the will to desperate undertakings,
    As oft as any passion under heaven
    That does afflict our natures. I am sorry.   105
    What, have you given him any hard words of late?
Ophelia. No, my good lord; but, as you did command,
    I did repel his letters and denied
    His access to me.

101. **Ecstasy**—Madness.

"I have been so affrighted!"

*Ophelia as played by Pamela Stanley
in the Howard Production*

Polonius.   That hath made him mad.
    I am sorry that with better heed and judgment   110
    I had not quoted him. I fear'd he did but trifle,
    And meant to wreck thee; but beshrew my jealousy!
    By heaven, it is as proper to our age
    To cast beyond ourselves in our opinions
    As it is common for the younger sort   115
    To lack discretion. Come, go we to the king:
    This must be known; which, being kept close, might
        move
    More grief to hide than hate to utter love.
    Come.
                                        [*Exeunt.*

Scene II

A room in the castle. Flourish. Enter King, Queen, Rosencrantz, Guildenstern, *and* Attendants.

King. Welcome, dear Rosencrantz and Guildenstern!
    Moreover that we much did long to see you,
    The need we have to use you did provoke
    Our hasty sending. Something have you heard
    Of Hamlet's transformation; so I call it,   5
    Since not th' exterior nor the inward man
    Resembles that it was. What it should be,
    More than his father's death, that thus hath put him

112. **Beshrew**—Curse.
117. **Being kept close . . . love**—More trouble would come from hiding
     it, than displeasure from telling it.

So much from th' understanding of himself,
I cannot dream of. I entreat you both,   10
That, being of so young days brought up with him,
And since so neighbour'd to his youth and humour,
That you vouchsafe your rest here in our court
Some little time; so by your companies
To draw him on to pleasures, and to gather,   15
So much as from occasions you may glean,
Whether aught, to us unknown, afflicts him thus,
That, open'd, lies within our remedy.

Queen. Good gentlemen, he hath much talk'd of you;
And sure I am two men there are not living   20
To whom he more adheres. If it will please you
To show us so much gentry and good-will
As to expend your time with us awhile
For the supply and profit of our hope,
Your visitation shall receive such thanks   25
As fits a king's remembrance.

Rosencrantz.   Both your majesties
Might, by the sovereign power you have of us,
Put your dread pleasures more into command
Than to entreaty.

Guildenstern. We both obey,
And here give up ourselves, in the full bent   30
To lay our services freely at your feet,
To be commanded.

King. Thanks, Rosencrantz and gentle Guildenstern.

22. **Gentry**—Courtesy.

Queen. Thanks, Guildenstern and gentle Rosencrantz:
    And I beseech you instantly to visit   35
    My too much changed son. Go, some of ye,
    And bring the gentlemen where Hamlet is.
Guildenstern. Heavens make our presence and our prac-
        tices
    Pleasant and helpful to him!
Queen.   Ay, amen!   39

    [*Exeunt* ROSENCRANTZ, GUILDENSTERN, *and some* Attendants.
             Enter POLONIUS.

Polonius. Th' ambassadors from Norway, my good lord,
    Are joyfully return'd.   41
King. Thou still hast been the father of good news.
Polonius. Have I, my lord? Assure you, my good liege,
    I hold my duty, as I hold my soul,
    Both to my God and to my gracious king;   45
    And I do think, or else this brain of mine
    Hunts not the trail of policy so sure
    As it hath us'd to do, that I have found
    The very cause of Hamlet's lunacy.
King. O, speak of that; that I do long to hear.   50
Polonius. Give first admittance to th' ambassadors;
    My news shall be the fruit to that great feast.
King. Thyself do grace to them, and bring them in.
                      [*Exit* POLONIUS.
    He tells me, my dear Gertrude, he hath found
    The head and source of all your son's distemper.   55

Queen. I doubt it is no other but the main;
His father's death, and our o'erhasty marriage.
King. Well, we shall sift him.

Re-enter POLONIUS, *with* VOLTIMAND *and* CORNELIUS.

Welcome, my good friends!
Say, Voltimand, what from our brother Norway?
Voltimand. Most fair return of greetings and desires.   60
Upon our first, he sent out to suppress
His nephew's levies, which to him appear'd
To be a preparation 'gainst the Polack;
But better look'd into, he truly found
It was against your highness: whereat griev'd,   65
That so his sickness, age, and impotence
Was falsely borne in hand, sends out arrests
On Fortinbras; which he, in brief, obeys;
Receives rebuke from Norway, and in fine
Makes vow before his uncle never more   70
To give th' assay of arms against your majesty.
Whereon old Norway, overcome with joy,
Gives him three thousand crowns in annual fee,
And his commission to employ those soldiers,
So levied as before, against the Polack;   75
With an entreaty, herein further shown,   [*Giving a paper.*
That it might please you to give quiet pass
Through your dominions for this enterprise,
On such regards of safety and allowance
As therein are set down.

King.   It likes us well;   80
    And at our more consider'd time we'll read,
    Answer, and think upon this business.
    Meantime we thank you for your well-took labour.
    Go to your rest; at night we'll feast together:
    Most welcome home! [*Exeunt* VOLTIMAND *and* CORNELIUS.
Polonius.   This business is well ended.   85
    My liege, and madam, to expostulate
    What majesty should be, what duty is,
    Why day is day, night night, and time is time,
    Were nothing but to waste night, day, and time.
    Therefore, since brevity is the soul of wit,   90
    And tediousness the limbs and outward flourishes,
    I will be brief. Your noble son is mad:
    Mad call I it; for, to define true madness,
    What is 't but to be nothing else but mad?
    But let that go.
Queen.   More matter, with less art.   95
Polonius. Madam, I swear I use no art at all.
    That he is mad, 't is true; 't true 't is pity,
    And pity 't is 't is true: a foolish figure!
    But farewell it, for I will use no art.
    Mad let us grant him then; and now remains   100
    That we find out the cause of this effect,
    Or rather say, the cause of this defect,
    For this effect defective comes by cause:
    Thus it remains, and the remainder thus.

  86. **Expostulate**—Discuss.

Perpend.   105

I have a daughter—have whilst she is mine—

Who, in her duty and obedience, mark,

Hath given me this; now gather, and surmise.

[*Reads the letter*.

    To the celestial and my soul's idol, the most beau-

    tified Ophelia,—   110

That's an ill phrase, a vile phrase; 'beautified' is a vile

phrase. But you shall hear. Thus:

    In her excellent white bosom, these, etc.

Queen.   Came this from Hamlet to her?

Polonius.   Good madam, stay awhile. I will be faithful.

[*Reads*.

      Doubt thou the stars are fire,   116

        Doubt that the sun doth move,

        Doubt truth to be a liar,

        But never doubt I love.

    O dear Ophelia, I am ill at these numbers. I have

not art to reckon my groans; but that I love thee

best, O most best, believe it. Adieu.   122

      Thine evermore, most dear lady,

        Whilst this machine is to him, HAMLET.

This in obedience hath my daughter shown me,   125

And more above, hath his solicitings,

As they fell out by time, by means, and place,

All given to mine ear.

105. **Perpend**—Consider this.
120. **Ill at these numbers**—Not good at writing poetry.
124. **Whilst this machine is to him**—While this body is his.

King.   But how hath she
    Receiv'd his love?
Polonius.   What do you think of me?
King. As of a man faithful and honourable.   130
Polonius. I would fain prove so. But what might you
    think,
    When I had seen this hot love on the wing—
    As I perceiv'd it, I must tell you that,
    Before my daughter told me—what might you,
    Or my dear majesty your queen here, think,   135
    If I had play'd the desk or table-book,
    Or given my heart a winking, mute and dumb,
    Or look'd upon this love with idle sight;
    What might you think? No, I went round to work,
    And my young mistress thus I did bespeak: 140
    'Lord Hamlet is a prince, out of thy star;
    This must not be.' And then I precepts gave her,
    That she should lock herself from his resort,
    Admit no messengers, receive no tokens.
    Which done, she took the fruits of my advice;   145
    And he, repulsed—a short tale to make—
    Fell into a sadness, then into a fast,
    Thence to a watch, thence into a weakness,
    Thence to a lightness, and by this declension
    Into the madness wherein now he raves,   150
    And all we mourn for.
King.   Do you think 't is this?

143. **Resort**—Company.

Queen. It may be, very likely.

Polonius. Hath there been such a time—I'd fain know
    that—

    That I have positively said ' 'T is so,'

    When it prov'd otherwise?

King.   Not that I know.   155

Polonius. Take this from this, if this be otherwise.

    If circumstances lead me, I will find

    Where truth is hid, though it were hid indeed

    Within the centre.

King.   How may we try it further?

Polonius. You know, sometimes he walks four hours
    together   160

    Here in the lobby.

Queen.   So he does, indeed.

Polonius. At such a time I'll loose my daughter to him:

    Be you and I behind an arras then;

    Mark the encounter: if he love her not,

    And be not from his reason fall'n thereon,   165

    Let me be no assistant for a state,

    But keep a farm and carters.

King.   We will try it.

156. **This from this**—My head from my body.

159. **Centre**—Centre (of earth). He'll go to great lengths to discover the
truth.

160. **Four**—For. In Shakespeare's time *four* was used for an indefinite
number as we use *for* today.

163. **Arras**—Curtain, tapestry hangings, named after Arras, a town in
France where they were made.

167. **Carters**—Those who drive carts, teamsters.

Enter HAMLET, *reading on a book.*

Queen.   But look where sadly the poor wretch comes
        reading.

Polonius.   Away, I do beseech you, both away;
        I'll board him presently.

                    [*Exeunt* KING, QUEEN, *and* Attendants.
                        O, give me leave.   170
        How does my good Lord Hamlet?

Hamlet.   Well, God-a-mercy.

Polonius.   Do you know me, my lord?

Hamlet.   Excellent well; you're a fishmonger.

Polonius.   Not I, my lord.   175

Hamlet.   Then I would you were so honest a man.

Polonius.   Honest, my lord!

Hamlet.   Ay, sir; to be honest, as this world goes, is to be
        one man pick'd out of ten thousand.

Polonius.   That 's very true, my lord.   180

Hamlet.   For if the sun breed maggots in a dead dog,
        being a good kissing carrion,—Have you a daughter?

Polonius.   I have, my lord.

Hamlet.   Let her not walk i' th' sun; conception is a
        blessing, but not as your daughter may conceive.
        Friend, look to 't.   186

Polonius.   [*Aside*] How say you by that? Still harping
        on my daughter: yet he knew me not at first; he said

170. **Board him presently**—Speak to him at once.
174. **Fishmonger**—Fish dealer.
182. **Carrion**—Rotting flesh of a dead animal.

I was a fishmonger; he is far gone, far gone: and
truly in my youth I suffer'd much extremity for love;
very near this. I'll speak to him again. What do you
read, my lord?   191

Hamlet. Words, words, words.

Polonius. What is the matter, my lord?

Hamlet. Between who?

Polonius. I mean, the matter that you read, my lord.   195

Hamlet. Slanders, sir; for the satirical rogue says here
that old men have gray beards, that their faces are
wrinkl'd, their eyes purging thick amber and plum-
tree gum, and that they have a plentiful lack of wit,
together with most weak hams; all which, sir, though
I most powerfully and potently believe, yet I hold it
not honesty to have it thus set down; for you yourself, sir, should be old as I am, if, like a crab, you
could go backward.   204

Polonius. [*Aside*] Though this be madness, yet there is
method in 't. Will you walk out of the air, my lord?

Hamlet. Into my grave?

Polonius. Indeed, that is out o' th' air. [*Aside*] How
pregnant sometimes his replies are! a happiness that
often madness hits on, which reason and sanity could
not so prosperously be deliver'd of. I will leave him,
and suddenly contrive the means of meeting between
him and my daughter. My honourable lord, I will
most humbly take my leave of you.   214

Hamlet. You cannot, sir, take from me any thing that I

will more willingly part withal,—[*Aside*] except my
life, except my life, except my life.   217

Polonius. Fare you well, my lord.

Hamlet. These tedious old fools!

    Enter ROSENCRANTZ *and* GUILDENSTERN.

Polonius. You go to seek the Lord Hamlet; there he is. 220

Rosencrantz. [*To* POLONIUS] God save you, sir!

            [*Exit* POLONIUS.

Guildenstern. Mine honour'd lord!

Rosencrantz. My most dear lord!

Hamlet. My excellent good friends! How dost thou,
  Guildenstern? Ah, Rosencrantz! Good lads, how do 225
  ye both?

Rosencrantz. As the indifferent children of the earth.

Guildenstern. Happy, in that we are not overhappy;
  On Fortune's cap we are not the very button.

Hamlet. Nor the soles of her shoe?   230

Rosencrantz. Neither, my lord.

Hamlet. Then you live about her waist, or in the middle
  of her favours? What's the news?

Rosencrantz. None, my lord, but that the world's grown
  honest.

Hamlet. Then is doomsday near; but your news is not
  true. Let me question more in particular. What have
  you, my good friends, deserv'd at the hands of For- 238
  tune, that she sends you to prison hither?

227. **Indifferent**—Average, ordinary.
229. **Button**—Possibly, the button at the very top of Fortune's cap.

Guildenstern. Prison, my lord!   240
Hamlet. Denmark's a prison.
Rosencrantz. Then is the world one.
Hamlet. A goodly one; in which there are many con-
    fines, wards, and dungeons, Denmark being one o'
    th' worst.
Rosencrantz. We think not so, my lord.
Hamlet. Why, then 't is none to you; for there is noth-
    ing either good or bad, but thinking makes it so: to
    me it is a prison.   249
Rosencrantz. Why, then your ambition makes it one;
    't is too narrow for your mind.
Hamlet. O God, I could be bounded in a nut-shell and
    count myself a king of infinite space, were it not that
    I have bad dreams.   254
Guildenstern. Which dreams, indeed, are ambition; for
    the very substance of the ambitious is merely the
    shadow of a dream.   257
Hamlet. A dream itself is but a shadow.
Rosencrantz. Truly, and I hold ambition of so airy and
    light a quality that it is but a shadow's shadow.
Hamlet. Then are our beggars bodies, and our mon-
    archs and outstretch'd heroes the beggars' shadows.
    Shall we to the court? for, by my fay, I cannot reason. 263
Rosencrantz. ⎫
Guildenstern. ⎭ We'll wait upon you.

261. **Beggars bodies . . . shadows**—If ambition is only a shadow, then
    unambitious men, like beggars, are the reality; and monarchs and he-
    roes only the shadow. 263. **By my fay**—By my faith. See page
    429.

Hamlet. No such matter: I will not sort you with the rest of my servants; for, to speak to you like an honest man, I am most dreadfully attended. But, in the beaten way of friendship, what make you at Elsinore? 269

Rosencrantz. To visit you, my lord; no other occasion.

Hamlet. Beggar that I am, I am even poor in thanks; but I thank you: and sure, dear friends, my thanks are too dear a halfpenny. Were you not sent for? Is it your own inclining? Is it a free visitation? Come, deal justly with me: come, come; nay, speak. 275

Guildenstern. What should we say, my lord?

Hamlet. Why, any thing, but to the purpose. You were sent for; and there is a kind of confession in your looks which your modesties have not craft enough to colour. I know the good king and queen have sent for you. 280

Rosencrantz. To what end, my lord?

Hamlet. That you must teach me. But let me conjure you, by the rights of our fellowship, by the consonancy of our youth, by the obligation of our ever-preserv'd love, and by what more dear a better proposer could charge you withal, be even and direct with me, whether you were sent for, or no. 287

Rosencrantz. [*Aside to* GUILDENSTERN] What say you?

Hamlet. [*Aside*] Nay, then, I have an eye of you. If you love me, hold not off. 290

282. **Conjure**—Beg of you, entreat you.
283. **Consonancy**—Happy or harmonious friendship.

Guildenstern. My lord, we were sent for.

Hamlet. I will tell you why; so shall my anticipation prevent your discovery, and your secrecy to the king and
queen moult no feather. I have of late—but wherefore 294
I know not—lost all my mirth, forgone all custom of
exercises; and indeed it goes so heavily with my disposition that this goodly frame, the earth, seems to me
a sterile promontory; this most excellent canopy, the
air, look you, this brave o'erhanging firmament, this
majestical roof fretted with golden fire, why, it appears
no other thing to me than a foul and pestilent congre-
gation of vapours. What a piece of work is a man!
how noble in reason! how infinite in faculty! in form
and moving how express and admirable! in action
how like an angel! in apprehension how like a god!
the beauty of the world! the paragon of animals! And 306
yet, to me, what is this quintessence of dust? man delights not me; no, nor woman neither, though by your
smiling you seem to say so.   309

Rosencrantz. My lord, there was no such stuff in my
thoughts.

Hamlet. Why did you laugh then, when I said 'man
delights not me?'

Rosencrantz. To think, my lord, if you delight not in
man, what lenten entertainment the players shall re- 315
ceive from you; we coted them on the way, and hither

294. **Moult no feather**—Remain untouched.
306. **Paragon**—Model of perfection. 307. **Quintessence**—Essential.
315. **Lenten**—Scanty.   316. **Coted**—Passed.

are they coming to offer you service.　　　　　　　 317

Hamlet.　He that plays the king shall be welcome; his
majesty shall have tribute of me; the adventurous
knight shall use his foil and target; the lover shall not
sigh gratis; the humorous man shall end his part in
peace; the clown shall make those laugh whose lungs
are tickle o' the sere; and the lady shall say her mind
freely, or the blank verse shall halt for 't. What
players are they?　　　　　　　　　　　　　　 325

Rosencrantz.　Even those you were wont to take such
delight in, the tragedians of the city.

Hamlet.　How chances it they travel? their residence,
both in reputation and profit, was better both ways.

Rosencrantz.　I think their inhibition comes by the means
of the late innovation.　　　　　　　　　　　　 331

Hamlet.　Do they hold the same estimation they did when
I was in the city? are they so follow'd?

Rosencrantz.　No, indeed, they are not.

Hamlet.　How comes it? do they grow rusty?　　　 335

Rosencrantz.　Nay, their endeavour keeps in the wonted
pace; but there is, sir, an aerie of children, little eyases, that cry out on the top of question, and are most
tyrannically clapp'd for 't: these are now the fashion,

321. **Gratis**—For nothing.
323. **Tickle o' the sere**—Easily moved to laughter. (The sere was the
　　　trigger bar. If it were ticklish or lightly hung, the gun would go
　　　off easily.)　331. **Late innovation**—See page 429.
332. **Do they hold the same estimation**—Are they as popular as ever?
337. **Aerie . . . eyases**—A group of children like a brood of little un-
　　　trained falcons.
338. **Top of the question**—At the top of their lungs.

and so berattle the common stages—so they call them
—that many wearing rapiers are afraid of goose-quills
and dare scarce come thither.   342

Hamlet. What, are they children? who maintains 'em?
how are they escoted?   Will they pursue the quality
no longer than they can sing? will they not say afterwards, if they should grow themselves to common
players—as it is most like, if their means are no better
—their writers do them wrong, to make them exclaim
against their own succession?

Rosencrantz. Faith, there has been much to do on both
sides; and the nation holds it no sin to tarre them to   351
controversy; there was for a while no money bid for
argument, unless the poet and the player went to cuffs
in the question.

Hamlet. Is 't possible?   355

Guildenstern. O, there has been much throwing about of
brains.

Hamlet. Do the boys carry it away?

Rosencrantz. Ay, that they do, my lord; Hercules and his
load, too.   360

Hamlet. It is not very strange; for mine uncle is king of

344. **Escoted**—Provided for.
344. **Will they pursue . . . own succession**—Will they be actors only
      while they keep their boyish voices? Won't they finally become regu-
      lar actors, themselves, and then think the playwright wronged them
      in making them criticize their own profession?
351. **Tarre**—Encourage.   353. **Argument**—The plot of the play.
359. **Hercules**—An allusion to the figure of Hercules in front of the Globe
      Theater.   (Yes, they are even playing at the Globe.)

Denmark, and those that would make mows at him   362
while my father liv'd, give twenty, forty, fifty, an hundred ducats apiece for his picture in little. 'S blood,
there is something in this more than natural, if philosophy could find it out.

                    [*Flourish of trumpets within.*

Guildenstern. There are the players.   367

Hamlet. Gentlemen, you are welcome to Elsinore. Your
hands, come; the appurtenance of welcome is fashion
and ceremony: let me comply with you in this garb,
lest my extent to the players, which, I tell you, must
show fairly outward, should more appear like entertainment than yours. You are welcome; but my
uncle-father and aunt-mother are deceiv'd.   374

Guildenstern. In what, my dear lord?

Hamlet. I am but mad north-north-west; when the wind
is southerly I know a hawk from a handsaw.

                    Re-enter POLONIUS.

Polonius. Well be with you, gentlemen!

Hamlet. Hark you, Guildenstern; and you too; at each
ear a hearer: that great baby you see there is not yet
out of his swaddling clouts.

Rosencrantz. Happily he's the second time come to them,
for they say an old man is twice a child.   383

362. **Make mows**—Make faces.
369. **Appurtenance . . . garb**—What properly belongs to a welcome is
    fashion and ceremony. Let me greet you in this fashion.
377. **Hawk from a handsaw**—See Notes, page 430.
381. **Clouts**—Clothes.

Hamlet. I will prophesy he comes to tell me of the play-
    ers; mark it. You say right, sir: o' Monday morning;
    't was so, indeed.

Polonius. My lord, I have news to tell you.   387

Hamlet. My lord, I have news to tell you. When Roscius
    was an actor in Rome,—

Polonius. The actors are come hither, my lord.

Hamlet. Buz, buz!

Polonius. Upon mine honour,—   392

Hamlet. Then came each actor on his ass,—

Polonius. The best actors in the world, either for tragedy,
    comedy, history, pastoral, pastoral-comical, historical-
    pastoral, tragical-historical, tragical-comical-historical-
    pastoral, scene individable, or poem unlimited; Seneca
    cannot be too heavy, nor Plautus too light. For the
    law of writ and the liberty, these are the only men.   399

Hamlet. O Jephthah, judge of Israel, what a treasure
    hadst thou!

Polonius. What a treasure had he, my lord?   402

Hamlet. Why,
        One fair daughter, and no more,
        The which he loved passing well.

Polonius. [*Aside*] Still on my daughter.

Hamlet. Am I not i' th' right, old Jephthah?   407

385. **You say right**—This is said merely to confuse Polonius.
397. **Seneca, Plautus**—Latin writers of tragedy and comedy, respectively.
400. **Jephthah**—Referring to a popular Elizabethan ballad based on the
    Bible story. Jephthah, a judge in Israel, vowed to sacrifice his first-
    born if he were victorious over his enemies. His only child, a daugh-
    ter, was sacrificed.

Polonius. If you call me Jephthah, my lord, I have a
daughter that I love passing well.

Hamlet. Nay, that follows not.

Polonius. What follows, then, my lord?

Hamlet. Why,   412

As by lot, God wot,

and then you know,

It came to pass, as most like it was,—

the first row of the pious chanson will show you more;

for look where my abridgments come.   417

Enter four or five PLAYERS.

You're welcome, masters; welcome, all. I am glad to
see thee well. Welcome, good friends. O, my old
friend! Thy face is valanc'd since I saw thee last;
com'st thou to beard me in Denmark? What, my
young lady and mistress! By 'r lady, your ladyship
is nearer to heaven than when I saw you last, by the
altitude of a chopine. Pray God, your voice, like a   424
piece of uncurrent gold, be not crack'd within the
ring. Masters, you are all welcome. We'll e'en to 't
like French falconers, fly at any thing we see; we 'll

416. **Pious chanson**—The song or ballad dealing with the Bible story.
417. **Abridgments**—Those who would cut short my speech.
420. **Valanc'd**—Covered with a beard.
422. **My young lady**—The boy who was to play the woman's part.
424. **Chopine**—A high-heeled shoe.
424. **Voice**—Boys took the part of women until their voices changed.
425. **Cracked**—When an Elizabethan gold coin had become cracked too
far toward the center, it was withdrawn from circulation. (Uncurrent gold.)

have a speech straight. Come, give us a taste of your
quality; come, a passionate speech.   429

1 Player. What speech, my lord?

Hamlet. I heard thee speak me a speech once, but it was
never acted; or, if it was, not above once; for the play,
I remember, pleas'd not the million; 't was caviare to 433
the general: but it was—as I receiv'd it, and others,
whose judgments in such matters cried in the top of
mine—an excellent play, well digested in the scenes,
set down with as much modesty as cunning. I remember, one said there were no sallets in the lines to 438
make the matter savoury; nor no matter in the phrase
that might indict the author of affectation; but call'd
it an honest method, as wholesome as sweet, and by
very much more handsome than fine. One speech in
it I chiefly lov'd: 't was Æneas' tale to Dido, and there- 443
about of it especially where he speaks of Priam's
slaughter. If it live in your memory, begin at this
line; let me see, let me see—   446

'The rugged Pyrrhus, like th' Hyrcanian beast,'—

it is not so; it begins with Pyrrhus:

433. **Caviare**—This Russian delicacy, recently introduced into England,
did not appeal to the uneducated taste. Hence—anything too fine
or unusual for the common people was "caviare to the general."
438. **Sallets**—Highly seasoned salads. Here, something attractive.
443. **Æneas' tale**—This refers, of course, to the story of the fall of Troy
where both King Priam and his wife Hecuba perished. The Trojan
hero Æneas escaped and took refuge for a while with Dido, Queen
of Carthage.   447. **Pyrrhus**—A Greek hero of the Trojan War.
447. **Hyrcanian beast**—Tiger.

'The rugged Pyrrhus, he whose sable arms,
Black as his purpose, did the night resemble   450
When he lay couched in the ominous horse,
Hath now this dread and black complexion smear'd
With heraldry more dismal; head to foot
Now is he total gules, horribly trick'd
With blood of fathers, mothers, daughters, sons,   455
Bak'd and impasted with the parching streets,
That lend a tyrannous and damned light
To their lord's murder. Roasted in wrath and fire,
And thus o'ersized with coagulate gore,
With eyes like carbuncles, the hellish Pyrrhus   460
Old grandsire Priam seeks.'
So, proceed you.

Polonius. 'Fore God, my lord, well spoken, with good
accent and good discretion.

1 Player.   'Anon he finds him   465
Striking too short at Greeks; his antique sword,
Rebellious to his arm, lies where it falls,
Repugnant to command: unequal match'd,
Pyrrhus at Priam drives; in rage strikes wide;
But with the whiff and wind of his fell sword   470
Th' unnerved father falls. Then senseless Ilium,
Seeming to feel this blow, with flaming top
Stoops to his base, and with a hideous crash
Takes prisoner Pyrrhus' ear; for, lo! his sword,

---

451. **Ominous horse**—The horse that brought disaster. What trick did
the Greeks use to win the Trojan War? 454. **Gules**—Red.

Which was declining on the milky head   475
Of reverend Priam, seem'd i' the air to stick:
So, as a painted tyrant, Pyrrhus stood;
And like a neutral to his will and matter,
Did nothing.
But, as we often see, against some storm,   480
A silence in the heavens, the rack stand still,
The bold winds speechless and the orb below
As hush as death, anon the dreadful thunder
Doth rend the region; so, after Pyrrhus' pause,
Aroused vengeance sets him new a-work,   485
And never did the Cyclops' hammers fall
On Mars' armour, forg'd for proof eterne,
With less remorse than Pyrrhus' bleeding sword
Now falls on Priam.
Out, out, thou strumpet, Fortune! All you gods,   490
In general synod take away her power;
Break all the spokes and fellies from her wheel,
And bowl the round nave down the hill of heaven
As low as to the fiends!'

Polonius.   This is too long.   495

Hamlet.   It shall to the barber's with your beard. Prithee,
    say on; come to Hecuba.

1 Player.   'But who, O, who had seen the mobled
        queen—'

486. **Cyclops**—One-eyed giants who helped Vulcan, the god of fire, in his
    workshop.   491. **Synod**—Council or conference.
492. **Fellies**—The parts of the outside rim of a wheel.
493. **Nave**—The hub.

Hamlet. 'The mobled queen?'

Polonius. That's good; 'mobled queen' is good.   500

1 Player. 'Run barefoot up and down, threatening the
     flames
     With bisson rheum; a clout upon that head
     Where late the diadem stood; and for a robe,
     About her lank and all o'er-teemed loins
     A blanket, in th' alarm of fear caught up;   505
     Who this had seen, with tongue in venom steep'd
     'Gainst Fortune's state would treason have pro-
         nounc'd:
     But if the gods themselves did see her then,
     When she saw Pyrrhus make malicious sport
     In mincing with his sword her husband's limbs,   510
     The instant burst of clamour that she made,
     Unless things mortal move them not at all,
     Would have made milch the burning eyes of heaven
     And passion in the gods.'

Polonius. Look, where he has not turn'd his colour and
     has tears in 's eyes. Pray you, no more.   516

Hamlet. 'T is well; I 'll have thee speak out the rest of
     this soon. Good my lord, will you see the players well
     bestow'd? Do ye hear, let them be well us'd, for they
     are the abstracts and brief chronicles of the time; after

499. **Mobled**—Muffled.
502. **Bisson rheum**—Blinding tears.   515. **Where**—Whether.
519. **Bestow'd**—Taken care of.
520. **Abstracts**—The stage presented important events of the times. (Eliza-
     bethan players were sometimes fined for attacking current abuses
     and satirizing persons or events.)

your death you were better have a bad epitaph than
their ill report while you liv'd.   522

Polonius.   My lord, I will use them according to their
desert.

Hamlet.   God's bodykins, man, much better! use every
man after his desert, and who should scape whipping?   Use them after your own honour and dignity;
the less they deserve, the more merit is in your
bounty. Take them in.   529

Polonius.   Come, sirs.

Hamlet.   Follow him, friends; we 'll hear a play tomorrow.

> [*Exit* Polonius *with all the* Players *but the First.*

Dost thou hear me, old friend? can you play the Murder of Gonzago?

1 Player.   Ay, my lord.   535

Hamlet.   We 'll ha 't to-morrow night. You could, for a
need, study a speech of some dozen or sixteen lines,
which I would set down and insert in 't, could ye not?

1 Player.   Ay, my lord.

Hamlet.   Very well. Follow that lord; and look you
mock him not. [*Exit the* Player] My good friends,
I'll leave you till night; you are welcome to Elsinore. 542

Rosencrantz.   Good my lord!

Hamlet.   Ay, so, God be wi' ye!

> [*Exeunt* Rosencrantz *and* Guildenstern.
> Now I am alone.

524. **Desert**—Worth, reward or punishment due.

O, what a rogue and peasant slave am I!   545
Is it not monstrous that this player here,
But in a fiction, in a dream of passion,
Could force his soul so to his own conceit
That from her working all his visage wann'd,
Tears in his eyes, distraction in 's aspect,   550
A broken voice, and his whole function suiting
With forms to his conceit? and all for nothing!
For Hecuba!
What 's Hecuba to him, or he to Hecuba,
That he should weep for her? What would he do,   555
Had he the motive and the cue for passion
That I have?   He would drown the stage with tears
And cleave the general ear with horrid speech,
Make mad the guilty and appall the free,
Confound the ignorant, and amaze indeed   560
The very faculty of eyes and ears. Yet I,
A dull and muddy-mettl'd rascal, peak,
Like John-a-dreams, unpregnant of my cause,
And can say nothing; no, not for a king,
Upon whose property and most dear life   565
A damn'd defeat was made. Am I a coward?
Who calls me villain? breaks my pate across?
Plucks off my beard, and blows it in my face?

548. **Conceit**—Idea.   549. **Visage wann'd**—His face grew pale.
562. **Muddy-mettl'd rascal**—Slow-witted member of the rabble.   (Early
        meaning of *rascal*.)   562. **Peak**—Grown thin.
563. **John-a-dreams**—An idler, a dreamer.
563. **Unpregnant of**—Not inspired with.   567. **Pate**—Crown of the head.

Tweaks me by th' nose? gives me the lie i' the throat,
As deep as to the lungs? who does me this?   570
Ha!
'Swounds, I should take it; for it cannot be
But I am pigeon-liver'd and lack gall
To make oppression bitter, or ere this
I should have fatted all the region kites   575
With this slave's offal. Bloody, bawdy villain!
Remorseless, treacherous, lecherous, kindless villain!
O, vengeance!
Why, what an ass am I! Sure, this is most brave,
That I, the son of a dear father murder'd,   580
Prompted to my revenge by heaven and hell,
Must unpack my heart with words,
And fall a-cursing, like a very drab,
A scullion!
Fie upon 't! foh! About, my brain! I have heard   585
That guilty creatures sitting at a play
Have by the very cunning of the scene
Been struck so to the soul that presently
They have proclaim'd their malefactions;
For murder, though it have no tongue, will speak   590
With most miraculous organ. I 'll have these players
Play something like the murder of my father
Before mine uncle: I 'll observe his looks;
I 'll tent him to the quick: if he but blench,

575. **Kites**—Birds of the hawk family.   577. **Kindless**—Unnatural.
594. **Tent**—Probe, try.

I know my course. The spirit that I have seen   595
May be the devil; and the devil hath power
T' assume a pleasing shape; yea, and perhaps
Out of my weakness and my melancholy,
As he is very potent with such spirits,
Abuses me to damn me. I'll have grounds   600
More relative than this. The play 's the thing
Wherein I 'll catch the conscience of the king.   [*Exit.*

601. **Relative**—Conclusive.

ACT THREE

Scene I

A room in the castle. Enter King, Queen, Polonius,
Ophelia, Rosencrantz, *and* Guildenstern.

King. And can you, by no drift of circumstance,
   Get from him why he puts on this confusion,
   Grating so harshly all his days of quiet
   With turbulent and dangerous lunacy?
Rosencrantz. He does confess he feels himself distracted;
   But from what cause he will by no means speak.   6
Guildenstern. Nor do we find him forward to be sounded,
   But, with a crafty madness, keeps aloof,
   When we would bring him on to some confession
   Of his true state.
Queen.   Did he receive you well?   10
Rosencrantz. Most like a gentleman.
Guildenstern. But with much forcing of his disposition.
Rosencrantz. Niggard of question, but of our demands
   Most free in his reply.
Queen.   Did you assay him
   To any pastime?   15

1. **Drift of circumstance**—Roundabout means.
7. **Forward to be sounded**—Inclined to be questioned.
13. **Niggard**—Stingy.   14. **Assay**—Try, tempt.

Rosencrantz. Madam, it so fell out that certain players
    We o'er-raught on the way; of these we told him,   17
    And there did seem in him a kind of joy
    To hear of it. They are about the court,
    And, as I think, they have already order   20
    This night to play before him.

Polonius.   'T is most true;
    And he beseech'd me to entreat your majesties
    To hear and see the matter.

King. With all my heart; and it doth much content me
    To hear him so inclin'd.
    Good gentlemen, give him a further edge,   26
    And drive his purpose on to these delights.

Rosencrantz. We shall, my lord.

                [*Exeunt* ROSENCRANTZ *and* GUILDENSTERN.

King.   Sweet Gertrude, leave us too;
    For we have closely sent for Hamlet hither,
    That he, as 't were by accident, may here   30
    Affront Ophelia.
    Her father and myself, lawful espials,
    Will so bestow ourselves that, seeing unseen,
    We may of their encounter frankly judge,
    And gather by him, as he is behav'd,   35
    If 't be th' affliction of his love or no
    That thus he suffers for.

17. **O'er-raught**—Overtook.
26. **Give him a further edge**—Urge him still further.
29. **Closely**—Secretly. 31. **Affront**—Meet. 32. **Espials**—Spies.
33. **Bestow**—Hide.

Queen.   I shall obey you.
    And for your part, Ophelia, I do wish
    That your good beauties be the happy cause
    Of Hamlet's wildness; so shall I hope your virtues   40
    Will bring him to his wonted way again,
    To both your honours.
Ophelia.   Madam, I wish it may.

                                            [*Exit* Queen.

Polonius.   Ophelia, walk you here.   Gracious, so please
        you,
    We will bestow ourselves.   [*To* Ophelia]   Read on
        this book;
    That show of such an exercise may colour   45
    Your loneliness.   We are oft to blame in this—
    'T is too much prov'd—that with devotion's visage
    And pious action we do sugar o'er
    The devil himself.
King.   [*Aside*]   O, 't is too true!
    How smart a lash that speech doth give my con-
        science!   50
    The harlot's cheek, beautied with plastering art,
    Is not more ugly to the thing that helps it
    Than is my deed to my most painted word.
    A heavy burden!
Polonius.   I hear him coming; let 's withdraw, my lord.

                            [*Exeunt* King *and* Polonius.

                Enter Hamlet.

Hamlet.   To be, or not to be,—that is the question;
  Whether 't is nobler in the mind to suffer
  The slings and arrows of outrageous fortune,
  Or to take arms against a sea of troubles,
  And by opposing end them. To die,—to sleep,—   60
  No more; and by a sleep to say we end
  The heart-ache and the thousand natural shocks
  That flesh is heir to,—'t is a consummation
  Devoutly to be wish'd. To die,—to sleep,—
  To sleep! perchance to dream! ay, there, there 's the
    rub;   65
  For in that sleep of death what dreams may come
  When we have shuffl'd off this mortal coil,
  Must give us pause: there 's the respect
  That makes calamity of so long life;
  For who would bear the whips and scorns of time,   70
  The oppressor's wrong, the proud man's contumely,
  The pangs of dispriz'd love, the law's delay,
  The insolence of office, and the spurns
  That patient merit of the unworthy takes,
  When he himself might his quietus make   75
  With a bare bodkin? who would these fardels bear,
  To grunt and sweat under a weary life,
  But that the dread of something after death,
  The undiscover'd country from whose bourn
  No traveller returns, puzzles the will,   80

63. **Consummation**—Outcome.
71. **Contumely**—Contempt, rudeness. 76. **Bodkin**—Dagger.
76. **Fardels**—Burdens. 79. **Bourn**—Boundaries.

"To be, or not to be, —"
*Laurence Olivier as Hamlet in
the Screen Production*

And makes us rather bear those ills we have
Than fly to others that we know not of?
Thus conscience does make cowards of us all;
And thus the native hue of resolution
Is sicklied o'er with the pale cast of thought,   85
And enterprises of great pith and moment
With this regard their currents turn awry,
And lose the name of action. Soft you now!
The fair Ophelia! Nymph, in thy orisons
Be all my sins remember'd.

Ophelia.   Good my lord,   90
How does your honour for this many a day?

Hamlet. I humbly thank you; well, well, well.

Ophelia. My lord, I have remembrances of yours,
That I have longed long to re-deliver;
I pray you, now receive them.

Hamlet.   No, not I;   95
I never gave you aught.

Ophelia. My honour'd lord, I know right well you did;
And with them words of so sweet breath compos'd
As made the things more rich: their perfume lost,
Take these again; for to the noble mind   100
Rich gifts wax poor when givers prove unkind.
There, my lord.

Hamlet. Ha, ha! are you honest?

Ophelia. My lord!

Hamlet. Are you fair?   105

89. **Orisons**—Prayers.

Ophelia.   What means your lordship?

Hamlet.   That if you be honest and fair, your honesty
should admit no discourse to your beauty.

Ophelia.   Could beauty, my lord, have better commerce
than with honesty?   110

Hamlet.   Ay, truly; for the power of beauty will sooner
transform honesty from what it is to a bawd than the
force of honesty can translate beauty into his likeness:
this was sometime a paradox, but now the time gives
it proof.   I did love you once.   115

Ophelia.   Indeed, my lord, you made me believe so.

Hamlet.   You should not have believ'd me, for virtue
cannot so inoculate our old stock but we shall relish of
it; I lov'd you not.

Ophelia.   I was the more deceiv'd   120

Hamlet.   Get thee to a nunnery; why wouldst thou be
a breeder of sinners?   I am myself indifferent honest,
but yet I could accuse me of such things that it were
better my mother had not borne me.   I am very proud,
revengeful, ambitious, with more offences at my beck
than I have thoughts to put them in, imagination to
give them shape, or time to act them in.   What should
such fellows as I do crawling between heaven and
earth?   We are arrant knaves all; believe none of
us.   Go thy ways to a nunnery.   Where 's your father? 130

Ophelia.   At home, my lord.

Hamlet.   Let the doors be shut upon him, that he may

109. **Commerce**—Dealings with.

play the fool no where but in 's own house. Farewell.

Ophelia. O, help him, you sweet heavens!   134

Hamlet. If thou dost marry, I'll give thee this plague
for thy dowry: be thou as chaste as ice, as pure as
snow, thou shalt not escape calumny. Get thee to a
nunnery, go; farewell. Or, if thou wilt needs marry,
marry a fool; for wise men know well enough what
monsters you make of them. To a nunnery, go;
and quickly too. Farewell.   141

Ophelia. O heavenly powers, restore him!

Hamlet. I have heard of your paintings too, well enough;
God has given you one face, and you make yourselves
another: you jig, you amble, and you lisp, and nick-
name God's creatures, and make your wantonness 146
your ignorance. Go to, I'll no more on 't; it hath
made me mad. I say, we will have no more mar-
riages: those that are married already, all but one,
shall live; the rest shall keep as they are. To a
nunnery, go.   [*Exit.*

Ophelia. O, what a noble mind is here o'erthrown!   152
The courtier's, soldier's, scholar's, eye, tongue, sword;
Th' expectancy and rose of the fair state,
The glass of fashion and the mould of form,
Th' observ'd of all observers, quite, quite down!
And I, of ladies most deject and wretched,
That suck'd the honey of his music vows,

137. **Calumny**—Evil gossip, slander.   143. **Paintings**—See page 430.
146. **Make your wantonness your ignorance**—Perhaps, pretend that
what you do intentionally is done unknowingly.

Now see that noble and most sovereign reason,
Like sweet bells jangled out of tune and harsh;   160
That unmatch'd form and feature of blown youth
Blasted with ecstasy   O, woe is me,
T' have seen what I have seen, see what I see!

Re-enter KING *and* POLONIUS.

King. Love! his affections do not that way tend;
Nor what he spake, though it lack'd form a little,   165
Was not like madness. There 's something in his soul
O'er which his melancholy sits on brood,
And I do doubt the hatch and the disclose
Will be some danger; which for to prevent,
I have in quick determination   170
Thus set it down: he shall with speed to England,
For the demand of our neglected tribute.
Haply the seas and countries different
With variable objects shall expel
This something-settled matter in his heart,   175
Whereon his brains still beating puts him thus
From fashion of himself. What think you on 't?
Polonius. It shall do well; but yet do I believe
The origin and commencement of his grief
Sprung from neglected love. How now, Ophelia!   180
You need not tell us what Lord Hamlet said;
We heard it all. My lord, do as you please,

168. **Doubt the hatch and the disclose**—I fear that when this hidden
purpose is revealed there will be danger.

But, if you hold it fit, after the play
Let his queen mother all alone entreat him
To show his grief: let her be round with him;   185
And I'll be plac'd, so please you, in the ear
Of all their conference. If she find him not,
To England send him, or confine him where
Your wisdom best shall think.

King.   It shall be so;
Madness in great ones must not unwatch'd go.   [*Exeunt.*

Scene II

A hall in the castle. Enter Hamlet *and* Players.

Hamlet. Speak the speech, I pray you, as I pronounc'd   1
it to you, trippingly on the tongue; but if you mouth
it, as many of your players do, I had as lief the town-
crier spoke my lines. Nor do not saw the air too
much with your hand, thus, but use all gently; for
in the very torrent, tempest, and, as I may say, the
whirlwind of passion, you must acquire and beget a
temperance that may give it smoothness. O, it offends
me to the soul to hear a robustious periwig-pated fel-   9
low tear a passion to tatters, to very rags, to split
the ears of the groundlings, who for the most part are

9. **Robustious**—Noisy.
9. **Periwig-pated**—Wigged. (In Shakespeare's time, only actors wore wigs.)
11. **Groundlings**—The rabble who stood just below the stage, in what is now the orchestra.

capable of nothing but inexplicable dumb-shows and
noise. I would have such a fellow whipp'd for o'er-
doing Termagant; it out-herods Herod; pray you,
avoid it.   15

1 Player. I warrant your honour.

Hamlet. Be not too tame neither, but let your own discretion be your tutor; suit the action to the word, the
word to the action; with this special observance, that
you o'erstep not the modesty of nature; for any thing
so overdone is from the purpose of playing, whose end,
both at the first and now, was and is, to hold, as 't were,
the mirror up to nature; to show virtue her own feature, scorn her own image, and the very age and body
of the time his form and pressure. Now this overdone, or come tardy off, though it make the unskilful
laugh, cannot but make the judicious grieve; the
censure of the which one must in your allowance
o'erweigh a whole theater of others. O, there be
players that I have seen play, and heard others
praise, and that highly, not to speak it profanely,
that, neither having the accent of Christians nor the
gait of Christian, pagan, nor man, have so strutted
and bellow'd that I have thought some of nature's
journeymen had made men and not made them well,
they imitated humanity so abominably.   36

14. **Termagant**—A Saracen god, represented as a violent character.
14. **Herod**—In the miracle plays, the Herod from the New Testament was
always a loud, boastful person.

1 Player. I hope we have reform'd that indifferently
with us, sir.

Hamlet. O, reform it altogether. And let those that play
your clowns speak no more than is set down for them;
for there be of them that will themselves laugh to set
on some quantity of barren spectators to laugh too,
though in the meantime some necessary question of   43
the play be then to be consider'd: that's villainous, and
shows a most pitiful ambition in the fool that uses
it. Go, make you ready.   46

                               [Exeunt PLAYERS.

  Enter POLONIUS, ROSENCRANTZ, *and* GUILDENSTERN.

How now, my lord! will the king hear this piece of
work?

Polonius. And the queen too, and that presently.

Hamlet. Bid the players make haste.   *[Exit* POLONIUS.
Will you two help to hasten them?   51

Rosencrantz. }
Guildenstern. } We will, my lord.

        [Exeunt ROSENCRANTZ *and* GUILDENSTERN.

Hamlet. What, ho, Horatio!

              Enter HORATIO.

Horatio. Here, sweet lord, at your service.

Hamlet. Horatio, thou art e'en as just a man   55
As e'er my conversation cop'd withal.

Horatio. O, my dear lord,—

Hamlet.   Nay, do not think I flatter,

  43. **Question**—Speech.

For what advancement may I hope from thee
That no revenue hast but thy good spirits
To feed and clothe thee? Why should the poor be
    flatter'd?   60
No, let the candied tongue lick absurd pomp,
And crook the pregnant hinges of the knee
Where thrift may follow fawning. Dost thou hear?
Since my dear soul was mistress of her choice
And could of men distinguish, her election   65
Hath seal'd thee for herself; for thou hast been
As one, in suffering all, that suffers nothing,
A man that fortune's buffets and rewards
Hast ta'en with equal thanks; and blest are those
Whose blood and judgment are so well commingl'd,   70
That they are not a pipe for fortune's finger
To sound what stop she please. Give me that man
That is not passion's slave, and I will wear him
In my heart's core, ay, in my heart of heart,
As I do thee. Something too much of this.   75
There is a play to-night before the king;
One scene of it comes near the circumstance
Which I have told thee of my father's death.
I prithee, when thou seest that act afoot,
Even with the very comment of thy soul   80
Observe my uncle. If his occulted guilt
Do not itself unkennel in one speech,

59. **Revenue**—Income.
81. **Occulted**—Hidden.   82. **Unkennel**—Disclose, reveal.

It is a damned ghost that we have seen,
And my imaginations are as foul
As Vulcan's stithy. Give him heedful note;   85
For I mine eyes will rivet to his face,
And after we will both our judgments join
In censure of his seeming.

Horatio.   Well, my lord;
If he steal aught the whilst this play is playing,
And 'scape detecting, I will pay the theft.   .   90

Danish march. A flourish. Enter KING, QUEEN, POLONIUS,
OPHELIA, ROSENCRANTZ, GUILDENSTERN, *and other* Lords
attendant, with the Guard *carrying torches.*

Hamlet. They are coming to the play; I must be idle.
Get you a place.

King. How fares our cousin Hamlet?

Hamlet. Excellent, i' faith; of the chameleon's dish. I
eat the air, promise-cramm'd; you cannot feed capons
so.   96

King. I have nothing with this answer, Hamlet; these
words are not mine.

Hamlet. No, nor mine now. [*To* POLONIUS] My lord,
you play'd once i' th' university, you say?   100

Polonius. That did I, my lord, and was accounted a good
actor.

Hamlet. And what did you enact?

Polonius. I did enact Julius Cæsar; I was kill'd i' th'

---

85. **Vulcan's stithy**—The anvil or forge of Vulcan (god of fire).
91. **Must be idle**—Must seem to be disengaged.
94. **Chameleon's dish**—The chameleon was supposed to live on air.

Capitol; Brutus kill'd me.

Hamlet. It was a brute part of him to kill so capital a
  calf there. Be the players ready?

Rosencrantz. Ay, my lord; they stay upon your patience.

Queen. Come hither, my dear Hamlet, sit by me.   109

Hamlet. No, good mother, here 's metal more attractive.

                    [*Lying down at* Ophelia's *feet.*

Polonius. [*To the* King] Oh, ho! do you mark that?

Ophelia. You are merry, my lord.

Hamlet. Who, I?

Ophelia. Ay, my lord.   114

Hamlet. O God, your only jig-maker. What should a
  man do but be merry? for, look you, how cheerfully
  my mother looks, and my father died within 's two
  hours.   118

Ophelia. Nay, 't is twice two months, my lord.

Hamlet. So long? Nay then, let the devil wear black,
  for I 'll have a suit of sables. O heavens! die two
  months ago, and not forgotten yet? Then there 's
  hope a great man's memory may outlive his life half
  a year; but, by 'r lady, he must build churches then,
  or else shall he suffer not thinking on, with the
  hobby-horse, whose epitaph is, 'For, O, for, O, the
  hobby-horse is forgot.'   127

          Hautboys Play. The dumb-show enters.

120. **Wear black ... sables**—I will put aside my mourning garb and wear
     rich furs.
126. **Hobby-horse**—A figure used in the morris dances. See page 431.

"The play's the thing wherein I'll catch the conscience of the king."

From Leslie Howard's Hamlet

Enter a King *and* Queen *very lovingly; the* Queen *embracing him. She kneels and makes show of protestation unto him. He takes her up, and declines his head upon her neck; lays him down upon a bank of flowers. She, seeing him asleep, leaves him. Anon comes in a fellow, takes off his crown, kisses it, and pours poison in the* King's *ears, and exit. The* Queen *returns, finds the* King *dead, and makes passionate action. The poisoner, with some two or three Mutes, comes in again, seeming to lament with her. The dead body is carried away. The poisoner woos the* Queen *with gifts; she seems unwilling awhile, but in the end accepts his love.* [*Exeunt.*

Ophelia. What means this, my lord?

Hamlet. Marry, this is miching mallecho; it means mischief. 130

Ophelia. Belike this show imports the argument of the play.

Enter Prologue.

Hamlet. We shall know by this fellow. The players cannot keep counsel; they 'll tell all.

Ophelia. Will he tell us what this show meant? 135

Hamlet. Ay, or any show that you 'll show him; be not you asham'd to show, he 'll not shame to tell you what it means.

Ophelia. You are naught, you are naught. I 'll mark the play. 140

129. **Miching mallecho**—Secret mischief. 132. **Prologue**—See page 431.

Prologue. For us, and for our tragedy,
          Here stooping to your clemency,
          We beg your hearing patiently.   [*Exit.*
Hamlet. Is this a prologue, or the posy of a ring?
Ophelia. 'T is brief, my lord.   145
Hamlet. As woman's love.

          Enter two PLAYERS, KING *and* QUEEN.

Player King. Full thirty times hath Phœbus' cart gone
          round
     Neptune's salt wash and Tellus' orbed ground,
     And thirty dozen moons with borrowed sheen
     About the world have times twelve thirties been,   150
     Since love our hearts and Hymen did our hands
     Unite commutual in most sacred bands.
Player Queen. So many journeys may the sun and moon
     Make us again count o'er ere love be done!
     But, woe is me! you are so sick of late,   155
     So far from cheer and from your former state,
     That I distrust you. Yet, though I distrust,
     Discomfort you, my lord, it nothing must;
     For women's fear and love holds quantity,
     In neither aught, or in extremity.   160
     Now, what my love is, proof hath made you know;

147. **Phœbus' cart**—The sun.
148. **Neptune's salt wash**—The sea.
148. **Tellus' orbed ground**—The earth.
151. **Hymen**—Greek god of marriage.
152. **Commutual**—Emphatic form of mutual.

And as my love is siz'd, my fear is so:
Where love is great, the littlest doubts are fear;
Where little fears grow great, great love grows there.

Player King. Faith, I must leave thee, love, and shortly
      too;   165
My operant powers their functions leave to do:
And thou shalt live in this fair world behind,
Honour'd, belov'd; and haply one as kind
For husband shalt thou—

Player Queen.   O, confound the rest!
Such love must needs be treason in my breast;   170
In second husband let me be accurst!
None wed the second but who kill'd the first.

Hamlet. [*Aside*] Wormwood, wormwood.

Player Queen. The instances that second marriage move
Are base respects of thrift, but none of love.   175
A second time I kill my husband dead
When second husband kisses me in bed.

Player King. I do believe you think what now you speak,
But what we do determine oft we break.
Purpose is but the slave to memory,   180
Of violent birth, but poor validity;
Which now, like fruit unripe, sticks on the tree,
But fall unshaken when they mellow be.
Most necessary 't is that we forget
To pay ourselves what to ourselves is debt;   185

166 **Operant powers**—Active powers.

What to ourselves in passion we propose,
The passion ending, doth the purpose lose.
The violence of either grief or joy
Their own enactures with themselves destroy:
Where joy most revels, grief doth most lament;   190
Grief joys, joy grieves, on slender accident.
This world is not for aye, nor 't is not strange
That even our loves should with our fortunes change;
For 't is a question left us yet to prove,
Whether love lead fortune, or else fortune love.   195
The great man down, you mark his favourite flies;
The poor advanc'd makes friends of enemies:
And hitherto doth love on fortune tend;
For who not needs shall never lack a friend,
And who in want a hollow friend doth try,   200
Directly seasons him his enemy.
But, orderly to end where I begun,
Our wills and fates do so contrary run
That our devices still are overthrown;
Our thoughts are ours, their ends none of our own.
So think thou wilt no second husband wed;   206
But die thy thoughts when thy first lord is dead.
Player Queen. Nor earth to me give food, nor heaven
        light!
Sport and repose lock from me day and night!
To desperation turn my trust and hope!   210
An anchor's cheer in prison be my scope!

201. **Seasons**—Makes. 211. **Anchor**—Hermit.

Each opposite that blanks the face of joy
Meet what I would have well, and it destroy!
Both here and hence pursue me lasting strife,
If, once a widow, ever I be wife!   215

Hamlet. If she should break it now!

Player King. 'T is deeply sworn. Sweet, leave me here
    awhile.
My spirits grow dull, and fain I would beguile
The tedious day with sleep.   [*Sleeps.*
Player Queen.   Sleep rock thy brain;
    And never come mischance between us twain!   [*Exit.*
Hamlet. Madam, how like you this play?   221
Queen. The lady doth protest too much, methinks.
Hamlet. O, but she 'll keep her word.
King. Have you heard the argument? Is there no
    offence in 't?
Hamlet. No, no, they do but jest, poison in jest; no of-
    fence i' th' world.
King. What do you call the play?   228
Hamlet. The Mouse-trap. Marry, how? Tropically.
This play is the image of a murder done in Vienna.
Gonzago is the duke's name; his wife, Baptista. You
shall see anon; 't is a knavish piece of work, but what
o' that? your majesty and we that have free souls, it

218. **Fain I would beguile**—I would be happy to relieve the tiresome day.
224. **Argument**—Summary of the plot. 229. **Tropically**—Figuratively.

touches us not. Let the gall'd jade wince, our withers
are unwrung.   235

Enter LUCIANUS.

This is one Lucianus, nephew to the king.

Ophelia. You are as good as a chorus, my lord.

Hamlet. I could interpret between you and your love,
if I could see the puppets dallying.

Ophelia. You are keen, my lord, you are keen.   240

Hamlet. Begin, murderer; pox! leave thy damnable faces,
and begin. Come: 'The croaking raven doth bellow
for revenge.'

Lucianus. Thoughts black, hands apt, drugs fit, and time
agreeing;

Confederate season, else no creature seeing.   245
Thou mixture rank, of midnight weeds collected,
With Hecate's ban thrice blasted, thrice infected,
Thy natural magic and dire property
On wholesome life usurp immediately.

[Pours the poison into the sleeper's ears.

Hamlet. He poisons him i' th' garden for 's estate. His
name's Gonzago; the story is extant, and writ in choice 251
Italian. You shall see anon how the murderer gets

---

234. **Gall'd jade**—Horse with sores. A jade also refers to a worthless man.
This is another of Shakespeare's puns. 235. **Unwrung**—Untouched.
237. **Chorus**—The chorus of a play often explained the action.
239. **Puppets dallying**—In a puppet show, the interpreter sat on the stage
and explained the actions of the puppets. If Ophelia and her love
were to act such a play, Hamlet could explain it.
247. **Hecate**—Dark goddess of magic. 251. **Extant**—Still in existence.

the love of Gonzago's wife.   253
Ophelia. The king rises!
Hamlet. What, frighted with false fire!
Queen. How fares my lord?
Polonius. Give o'er the play.
King. Give me some light! Away!
All. Lights, lights, lights!

[*Exeunt all but* Hamlet *and* Horatio.

Hamlet. Why, let the strucken deer go weep,   260
    The hart ungalled play;
  For some must watch while some must sleep:
    So runs the world away.
Would not this, sir, and a forest of feathers—if the
rest of my fortunes turn Turk with me—with two
Provincial roses on my raz'd shoes, get me a fellow-
ship in a cry of players, sir?   267

Horatio. Half a share.

Hamlet. A whole one, I.
    For thou dost know, O Damon dear,
      This realm dismantl'd was
    Of Jove himself; and now reigns here
      A very, very—pajock.

Horatio. You might have rhym'd.   274

Hamlet. O good Horatio, I 'll take the ghost's word for a
thousand pound. Didst perceive?

261. **Hart ungalled**—The uninjured stag.
264. **Would not this . . . players**—If my fortunes should fare badly,
    would not this dramatizing of mine, combined with the extravagant
    dress of an actor, admit me to a company of players?
273. **Pajock**—Possibly, peacock.

Horatio. Very well, my lord.

Hamlet. Upon the talk of the poisoning?

Horatio. I did very well note him.

Hamlet. Ah, ha! Come, some music! Come, the re-
corders!   281

>   For if the king like not the comedy,
>   Why, then, belike, he likes it not, perdy.

Come, some music!

Re-enter ROSENCRANTZ *and* GUILDENSTERN.

Guildenstern. Good my lord, vouchsafe me a word with
you.   286

Hamlet. Sir, a whole history.

Guildenstern. The king, sir,—

Hamlet. Ay, sir, what of him?

Guildenstern. Is in his retirement marvellous distem-
per'd.   291

Hamlet. With drink, sir?

Guildenstern. No, my lord, rather with choler.

Hamlet. Your wisdom should show itself more richer
to signify this to his doctor; for, for me to put him to
his purgation would perhaps plunge him into far 296
more choler.

Guildenstern. Good my lord, put your discourse into
some frame, and start not so wildly from my affair.

280. **Recorders**—A kind of flute.
283. **Perdy**—A shortened form of *par Dieu,* a curse.
290. **Distemper'd**—Disturbed.   293. **Choler**—Anger.
296. **Purgation**—Cleansing.

Hamlet. I am tame, sir; pronounce.   300

Guildenstern. The queen, your mother, in most great
  affliction of spirit, hath sent me to you.

Hamlet. You are welcome.

Guildenstern. Nay, good my lord, this courtesy is not of
  the right breed. If it shall please you to make me a
  wholesome answer, I will do your mother's commandment; if not, your pardon and my return shall
  be the end of my business.

Hamlet. Sir, I cannot.

Guildenstern. What, my lord?   310

Hamlet. Make you a wholesome answer; my wit 's dis-
  eas'd: but, sir, such answer as I can make, you shall
  command; or, rather, as you say, my mother: therefore no more, but to the matter. My mother, you
  say,—   315

Rosencrantz. Then thus she says: your behaviour hath
  struck her into amazement and admiration.

Hamlet. O wonderful son, that can so astonish a mother!
  But is there no sequel at the heels of this mother's
  admiration? Impart.   320

Rosencrantz. She desires to speak with you in her closet
  ere you go to bed.

Hamlet. We shall obey, were she ten times our mother.
  Have you any further trade with us?

Rosencrantz. My lord, you once did love me.   325

Hamlet. So I do still, by these pickers and stealers.

300. **Tame**—Composed, quiet.   326. **Pickers and stealers**—His hands.

Rosencrantz. Good my lord, what is your cause of distemper? you do surely bar the door upon your own
liberty, if you deny your griefs to your friend.

Hamlet. Sir, I lack advancement.   330

Rosencrantz. How can that be, when you have the voice
of the king himself for your succession in Denmark?

Hamlet. Ay, sir, but, 'While the grass grows,'—the
proverb is something musty.

Re-enter PLAYERS *with recorders.*

O, the recorders! let me see one.—To withdraw with
you:—why do you go about to recover the wind of
me, as if you would drive me into a toil?   337

Guildenstern. O, my lord, if my duty be too bold, my
love is too unmannerly.

Hamlet. I do not well understand that. Will you play
upon this pipe?   341

Guildenstern. My lord, I cannot.

Hamlet. I pray you.

Guildenstern. Believe me, I cannot.

Hamlet. I do beseech you.

Guildenstern. I know no touch of it, my lord.

Hamlet. 'T is as easy as lying. Govern these ventages 347
with your fingers and thumb, give it breath with your

333. **While the grass grows**—The proverb is, "While the grass grows, the
horse starves." (Hamlet must wait for the king's death before he
can have the throne.)

336. **Why . . . recover the wind of me . . . toil**—Why do you try to
get on the windward side, as if you were driving me into a trap?

347. **Ventages**—Holes of the pipe.

mouth, and it will discourse most eloquent music.
Look you, these are the stops.   350

Guildenstern. But these cannot I command to any utter-
ance of harmony; I have not the skill.

Hamlet. Why, look you now, how unworthy a thing you
make of me! You would play upon me; you would
seem to know my stops; you would pluck out the
heart of my mystery; you would sound me from my
lowest note to the top of my compass: and there is 357
much music, excellent voice, in this little organ; yet
cannot you make it speak. 'Sblood, do you think I am
easier to be play'd on than a pipe? Call me what
instrument you will, though you can fret me, you
cannot play upon me.   362

Re-enter Polonius.

God bless you, sir!

Polonius. My lord, the queen would speak with you, and
presently.

Hamlet. Do you see yonder cloud that 's almost in shape
of a camel?

Polonius. By th' mass, and 't is like a camel, indeed.

Hamlet. Methinks it is like a weasel.   370

Polonius. It is back'd like a weasel.

Hamlet. Or like a whale?

Polonius. Very like a whale.

357. **Compass**—Range.
361. **Fret**—Here is another pun. Fret, to vex; fret is also a bar on the fin-
    ger board of certain musical instruments to mark the fingering.

Hamlet.   Then will I come to my mother by and by.
   [*Aside*] They fool me to the top of my bent.—I will
   come by and by.   375
Polonius.   I will say so.   [*Exit* Polonius.
Hamlet.   'By and by' is easily said.   Leave me, friends.
                      [*Exeunt all but* Hamlet.
   'T is now the very witching time of night,
   When churchyards yawn and hell itself breathes out
   Contagion to this world. Now could I drink hot blood,
   And do such bitter business as the day   381
   Would quake to look on.   Soft! now to my mother.
   O heart, lose not thy nature; let not ever
   The soul of Nero enter this firm bosom;
   Let me be cruel, not unnatural.   385
   I will speak daggers to her, but use none;
   My tongue and soul in this be hypocrites;
   How in my words soever she be shent,
   To give them seals never, my soul, consent!   [*Exit.*

Scene III

A room in the castle.   Enter King, Rosencrantz, *and*
  Guildenstern.

King.   I like him not, nor stands it safe with us
   To let his madness range.   Therefore prepare you.

374. **Top of my bent**—To the utmost.
384. **Soul of Nero**—A very cruel Roman emperor who murdered his mother.
388. **Shent**—Reproached.   389. **Give seals**—Confirm by action.

I your commission will forthwith dispatch,
And he to England shall along with you.
The terms of our estate may not endure   5
Hazard so dangerous as doth hourly grow
Out of his lunacies.

Guildenstern.   We will ourselves provide;
Most holy and religious fear it is
To keep those many many bodies safe
That live and feed upon your majesty.   10

Rosencrantz. The single and peculiar life is bound
With all the strength and armour of the mind
To keep itself from noyance, but much more
That spirit upon whose weal depends and rests
The lives of many. The cease of majesty   15
Dies not alone, but like a gulf doth draw
What's near it with it. It is a massy wheel,
Fix'd on the summit of the highest mount,
To whose huge spokes ten thousand lesser things
Are mortis'd and adjoin'd; which when it falls, 20
Each small annexment, petty consequence,
Attends the boisterous ruin. Never alone
Did the king sigh, but with a general groan.

King. Arm you, I pray you, to this speedy voyage;
For we will fetters put upon this fear,   25
Which now goes too free-footed.

Rosencrantz. ⎫
Guildenstern. ⎭   We will haste us.

[*Exeunt* Rosencrantz *and* Guildenstern.

13. **Noyance**—Injury.

Enter POLONIUS.

Polonius. My lord, he's going to his mother's closet.
      Behind the arras I 'll convey myself,
      To hear the process; I 'll warrant she 'll tax him home:
      And, as you said, and wisely was it said,   30
      'T is meet that some more audience than a mother,
      Since nature makes them partial, should o'erhear
      The speech, of vantage. Fare you well, my liege;
      I 'll call upon you ere you go to bed,
      And tell you what I know.

King.   Thanks, dear my lord. [*Exit* POLONIUS. 35
      O, my offence is rank, it smells to heaven;
      It hath the primal eldest curse upon 't,
      A brother's murder! Pray can I not;
      Though inclination be as sharp as will,
      My stronger guilt defeats my strong intent,   40
      And, like a man to double business bound,
      I stand in pause where I shall first begin,
      And both neglect. What if this cursed hand
      Were thicker than itself with brother's blood,
      Is there not rain enough in the sweet heavens   45
      To wash it white as snow? Whereto serves mercy
      But to confront the visage of offence?
      And what 's in prayer but this twofold force,
      To be forestalled ere we come to fall,
      Or pardon'd being down? Then I 'll look up;   50

29. **Tax him home**—Scold him soundly. 33. **Liege**—Lord.

My fault is past. But, O, what form of prayer
Can serve my turn? 'Forgive me my foul murder?'
That cannot be; since I am still possess'd
Of those effects for which I did the murder,
My crown, mine own ambition, and my queen.   55
May one be pardon'd and retain th' offence?
In the corrupted currents of this world
Offence's gilded hand may shove by justice;
And oft 't is seen the wicked prize itself
Buys out the law; but 't is not so above;   60
There is no shuffling, there the action lies
In his true nature, and we ourselves compell'd,
Even to the teeth and forehead of our faults,
To give in evidence. What then? what rests?
Try what repentance can. What can it not?   65
Yet what can it when one can not repent?
O wretched state! O bosom black as death!
O limed soul, that struggling to be free
Art more engag'd! Help, angels! Make assay!
Bow, stubborn knees, and, heart with strings of steel, 70
Be soft as sinews of the new-born babe!
All may be well.   [*Retires and kneels.*

Enter HAMLET.

Hamlet. Now might I do it pat, now he is praying;
And now I'll do 't. And so he goes to heaven;
And so am I reveng'd. That would be scann'd.   75

68. **Limed**—Trapped. (As birds are caught by lime.)
75. **That would be scann'd**—That must be considered.

A villain kills my father; and for that,
I, his sole son, do this same villain send
To heaven.
O, this is hire and salary, not revenge.
He took my father grossly, full of bread,   80
With all his crimes broad blown, as flush as May;
And how his audit stands who knows save heaven?
But in our circumstance and course of thought,
'T is heavy with him; and am I then reveng'd,
To take him in the purging of his soul,   85
When he is fit and season'd for his passage?
No!
Up, sword; and know thou a more horrid hent;
When he is drunk asleep, or in his rage,
Or in th' incestuous pleasure of his bed;   90
At gaming, swearing, or about some act
That has no relish of salvation in 't,—
Then trip him, that his heels may kick at heaven,
And that his soul may be as damn'd and black
As hell, whereto it goes. My mother stays.   95
This physic but prolongs thy sickly days.   [Exit.

King [*Rising*] My words fly up, my thoughts remain
        below;
    Words without thoughts never to heaven go.   [*Exit.*

88. **Up, sword . . . hent**—Hold, you know a more terrible way to slay
    him.
96. **Physic**—Medicine. (My temporary restraint is like a medicine that
    merely delays the fatal end of the disease.)

"And am I then reveng'd
To take him in the purging of his soul?"

Maurice Evans in the role of Hamlet

Scene IV

The Queen's *closet. Enter* Queen *and* Polonius.

Polonius. He will come straight. Look you lay home to
　　him;
　　Tell him his pranks have been too broad to bear with,
　　And that your grace hath screen'd and stood between
　　Much heat and him. I 'll silence me e'en here.
　　Pray you, be round with him.　　　　　　　　　　5

Hamlet. [*Within*] Mother, mother, mother!

Queen.　　　　　　　　　　　　I 'll warrant you;
　　Fear me not. Withdraw, I hear him coming.

　　　　　　　　　　[Polonius *hides behind the arras.*

Enter Hamlet.

Hamlet. Now, mother, what's the matter?

Queen. Hamlet, thou hast thy father much offended.

Hamlet. Mother, you have my father much offended.

Queen. Come, come, you answer with an idle tongue.

Hamlet. Go, go, you question with a wicked tongue.

Queen. Why, how now, Hamlet!

Hamlet.　　　　　　　　　　What's the matter now?

Queen. Have you forgot me?

Hamlet.　　　　　　　　No, by the rood, not so:
　　You are the queen, your husband's brother's wife;　15
　　And—would it were not so!—you are my mother.

Queen. Nay, then I 'll set those to you that can speak.

13. **Forgot me**—Forgotten who I am.　14. **By the rood**—By the cross.

Hamlet. Come, come, and sit you down; you shall not
        budge:
    You go not till I set you up a glass
    Where you may see the inmost part of you.   20
Queen. What wilt thou do? thou wilt not murder me?
    Help, help, ho!
Polonius. [*Behind*] What, ho! help, help, help!
Hamlet. [*Drawing*] How now! a rat? Dead for a ducat,
        dead!   [*Makes a pass through the arras.*
Polonius. [*Behind*] O, I am slain!   [*Falls and dies.*
Queen. O me! what hast thou done?
Hamlet.   Nay, I know not;   25
    Is it the king?
Queen. O, what a rash and bloody deed is this!
Hamlet. A bloody deed! almost as bad, good mother,
    As kill a king, and marry with his brother.
Queen. As kill a king!
Hamlet.   Ay, lady, 't was my word.   30
                [*Lifts up the arras and discovers* Polonius.
    Thou wretched, rash, intruding fool, farewell!
    I took thee for thy better; take thy fortune;
    Thou find'st to be too busy is some danger.
    Leave wringing of your hands. Peace! sit you down,
    And let me wring your heart: for so I shall   35
    If it be made of penetrable stuff;
    If damned custom have not braz'd it so

37. **Custom have not braz'd**—If your habits have not made your heart
    as hard as brass.

That it is proof and bulwark against sense.

Queen. What have I done, that thou dar'st wag thy
   tongue
  In noise so rude against me?

Hamlet.   Such an act   40
  That blurs the grace and blush of modesty,
  Calls virtue hypocrite, takes off the rose
  From the fair forehead of an innocent love,
  And sets a blister there, makes marriage-vows
  As false as dicers' oaths; O, such a deed   45
  As from the body of contraction plucks
  The very soul, and sweet religion makes
  A rhapsody of words! heaven's face doth glow,
  Yea, this solidity and compound mass,
  With tristful visage, as against the doom,   50
  Is thought-sick at the act.

Queen.   Ay me, what act,
  That roars so loud and thunders in the index?

Hamlet. Look here, upon this picture, and on this,
  The counterfeit presentment of two brothers.
  See, what a grace was seated on this brow;   55
  Hyperion's curls; the front of Jove himself,
  An eye like Mars, to threaten and command;
  A station like the herald Mercury
  New-lighted on a heaven-kissing hill;

---

45. **Dicers' oaths**—Oaths of those playing at dice—not to be trusted.
56. **Hyperion**—Apollo, god of manly beauty. 57. **Mars**—God of war.
58. **Station**—Manner of standing. 58. **Mercury**—Messenger of the gods.

A combination and a form indeed,   60
Where every god did seem to set his seal,
To give the world assurance of a man.
This was your husband. Look you now what follows:
Here is your husband; like a mildew'd ear,
Blasting his wholesome brother. Have you eyes?   65
Could you on this fair mountain leave to feed,
And batten on this moor? Ha! have you eyes?
You cannot call it love, for at your age
The hey-day in the blood is tame, it 's humble,
And waits upon the judgment; and what judgment   70
Would step from this to this? Sense, sure, you have,
Else could you not have motion; but sure, that sense
Is apoplex'd; for madness would not err,
Nor sense to ecstasy was ne'er so thrall'd,
But it reserv'd some quantity of choice,   75
To serve in such a difference. What devil was 't
That thus hath cozen'd you at hoodman-blind?
Eyes without feeling, feeling without sight,
Ears without hands or eyes, smelling sans all,
Or but a sickly part of one true sense   80
Could not so mope.
O shame! where is thy blush? Rebellious hell,
If thou canst mutine in a matron's bones,
To flaming youth let virtue be as wax,
And melt in her own fire; proclaim no shame   85

77. **Cozen'd . . . blind**—Cheated you at blindman's buff.
79. **Sans all**—Without all the senses.
83. **Mutine**—Revolt against authority.

When the compulsive ardour gives the charge,
Since frost itself as actively doth burn,
And reason panders will.

Queen.   O Hamlet, speak no more!
Thou turn'st mine eyes into my very soul,
And there I see such black and grained spots   90
As will not leave their tinct.

Hamlet.   Nay, but to live
Stew'd in corruption,—

Queen.   O, speak to me no more!
These words, like daggers, enter in mine ears.
No more, sweet Hamlet!

Hamlet.   A murderer and a villain;
A slave that is not twentieth part the tithe   95
Of your precedent lord; a vice of kings;
A cutpurse of the empire and the rule,
That from a shelf the precious diadem stole,
And put it in his pocket!

Queen.   No more!

Hamlet. A king of shreds and patches—   100

Enter GHOST.

Save me, and hover o'er me with your wings,
You heavenly guards! What would your gracious
    figure?

Queen. Alas, he's mad!

91. **Will not leave their tinct**—Will not fade.   95. **Tithe**—Small part.
97. **Cutpurse**—Robber. Purses in Elizabethan days were often worn on
    the outside, attached to the girdle.

Hamlet. Do you not come your tardy son to chide,
       That, laps'd in time and passion, lets go by   105
       Th' important acting of your dread command?
       O, say!

Ghost. Do not forget. This visitation
       Is but to whet thy almost blunted purpose.
       But, look, amazement on thy mother sits;   110
       O, step between her and her fighting soul!
       Conceit in weakest bodies strongest works.
       Speak to her, Hamlet.

Hamlet.   How is it with you, lady?

Queen. Alas, how is 't with you,
       That you do bend your eye on vacancy,   115
       And with th' incorporal air do hold discourse?
       Forth at your eyes your spirits wildly peep;
       And, as the sleeping soldiers in th' alarm,
       Your bedded hair, like life in excrements,
       Start up and stand an end. O gentle son,   120
       Upon the heat and flame of thy distemper
       Sprinkle cool patience. Whereon do you look?

Hamlet. On him, on him! Look you, how pale he glares!
       His form and cause conjoin'd, preaching to stones,
       Would make them capable. Do not look upon me;   125
       Lest with this piteous action you convert

104. **Chide**—Scold.
105. **Laps'd in time and passion**—Having let time slip and passion cool.
112. **Conceit**—Imagination.
116. **Incorporal air**—Air without form, empty space.
119. **Your bedded hair . . . stand an end**—Your hair stands up as if
       alive.

My stern effects. Then what I have to do
Will want true colour; tears, perchance, for blood.
Queen. To whom do you speak this?
Hamlet.   Do you see nothing there?
Queen. Nothing at all; yet all that is I see.   130
Hamlet. Nor did you nothing hear?
Queen.   No, nothing but ourselves.
Hamlet. Why, look you there! look, how it steals away!
    My father, in his habit as he liv'd!
    Look, where he goes, even now, out at the portal!
                                        [*Exit* Ghost.
Queen. This is the very coinage of your brain;   135
    This bodiless creation ecstasy
    Is very cunning in.
Hamlet.   Ecstasy!
    My pulse, as yours, doth temperately keep time,
    And makes as healthful music. It is not madness
    That I have uttered; bring me to the test,   140
    And I the matter will re-word, which madness
    Would gambol from. Mother, for love of grace,
    Lay not that flattering unction to your soul,
    That not your trespass but my madness speaks;
    It will but skin and film the ulcerous place,   145
    Whilst rank corruption, mining all within,
    Infects unseen. Confess yourself to heaven;
    Repent what's past, avoid what is to come;

143. **Unction**—Anything soothing.

"Lay not that flattering unction to your soul."
*Laurence Olivier and Eileen Herlie
in the Screen Production*

And do not spread the compost on the weeds,
To make them ranker. Forgive me this my virtue;   150
For in the fatness of these pursy times
Virtue itself of vice must pardon beg,
Yea, curb and woo for leave to do him good.
Queen. O Hamlet, thou hast cleft my heart in twain.
Hamlet. O, throw away the worser part of it,   155
And live the purer with the other half.
Good night: but go not to mine uncle's bed;
Assume a virtue, if you have it not.
That monster, custom, who all sense doth eat,
Of habits devil, is angel yet in this,   160
That to the use of actions fair and good
He likewise gives a frock or livery,
That aptly is put on. Refrain to-night,
And that shall lend a kind of easiness
To the next abstinence; the next more easy;   165
For use almost can change the stamp of nature,
And either master the devil or throw him out
With wondrous potency. Once more, good night;
And when you are desirous to be blest,
I'll blessing beg of you. For this same lord,   170
                    [*Pointing to* POLONIUS.
I do repent; but heaven hath pleas'd it so,
To punish me with this and this with me,
That I must be their scourge and minister.
I will bestow him, and will answer well

149. **Compost**—Mixture   151. **Pursy**—Fat, easy.

The death I gave him. So, again, good night.   175
I must be cruel, only to be kind;
Thus bad begins, and worse remains behind.
One word more, good lady.

Queen.   What shall I do?

Hamlet. Not this, by no means, that I bid you do:
Let the bloat king tempt you again to bed,   180
Pinch wanton on your cheek, call you his mouse;
And let him, for a pair of reechy kisses,
Or paddling in your neck with his damn'd fingers,
Make you to ravel all this matter out,
That I essentially am not in madness,   185
But mad in craft. 'T were good you let him know;
For who, that 's but a queen, fair, sober, wise,
Would from a paddock, from a bat, a gib,
Such dear concernings hide? who would do so?
No, in despite of sense and secrecy,   190
Unpeg the basket on the house's top,
Let the birds fly, and, like the famous ape,
To try conclusions, in the basket creep,
And break your own neck down.

Queen. Be thou assur'd, if words be made of breath,   195
And breath of life, I have no life to breathe
What thou hast said to me.

Hamlet. I must to England; you know that?

Queen.   Alack,

185. **Essentially . . . craft**—That I am not really mad, but pretending.
188. **Paddock**—Toad. 188. **Gib**—Tomcat.
189. **Dear concernings**—Important matters.

I had forgot; 't is so concluded on.

Hamlet.   There's letters seal'd; and my two schoolfellows,   200
    Whom I will trust as I will adders fang'd,
    They bear the mandate; they must sweep my way,
    And marshal me to knavery.   Let it work;
    For 't is the sport to have the enginer
    Hoist with his own petar; and 't shall go hard   205
    But I will delve one yard below the mines,
    And blow them at the moon.   O, 't is most sweet
    When in one line two crafts directly meet!
    This man shall set me packing.
    I 'll lug the guts into the neighbour room.   210
    Mother, good night.   Indeed, this counsellor
    Is now most still, most secret, and most grave,
    Who was in life a foolish prating knave.
    Come, sir, to draw toward an end with you.
    Good night, mother.   215

      [*Exeunt severally;* HAMLET *dragging in* POLONIUS.

201. **Adders**—Poisonous snakes.
205. **Petar**—A machine for breaking open gates.
213. **Prating**—Chattering.

ACT FOUR

Scene I

A room in the castle. Enter King, Queen, Rosencrantz, *and* Guildenstern.

King. There's matter in these sighs; these profound heaves
    You must translate; 't is fit we understand them.
    Where is your son?
Queen. Bestow this place on us a little while.
                [*Exeunt* Rosencrantz *and* Guildenstern.
    Ah, my good lord, what have I seen to-night!   5
King. What, Gertrude? How does Hamlet?
Queen. Mad as the sea and wind, when both contend
    Which is the mightier; in his lawless fit,
    Behind the arras hearing something stir,
    Whips out his rapier, cries 'A rat, a rat!'   10
    And in this brainish apprehension kills
    The unseen good old man.
King.   O heavy deed!
    It had been so with us, had we been there;
    His liberty is full of threats to all,
    To you yourself, to us, to every one.   15

  1. **Profound heaves**—Deep breaths or sighs.
  4. **Bestow . . . place**—Give us this place; please leave us alone.
11. **Brainish apprehension**—Imaginary idea.

Alas, how shall this bloody deed be answer'd?
It will be laid to us, whose providence
Should have kept short, restrain'd, and out of haunt,
This mad young man; but so much was our love,
We would not understand what was most fit,   20
But, like the owner of a foul disease,
To keep it from divulging, let it feed
Even on the pith of life. Where is he gone?

Queen. To draw apart the body he hath kill'd;
O'er whom his very madness, like some ore   25
Among a mineral of metals base,
Shows itself pure. He weeps for what is done.

King. O Gertrude, come away!
The sun no sooner shall the mountains touch,
But we will ship him hence; and this vile deed   30
We must, with all our majesty and skill,
Both countenance and excuse. Ho, Guildenstern!

    Re-enter Rosencrantz *and* Guildenstern.

Friends both, go join you with some further aid;
Hamlet in madness hath Polonius slain,
And from his mother's closet hath he dragg'd him.   35
Go seek him out; speak fair, and bring the body
Into the chapel. I pray you, haste in this.

      [*Exeunt* Rosencrantz *and* Guildenstern.

Come, Gertrude, we'll call up our wisest friends,
And let them know both what we mean to do,

17. **Providence**—Watchfulness, foresight.
18. **Out of haunt**—Away from the company of others.
32. **Countenance**—Approve.

And what's untimely done; so, haply slander,   40
Whose whisper o'er the world's diameter,
As level as the cannon to his blank,
Transports his poison'd shot, may miss our name,
And hit the woundless air. O, come away!   44
My soul is full of discord and dismay.   [*Exeunt.*

Scene II

Another room in the castle. Enter HAMLET.

Hamlet. Safely stowed.

Rosencrantz. ⎫
                ⎬ [*Within*] Hamlet! Lord Hamlet!
Guildenstern. ⎭

Hamlet. But soft, what noise? who calls on Hamlet?
    O, here they come.

                Enter ROSENCRANTZ *and* GUILDENSTERN.

Rosencrantz. What have you done, my lord, with the
        dead body?   5

Hamlet. Compounded it with dust, whereto 't is kin.

Rosencrantz. Tell us where 't is, that we may take it
        thence
    And bear it to the chapel.

Hamlet. Do not believe it.

Rosencrantz. Believe what?   10

Hamlet. That I can keep your counsel and not mine own.
    Besides, to be demanded of a sponge, what replication

12. **Replication**—Reply.

should be made by the son of a king?

Rosencrantz. Take you me for a sponge, my lord?

Hamlet. Ay, sir, that soaks up the king's countenance,
his rewards, his authorities. But such officers do the
king best service in the end. He keeps them, like an
ape, in the corner of his jaw; first mouth'd, to be
last swallow'd: when he needs what you have glean'd,
it is but squeezing you, and, sponge, you shall be dry
again.   20

Rosencrantz. I understand you not, my lord.

Hamlet. I am glad of it; a knavish speech sleeps in a foolish ear.

Rosencrantz. My lord, you must tell us where the body is,
and go with us to the king.   25

Hamlet. The body is with the king, but the king is not
with the body. The king is a thing—

Guildenstern. A thing, my lord!

Hamlet. Of nothing; bring me to him. Hide fox, and all
after.   [*Exeunt.*

SCENE III

Another room in the castle. Enter KING, *attended.*

King. I have sent to seek him, and to find the body.
How dangerous it is that this man goes loose!
Yet must not we put the strong law on him:
He 's lov'd of the distracted multitude,

Who like not in their judgment, but their eyes;   5
And, where 't is so, th' offender's scourge is weigh'd,
But never the offence. To bear all smooth and even,
This sudden sending him away must seem
Deliberate pause; diseases desperate grown
By desperate appliance are reliev'd,   10
Or not at all.

Enter ROSENCRANTZ.

How now! what hath befall'n?
Rosencrantz. Where the dead body is bestow'd, my lord,
We cannot get from him.
King.   But where is he?
Rosencrantz. Without, my lord; guarded, to know your
    pleasure.
King. Bring him before us.   15
Rosencrantz. Ho, Guildenstern! bring in my lord.

Enter HAMLET *and* GUILDENSTERN.

King. Now, Hamlet, where's Polonius?
Hamlet. At supper.
King. At supper! where?   19
Hamlet. Not where he eats, but where he is eaten; a
    certain convocation of politic worms are e'en at him.
    Your worm is your only emperor for diet; we fat all
    creatures else to fat us, and we fat ourselves for mag-
    gots. Your fat king and your lean beggar is but

---

5. **Who like . . . eyes**—The multitude form their opinion from outward appearances, not reason.

variable service, two dishes, but to one table; that's
the end.   26

King. Alas, alas!

Hamlet. A man may fish with the worm that hath eat of
a king, and eat of the fish that hath fed of that worm.

King. What dost thou mean by this?   30

Hamlet. Nothing but to show you how a king may go a
progress through the guts of a beggar.

King. Where is Polonius?

Hamlet. In heaven; send thither to see: if your messenger
find him not there, seek him i' th' other place yourself.
But indeed, if you find him not within this month,
you shall nose him as you go up the stairs into the
lobby.   38

King. Go seek him there. [*To some* Attendants]

Hamlet. He will stay till ye come.   [*Exeunt* Attendants.

King. Hamlet, this deed, for thine especial safety,
Which we do tender, as we dearly grieve   42
For that which thou hast done, must send thee hence
With fiery quickness; therefore prepare thyself.
The bark is ready, and the wind at help,
Th' associates tend, and every thing is bent
For England.

Hamlet. For England?

King.   Ay, Hamlet.

Hamlet.   Good.   47

King. So is it, if thou knew'st our purposes.

Hamlet. I see a cherub that sees them. But, come; for

England!   Farewell, dear mother.

King. Thy loving father, Hamlet.   51

Hamlet. My mother: father and mother is man and
wife; man and wife is one flesh; and so, my mother.
Come, for England!   [*Exit.*

King. Follow him at foot; tempt him with speed aboard;
Delay it not; I 'll have him hence to-night.
Away! for every thing is seal'd and done   57
That else leans on th' affair; pray you, make haste.

           [*Exeunt* Rosencrantz *and* Guildenstern.

And, England, if my love thou hold'st at aught—
As my great power thereof may give thee sense,
Since yet thy cicatrice looks raw and red
After the Danish sword, and thy free awe   62
Pays homage to us—thou mayst not coldly set
Our sovereign process; which imports at full,
By letters conjuring to that effect,
The present death of Hamlet. Do it, England;
For like the hectic in my blood he rages,   67
And thou must cure me. Till I know 't is done,
Howe'er my haps, my joys were ne'er begun.   [*Exit.*

61. **Cicatrice**—Scar.
64. **Process**—Procedure.   67. **Hectic**—Fever.
69. **Haps**—Luck or fortune.   Some scholars make this *hopes.*

Scene IV

A plain in Denmark. Enter Fortinbras, *a* Captain, *and*
   Soldiers, *marching.*

Fortinbras. Go, captain, from me greet the Danish king;
   Tell him that by his license Fortinbras
   Claims the conveyance of a promis'd march
   Over his kingdom. You know the rendezvous.
   If that his majesty would aught with us,   5
   We shall express our duty in his eye;
   And let him know so.

Captain.   I will do 't, my lord.

Fortinbras. Go softly on.

                              [*Exeunt* Fortinbras *and* Soldiers.

Enter Hamlet, Rosencrantz, Guildenstern, *and others.*

Hamlet. Good sir, whose powers are these?

Captain. They are of Norway, sir.   10

Hamlet. How purpos'd, sir, I pray you?

Captain. Against some part of Poland.

Hamlet. Who commands them, sir?

Captain. The nephew to old Norway, Fortinbras.

Hamlet. Goes it against the main of Poland, sir,   15
   Or for some frontier?

Captain. Truly to speak, and with no addition,
   We go to gain a little patch of ground

   11. **How purpos'd**—What is their purpose or destination?

That hath in it no profit but the name.
To pay five ducats, five, I would not farm it;   2c
Nor will it yield to Norway or the Pole
A ranker rate, should it be sold in fee.
Hamlet. Why, then the Polack never will defend it.
Captain. Yes, 't is already garrison'd.   24
Hamlet. Two thousand souls and twenty thousand ducats
Will not debate the question of this straw;
This is th' imposthume of much wealth and peace,
That inward breaks, and shows no cause without
Why the man dies. I humbly thank you, sir.
Captain. God be wi' you, sir.   [*Exit.*
Rosencrantz.   Will 't please you go, my lord? 30
Hamlet. I 'll be with you straight. Go a little before.
                    [*Exeunt all but* HAMLET.
How all occasions do inform against me,
And spur my dull revenge! What is a man,
If his chief good and market of his time
Be but to sleep and feed? a beast, no more.   35
Sure, he that made us with such large discourse,
Looking before and after, gave us not
That capability and godlike reason
To fust in us unus'd. Now, whether it be
Bestial oblivion, or some craven scruple   40
Of thinking too precisely on th' event—
A thought which, quarter'd, hath but one part wisdom,

22. **Ranker**—Greater, higher.   27. **Imposthume**—Inward sore.
39. **Fust**—Grow mouldy.   40. **Craven**—Cowardly.

And ever three parts coward—I do not know
Why yet I live to say 'This thing 's to do,'
Sith I have cause and will and strength and means   45
To do 't. Examples gross as earth exhort me;
Witness this army of such mass and charge,
Led by a delicate and tender prince,
Whose spirit with divine ambition puff'd
Makes mouths at the invisible event,   50
Exposing what is mortal and unsure
To all that fortune, death, and danger dare,
Even for an egg-shell. Rightly to be great
Is not to stir without great argument,
But greatly to find quarrel in a straw   55
When honour 's at the stake. How stand I then,
That have a father kill'd, a mother stain'd,
Excitements of my reason and my blood,
And let all sleep? while, to my shame, I see
The imminent death of twenty thousand men,   60
That for a fantasy and trick of fame
Go to their graves like beds, fight for a plot
Whereon the numbers cannot try the cause,
Which is not tomb enough and continent
To hide the slain? O, from this time forth,   65
My thoughts be bloody, or be nothing worth!   [*Exit.*

45. **Sith**—Since.

Scene V

Elsinore. A room in the castle. Enter Queen, Horatio, *and a* Gentleman.

Queen. I will not speak with her.

Gentleman. She is importunate, indeed distract;
    Her mood will needs be pitied.

Queen.   What would she have?

Gentleman. She speaks much of her father; says she hears   4
    There 's tricks i' th' world; and hems, and beats her
        heart;
    Spurns enviously at straws; speaks things in doubt,
    That carry but half sense: her speech is nothing,
    Yet the unshaped use of it doth move
    The hearers to collection; they aim at it,
    And botch the words up fit to their own thoughts;   10
    Which, as her winks and nods and gestures yield
        them,
    Indeed would make one think there might be thought,
    Though nothing sure, yet much unhappily.

Horatio. 'T were good she were spoken with; for she
    may strew
    Dangerous conjectures in ill-breeding minds.   15

Queen. Let her come in.   [*Exit* Gentleman.
[*Aside*] To my sick soul, as sin's true nature is,

---

6. **Spurns enviously**—Kicks angrily.
7. **Her speech . . . collection**—Her disconnected words cause her
    hearers to try to put them together to make sense.

Each toy seems prologue to some great amiss;
So full of artless jealousy is guilt,
It spills itself in fearing to be spilt.   20

Re-enter GENTLEMAN, *with* OPHELIA.

Ophelia. Where is the beauteous majesty of Denmark?
Queen. How now, Ophelia!
Ophelia. [*Sings*]

> How should I your true-love know
>   From another one?
> By his cockle hat and staff,   25
>   And his sandal shoon.

Queen. Alas, sweet lady, what imports this song?
Ophelia. Say you? nay, pray you, mark.

> [*Sings*] He is dead and gone, lady,
>   He is dead and gone;   30
> At his head a grass-green turf,
>   At his heels a stone.

O, ho!
Queen. Nay, but, Ophelia,—
Ophelia.   Pray you, mark.
     [*Sings*] White his shroud as the mountain snow,—
                    Enter KING.
Queen. Alas, look here, my lord.   35
Ophelia. [*Sings*]

26. **Shoon**—The old plural form for shoes. 27. **Imports**—Means.

>   Larded with sweet flowers;
>   Which bewept to the grave did not go,
>   With true-love showers.

King. How do you, pretty lady?

Ophelia. Well, God 'ild you! They say the owl was a
baker's daughter. Lord, we know what we are, but
know not what we may be. God be at your table!

King. Conceit upon her father.

Ophelia. Pray you, let's have no words of this; but, when
they ask you what it means, say you this: 45

>   [*Sings*] To-morrow is Saint Valentine's day,
>   All in the morning betime,
>   And I a maid at your window,
>   To be your Valentine.

King. How long hath she been thus?   50

Ophelia. I hope all will be well. We must be patient;
but I cannot choose but weep, to think they should lay
him i' th' cold ground. My brother shall know of
it; and so I thank you for your good counsel. Come,
my coach! Good night, ladies; good night, sweet
ladies; good night, good night.   [*Exit.*

King. Follow her close; give her good watch, I pray
you.   [*Exit* HORATIO.

40. **'Ild**—Yield or reward you.
40. **Owl . . . daughter**—An old legend says that Christ begged for bread
at a baker's shop. The daughter of the baker objected to her mother's
generosity and was transformed into an owl.
43. **Conceit . . . father**—Thoughts of her father.

O, this is the poison of deep grief; it springs
All from her father's death. O Gertrude, Gertrude,
When sorrows come, they come not single spies,   60
But in battalions! First, her father slain;
Next your son gone; and he most violent author
Of his own just remove: the people muddied,
Thick and unwholesome in their thoughts and whis-
    pers,   64
For good Polonius' death; and we have done but
    greenly,
In hugger-mugger to inter him; poor Ophelia
Divided from herself and her fair judgment,
Without the which we are pictures, or mere beasts;
Last, and as much containing as all these,
Her brother is in secret come from France,   70
Feeds on his wonder, keeps himself in clouds,
And wants not buzzers to infect his ear
With pestilent speeches of his father's death,
Wherein necessity, of matter beggar'd,
Will nothing stick our person to arraign   75
In ear and ear. O my dear Gertrude, this,
Like to a murdering-piece, in many places
Gives me superfluous death.   [*A noise within.*

Queen.   Alack, what noise is this?

65. **We have done . . . to inter him**—We have acted unwisely to bury
   him so unceremoniously. 72. **Buzzers**—Talebearers, whisperers.
74. **Necessity . . . arraign**—Lacking the truth of the matter, the ac-
   cusers will not hesitate to blame even us.

King. Where are my Switzers? Let them guard the
    door.

                Enter another Gentleman.

    What is the matter?
Gentleman.   Save yourself, my lord;   80
    The ocean, overpeering of his list,
    Eats not the flats with more impetuous haste
    Than young Laertes, in a riotous head,
    O'erbears your officers. The rabble call him lord;
    And, as the world were now but to begin,   85
    Antiquity forgot, custom not known,
    The ratifiers and props of every word,
    They cry, 'Choose we; Laertes shall be king!'
    Caps, hands, and tongues applaud it to the clouds,
    'Laertes shall be king, Laertes king!'   90
Queen. How cheerfully on the false trail they cry!
    O, this is counter, you false Danish dogs!
King. The doors are broke.   [*Noise within.*
        Enter Laertes, *armed;* Danes *following.*
Laertes. Where is this king? Sirs, stand you all without.
Danes. No, let 's come in.
Laertes.   I pray you, give me leave. 95
Danes. We will, we will.   [*They retire without the door.*

79. **Switzers**—The royal guards (from Switzerland).
81. **Overpeering of his list**—Rising above its boundary.
87. **Ratifiers and props**—Those who approve and support.
92. **Counter**—Hounds run *counter* when they trace the scent backward.

Laertes. I thank you; keep the door. O thou vile king,
 Give me my father!
Queen.   Calmly, good Laertes.

.   .   .   .   .

King.   What's the cause, Laertes,
 That thy rebellion looks so giant-like?   100
 Let him go, Gertrude; do not fear our person.
 There 's such divinity doth hedge a king
 That treason can but peep to what it would,
 Acts little of his will. Tell me, Laertes,
 Why thou art thus incens'd. Let him go, Gertrude.   105
 Speak, man.
Laertes. Where 's my father?
King.   Dead.
Queen.   But not by him.
King. Let him demand his fill.
Laertes. How came he dead? I 'll not be juggled with.   110
 To hell, allegiance! vows, to the blackest devil!
 Conscience and grace, to the profoundest pit!
 I dare damnation. To this point I stand,
 That both the worlds I give to negligence,
 Let come what comes; only I 'll be reveng'd   115
 Most throughly for my father.
King.   Who shall stay you?
Laertes. My will, not all the world;
 And, for my means, I 'll husband them so well
 They shall go far with little.   120
King.   Good Laertes,

If you desire to know the certainty
Of your dear father's death, is 't writ in your revenge,
That, swoopstake, you will draw both friend and foe,
Winner and loser?   125

Laertes.   None but his enemies.

King.   Will you know them, then?

Laertes.   To his good friends thus wide I 'll ope my arms,
   And, like the kind life-rendering pelican,
   Repast them with my blood.

King.   Why, now you speak
   Like a good child and a true gentleman.   130
   That I am guiltless of your father's death,
   And am most sensibly in grief for it,
   It shall as level to your judgment pierce
   As day does to your eye.

Danes.   [*Within*] Let her come in.

Laertes.   How now! what noise is that?   135

Re-enter OPHELIA.

O heat, dry up my brains! tears seven times salt,
Burn out the sense and virtue of mine eye!
By heaven, thy madness shall be paid by weight,
Till our scale turns the beam.   O rose of May!
Dear maid, kind sister, sweet Ophelia!   140
O heavens! is 't possible, a young maid's wits
Should be as mortal as an old man's life?
Nature is fine in love, and where 't is fine

---

128. **Pelican**—The pelican feeds its young by dropping the lower bill on to the breast.   Thus the young appear to be feeding on the breast itself.

It sends some precious instance of itself
After the thing it loves.   145
Ophelia. [*Sings*]

> They bore him barefac'd on the bier;
>   Hey non nonny, nonny, hey nonny;
> And on his grave rain'd many a tear.

Fare you well, my dove!
Laertes. Hadst thou thy wits, and didst persuade revenge,
It could not move thus.   151
Ophelia. You must sing, 'Down a-down, and you call
him a-down-a.' O, how the wheel becomes it! It is
the false steward that stole his master's daughter.
Laertes. This nothing 's more than matter.   155
Ophelia. There 's rosemary, that 's for remembrance;
pray you, love, remember; and there is pansies, that 's
for thoughts.
Laertes. A document in madness; thoughts and remem-
brance fitted.   160
Ophelia. There 's fennel for you, and columbines; there 's
rue for you, and here 's some for me; we may call it
herb of grace o' Sundays. O, you must wear your rue
with a difference. There 's a daisy. I would give you
some violets, but they wither'd all when my father
died. They say he made a good end,—   166

[*Sings*] For bonny sweet Robin is all my joy.

Laertes. Thought and affliction, passion, hell itself,
She turns to favour and to prettiness.

Ophelia.   [*Sings*]

> And will he not come again?   170
> And will he not come again?
>   No, no, he is dead,
>   Go to thy death-bed;
> He never will come again.
>
> His beard was as white as snow,   175
> All flaxen was his poll;
>   He is gone, he is gone,
>   And we cast away moan:
> God ha' mercy on his soul!

And of all Christian souls, I pray God. God be wi'
you.   [*Exit.*

Laertes. Do you see this, O God?

King. Laertes, I must commune with your grief,
Or you deny me right. Go but apart,
Make choice of whom your wisest friends you will,
And they shall hear and judge 'twixt you and me. 185
If by direct or by collateral hand
They find us touch'd, we will our kingdom give,
Our crown, our life, and all that we call ours,
To you in satisfaction; but if not,
Be you content to lend your patience to us,   190
And we shall jointly labour with your soul
To give it due content.

176. **Poll**—Head.   186. **Collateral**—Indirect.

Laertes.　　　　　　　Let this be so;
　His means of death, his obscure burial—
　No trophy, sword, nor hatchment o'er his bones,
　No noble rite nor formal ostentation—　　　　　　　195
　Cry to be heard, as 't were from heaven to earth,
　That I must call 't in question.
King.　　　　　　　　　　So you shall;
　And where th' offence is let the great axe fall.
　I pray you, go with me.　　　　　　　　　*[Exeunt.*

SCENE VI

Another room in the castle. Enter HORATIO *and a* SERVANT.
Horatio.　What are they that would speak with me?
Servant.　Sailors, sir; they say they have letters for you.
Horatio.　Let them come in.　　　　　　*[Exit* SERVANT.
　I do not know from what part of the world
　I should be greeted, if not from Lord Hamlet.　　　5

Enter SAILORS.

1 Sailor.　God bless you, sir.
Horatio.　Let him bless thee too.
1 Sailor.　He shall, sir, and 't please him. There 's a letter for you, sir—it comes from th' ambassador that was
bound for England—if your name be Horatio, as I am
let to know it is.　　　　　　　　　　　　　　11
Horatio.　[*Reads*] 'Horatio, when thou shalt have over-

look'd this, give these fellows some means to the
king; they have letters for him. Ere we were two days
old at sea, a pirate of very warlike appointment gave
us chase. Finding ourselves too slow of sail, we put
on a compell'd valour. In the grapple I boarded them.
On the instant they got clear of our ship; so I alone
became their prisoner. They have dealt with me like
thieves of mercy: but they knew what they did; I am
to do a good turn for them. Let the king have the
letters I have sent, and repair thou to me with as much
haste as thou wouldest fly death. I have words to
speak in thine ear will make thee dumb; yet are they
much too light for the bore of the matter. These
good fellows will bring thee where I am. Rosencrantz and Guildenstern hold their course for England; of them I have much to tell thee. Farewell. He
that thou knowest thine, HAMLET.'

Come, I will give you way for these your letters;   30
    And do 't the speedier, that you may direct me
To him from whom you brought them.   [*Exeunt.*

Scene VII

Another room in the castle. Enter King *and* Laertes.

King. Now must your conscience my acquittance seal,
    And you must put me in your heart for friend,
    Sith you have heard, and with a knowing ear,

That he which hath your noble father slain
Pursu'd my life.

Laertes.　　　　　It well appears.　But tell me, 5
Why you proceeded not against these feats,
So crimeful and so capital in nature,
As by your safety, wisdom, all things else,
You mainly were stirr'd up.

King.　　　　　　　　O, for two special reasons,
Which may to you, perhaps, seem much unsinew'd, 10
But yet to me they are strong.　The queen his mother
Lives almost by his looks; and for myself—
My virtue or my plague, be it either which—
She 's so conjunctive to my life and soul
That, as the star moves not but in his sphere, 15
I could not but by her.　The other motive
Why to a public count I might not go,
Is the great love the general gender bear him;
Who, dipping all his faults in their affection,
Would, like the spring that turneth wood to stone, 20
Convert his gyves to graces; so that my arrows,
Too lightly timber'd for so loud a wind,
Would have reverted to my bow again,
And not where I had aim'd them.

Laertes.　And so have I a noble father lost, 25
A sister driven into desperate terms,

10. **Unsinew'd**—Weak.　14. **Conjunctive**—Closely united.
18. **General gender**—Populace, the people.
21. **Convert his gyves to graces**—Make a martyr of him (turn his
　　bonds to reasons for favor.)

Whose worth, if praises may go back again,
Stood challenger on mount of all the age
For her perfections. But my revenge will come.

King. Break not your sleeps for that. You must not
  think   30
That we are made of stuff so flat and dull
That we can let our beard be shook with danger
And think it pastime. You shortly shall hear more.
I lov'd your father, and we love ourself,
And that, I hope, will teach you to imagine—   35

Enter a Messenger, *with letters.*

How now! what news?

Messenger.   Letters, my lord, from Hamlet:
  This to your majesty; this to the queen.

King. From Hamlet! who brought them?

Messenger. Sailors, my lord, they say; I saw them not:
  They were given me by Claudio; he receiv'd them   40
  Of him that brought them.

King.   Laertes, you shall hear them.
  Leave us.   [*Exit* Messenger.

[*Reads*] 'High and mighty: You shall know I am set
  naked on your kingdom. To-morrow shall I beg   44
  leave to see your kingly eyes, when I shall, first asking your pardon thereunto, recount the occasion of
  my sudden and more strange return.

                                        Hamlet.'

44. **Naked**—Alone, without attendants or equipment.

What should this mean?   Are all the rest come back?
Or is it some abuse, and no such thing?
Laertes.   Know you the hand?
King.   'T is Hamlet's character.   'Naked!'
And in a postscript here he says, 'alone.'   51
Can you advise me?
Laertes.   I 'm lost in it, my lord.   But let him come;
It warms the very sickness in my heart,
That I shall live and tell him to his teeth,   55
'Thus didest thou.'

King.   If it be so, Laertes—
As how should it be so?   How otherwise?—
Will you be rul'd by me?
Laertes.   Ay, my lord,
If so you 'll not o'errule me to a peace.
King.   To thine own peace.   If he be now return'd,   60
As checking at his voyage, and that he means
No more to undertake it, I will work him
To an exploit, now ripe in my device,
Under the which he shall not choose but fall;
And for his death no wind of blame shall breathe,   65
But even his mother shall uncharge the practice
And call it accident.
Laertes.   My lord, I will be rul'd;
The rather, if you could devise it so
That I might be the organ.

49. **Abuse**—Trick. 50. **Character**—Handwriting.
61. **Checking at**—Objecting to. (The falcon *checks* when it refuses to
     follow its prey.) 69. **Organ**—Means, instrument.

King.   It falls right.
    You have been talk'd of since your travel much,   70
    And that in Hamlet's hearing, for a quality
    Wherein, they say, you shine. Your sum of parts
    Did not together pluck such envy from him,
    As did that one, and that, in my regard,
    Of the unworthiest siege.

Laertes.   What part is that, my lord?   75

King.   A very riband in the cap of youth,
    Yet needful too; for youth no less becomes
    The light and careless livery that it wears
    Than settl'd age his sables and his weeds,
    Importing health and graveness. Two months since,   80
    Here was a gentleman of Normandy;—
    I 've seen myself, and serv'd against, the French,
    And they can well on horseback; but this gallant
    Had witchcraft in 't; he grew unto his seat,
    And to such wondrous doing brought his horse   85
    As had he been incorps'd and demi-natur'd
    With the brave beast. So far he topp'd my thought,
    That I, in forgery of shapes and tricks,
    Come short of what he did.

Laertes.   A Norman was 't?

King.   A Norman.   90

Laertes.   Upon my life, Lamond.

King.   The very same.

75. **Siege**—Rank. 83. **Can well**—Are skillful.
88. **I, in forgery . . . of what he did**—Perhaps, I could not even
    imagine (or describe) the things he did.

Laertes. I know him well; he is the brooch, indeed,
  And gem of all the nation.
King. He made confession of you,
  And gave you such a masterly report   95
  For art and exercise in your defence,
  And for your rapier most especially,
  That he cried out, 't would be a sight indeed,
  If one could match you. The scrimers of their nation,
  He swore, had neither motion, guard, nor eye,   100
  If you oppos'd them. Sir, this report of his
  Did Hamlet so envenom with his envy
  That he could nothing do but wish and beg
  Your sudden coming o'er, to play with him.
  Now, out of this—
Laertes.   What out of this, my lord?   105
King. Laertes, was your father dear to you?
  Or are you like the painting of a sorrow,
  A face without a heart?
Laertes.   Why ask you this?
King. Not that I think you did not love your father,
  But that I know love is begun by time,   110
  And that I see, in passages of proof,
  Time qualifies the spark and fire of it.
  There lives within the very flame of love
  A kind of wick or snuff that will abate it,
  And nothing is at a like goodness still;   115

92. **Brooch**—Ornament.
99. **Scrimers**—Fencers.   102. **Envenom**—Poison.

For goodness, growing to a plurisy,
Dies in his own too much.   That we would do,
We should do when we would; for this 'would'
    changes,
And hath abatements and delays as many
As there are tongues, are hands, are accidents;   120
And then this 'should' is like a spendthrift sigh,
That hurts by easing.   But, to th' quick o' the ulcer;
Hamlet comes back.   What would you undertake,
To show yourself your father's son in deed
More than in words?

Laertes.   To cut his throat i' th' church.   125

King.   No place, indeed, should murder sanctuarize;
Revenge should have no bounds.   But, good Laertes,
Will you do this, keep close within your chamber.
Hamlet return'd shall know you are come home.
We 'll put on those shall praise your excellence,   130
And set a double varnish on the fame
The Frenchman gave you; bring you, in fine, together,
And wager on your heads.   He, being remiss,
Most generous, and free from all contriving,
Will not peruse the foils, so that, with ease   135
Or with a little shuffling, you may choose
A sword unbated, and, in a pass of practice,
Requite him for your father.

116. **Plurisy**—Overabundance, excess.
137. **Unbated**—Unblunted.   (In fencing, the sharp point of the foil was
    usually covered by a button.)
138. **Requite . . . father**—Repay him for your father's death.

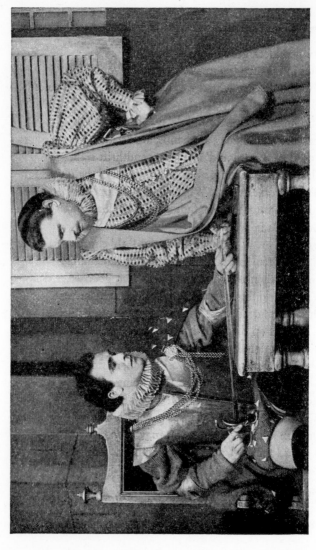

"With a little shuffling, you may choose a sword unbated."

Laertes and the King in the Evans Production

Laertes.   I will do 't;
  And for that purpose I 'll anoint my sword.
  I bought an unction of a mountebank,   140
  So mortal that but dip a knife in it,
  Where it draws blood no cataplasm so rare,
  Collected from all simples that have virtue
  Under the moon, can save the thing from death
  That is but scratch'd withal; I 'll touch my point   145
  With this contagion, that, if I gall him slightly,
  It may be death.
King.   Let 's further think of this;
  Weigh what convenience both of time and means
  May fit us to our shape. If this should fail,
  And that our drift look through our bad performance, 150
  'T were better not assay'd; therefore this project
  Should have a back or second, that might hold
  If this should blast in proof. Soft! let me see:
  We 'll make a solemn wager on your cunnings,—
  I ha 't!   155
  When in your motion you are hot and dry—
  As make your bouts more violent to that end—
  And that he calls for drink, I 'll have prepar'd him
  A chalice for the nonce, whereon but sipping,
  If he by chance escape your venom'd stuck,   160

140. **Unction**—Salve. 140. **Mountebank**—Quack doctor.
141. **Mortal**—Deadly. 142. **Cataplasm**—Poultice, medicine.
150. **Drift look through . . . performance**—If our purpose should be
    disclosed by our poor performance.
159. **For the nonce**—For the occasion.

Our purpose may hold there. But stay, what noise?

Enter QUEEN.

How now, sweet queen!

Queen. One woe doth tread upon another's heel,
    So fast they follow. Your sister 's drown'd, Laertes.
Laertes. Drown'd! O, where?   165
Queen. There is a willow grows aslant a brook,
    That shows his hoar leaves in the glassy stream;
    There with fantastic garlands did she come
    Of crow-flowers, nettles, daisies, and long purples,
    That liberal shepherds give a grosser name,   170
    But our cold maids do dead men's fingers call them;
    There, on the pendent boughs her coronet weeds
    Clambering to hang, an envious sliver broke,
    When down her weedy trophies and herself
    Fell in the weeping brook. Her clothes spread wide, 175
    And, mermaid-like, a while they bore her up;
    Which time she chanted snatches of old tunes,
    As one incapable of her own distress,
    Or like a creature native and indued
    Unto that element; but long it could not be   180
    Till that her garments, heavy with their drink,
    Pull'd the poor wretch from her melodious lay
    To muddy death.
Laertes.   Alas, then is she drown'd?
Queen. Drown'd, drown'd!

179. **Indued**—Fitted to, suited to. 182. **Lay**—Song.

Laertes.   Too much of water hast thou, poor Ophelia,
        And therefore I forbid my tears; but yet   186
        It is our trick; nature her custom holds,
        Let shame say what it will; when these are gone,
        The woman will be out.   Adieu, my lord;
        I have a speech of fire, that fain would blaze,   190
        But that this folly douts it.   [*Exit.*

King.   Let 's follow, Gertrude;
        How much I had to do to calm his rage!
        Now fear I this will give it start again;
        Therefore let 's follow.   [*Exeunt.*

189. **Woman will be out**—I shall be a man again.
191. **Douts it**—Puts it out.

ACT FIVE

Scene I

A churchyard. Enter two Clowns, *with spades, &c.*

1 Clown. Is she to be buried in Christian burial that wilfully seeks her own salvation?

2 Clown. I tell thee she is; and therefore make her grave straight. The crowner hath sat on her, and finds it   4 Christian burial.

1 Clown. How can that be, unless she drown'd herself in her own defence?

2 Clown. Why, 't is found so.

1 Clown. It must be 'se offendendo'; it cannot be else.   9 For here lies the point: If I drown myself wittingly, it argues an act, and an act hath three branches; it is, to act, to do, and to perform; argal she drown'd herself wittingly.   13

2 Clown. Nay, but hear you, goodman delver,—

1 Clown. Give me leave. Here lies the water; good. Here stands the man; good. If the man go to this water and drown himself, it is, will he nill he, he goes, —mark you that; but if the water come to him and

2. **Wilfully**—Suicides are not accorded the rites of the church.
4. **Crowner hath sat on her**—Coroner has given his decision on the case.
9. **Se offendendo**—For *defendendo*—self defense.
12. **Argal**—For *ergo,* meaning therefore.

drown him, he drowns not himself; argal he that is
not guilty of his own death shortens not his own life.

2 Clown. But is this law?   21

1 Clown. Ay, marry, is 't; crowner's quest law.

2 Clown. Will you ha' the truth on 't? If this had not
been a gentlewoman, she should have been buried out
o' Christian burial.   25

1 Clown. Why, there thou say'st; and the more pity that
great folk should have countenance in this world to
drown or hang themselves, more than their even
Christian. Come, my spade. There is no ancient
gentlemen but gardeners, ditchers, and grave-makers;
they hold up Adam's profession.

2 Clown. Was he a gentleman?   32

1 Clown. A' was the first that ever bore arms.

2 Clown. Why, he had none.

1 Clown. What, art a heathen? How dost thou understand the Scripture? The Scripture says, Adam
digg'd; could he dig without arms? I 'll put another
question to thee. If thou answerest me not to the purpose, confess thyself—

2 Clown. Go to.

1 Clown. What is he that builds stronger than either the
mason, the shipwright, or the carpenter?   42

2 Clown. The gallows-maker; for that frame outlives a
thousand tenants.

1 Clown. I like thy wit well, in good faith. The gallows

22. **Crowner's quest**—Coroner's inquest. 33. **A'**—He.

does well; but how does it well? It does well to those that do ill: now, thou dost ill to say the gallows is built stronger than the church; argal the gallows may do well to thee. To 't again; come.

2 Clown. Who builds stronger than a mason, a shipwright, or a carpenter?

1 Clown. Ay, tell me that, and unyoke.   52

2 Clown. Marry, now I can tell.

1 Clown. To 't.

2 Clown. Mass, I cannot tell.   55

    Enter HAMLET *and* HORATIO *afar off.*

1 Clown. Cudgel thy brains no more about it, for your dull ass will not mend his pace with beating; and, when you are ask'd this question next, say 'a gravemaker'; the houses that he makes last till doomsday. Go, get thee to Yaughan; fetch me a stoup of liquor. 60

           [*Exit 2* CLOWN.

     He digs and sings

  In youth, when I did love, did love,
   Methought it was very sweet,   62
  To contract, O the time, for-a my behove,
   O, methought there was nothing meet.

Hamlet. Has this fellow no feeling of his business, that he sings at grave-making?

Horatio. Custom hath made it in him a property of easiness.

 52. **Unyoke**—Your work is done. (Unyoke and go home.)
 60. **Stoup**—Drinking cup.

Hamlet. 'T is e'en so. The hand of little employment
　hath the daintier sense.

1 Clown. [*Sings*]

> But age, with his stealing steps,
> Hath claw'd me in his clutch,　　　　　　72
> And hath shipp'd me intil the land,
> 　As if I had never been such.

　　　　　　　　　　　　[*Throws up a skull.*

Hamlet. That skull had a tongue in it, and could sing
　once. How the knave jowls it to th' ground, as if it　76
　were Cain's jaw-bone, that did the first murder! It
　might be the pate of a politician, which this ass now
　o'er-reaches; one that would circumvent God, might
　it not?　　　　　　80

Horatio. It might, my lord.

Hamlet. Or of a courtier, which could say, 'Good mor-
　row, sweet lord! How dost thou, good lord?' This
　might be my lord such-a-one, that prais'd my lord
　such-a-one's horse, when he meant to beg it,—might
　it not?　　　　　　86

Horatio. Ay, my lord.

Hamlet. Why, e'en so; and now my Lady Worm's;
　chapless, and knock'd about the mazzard with a sex-　89
　ton's spade. Here's fine revolution, if we had the
　trick to see 't. Did these bones cost no more the

76. **Jowls**—Knocks.　78. **Pate**—Head.
8ρ. **Chapless**—Without a jaw.　89. **Mazzard**—Head.

breeding, but to play at loggats with 'em? mine ache   92
to think on 't.

1 Clown. [*Sings*]

> A pick-axe, and a spade, a spade,
>   For and a shrouding sheet;   95
> O, a pit of clay for to be made
>   For such a guest is meet.

[*Throws up another skull.*

Hamlet. There 's another; why may not that be the skull
of a lawyer? Where be his quiddits now, his quillets,
his cases, his tenures, and his tricks? why does he
suffer this rude knave now to knock him about the
sconce with a dirty shovel, and will not tell him of
his action of battery? Hum! This fellow might be 103
in 's time a great buyer of land, with his statutes, his
recognizances, his fines, his double vouchers, his recoveries. Is this the fine of his fines, and the recovery
of his recoveries, to have his fine pate full of fine dirt?
Will his vouchers vouch him no more of his pur-
chases, and double ones too, than the length and
breadth of a pair of indentures? The very convey- 110
ances of his lands will hardly lie in this box, and

92. **Did these . . . loggats with 'em**—Did it cost so little to breed these
    bones that one may play quoits with them?
97. **Meet**—Fitting, suitable.
99. **Quiddits . . . quillets**—Fine points of law and logic.
102. **Sconce**—Head. 103. **Action of battery**—Attack.
110. **Pair of indentures**—Indentures were agreements written in duplicate
    so that each person concerned could have a copy.

must the inheritor himself have no more, ha?   112
Horatio. Not a jot more, my lord.
Hamlet. Is not parchment made of sheep-skins?
Horatio. Ay, my lord, and of calf-skins too.
Hamlet. They are sheep and calves which seek out as-
surance in that. I will speak to this fellow. Whose
grave 's this, sirrah?
1 Clown. Mine, sir.

> [*Sings*] O, a pit of clay for to be made
>   For such a guest is meet.   121

Hamlet. I think it be thine indeed, for thou liest in 't.
1 Clown. You lie out on 't, sir, and therefore it is not
yours. For my part, I do not lie in 't, and yet it is
mine.
Hamlet. Thou dost lie in 't, to be in 't and say it is
thine. 'T is for the dead, not for the quick; therefore
thou liest.   128
1 Clown. 'T is a quick lie, sir; 't will away again, from
me to you.
Hamlet. What man dost thou dig it for?
1 Clown. For no man, sir.
Hamlet. What woman, then?   133
1 Clown. For none, neither.
Hamlet. Who is to be buried in 't?
1 Clown. One that was a woman, sir; but, rest her soul,
she 's dead.

Hamlet. How absolute the knave is! We must speak 138
    by the card, or equivocation will undo us. By the
    Lord, Horatio, these three years I have taken note of
    it; the age is grown so picked, that the toe of the
    peasant comes so near the heel of the courtier, he galls
    his kibe. How long hast thou been a grave-maker?   143
1 Clown. Of all the days i' th' year, I came to 't that day
    that our last king Hamlet o'ercame Fortinbras.
Hamlet. How long is that since?
1 Clown. Cannot you tell that? every fool can tell that.
    It was the very day that young Hamlet was born; he
    that is mad, and sent into England.
Hamlet. Ay, marry, why was he sent into England?
1 Clown. Why, because a' was mad. A' shall recover his
    wits there; or, if a' do not, it 's no great matter there.
Hamlet. Why?   153
1 Clown. 'T will not be seen in him there; there the men
    are as mad as he.
Hamlet. How came he mad?
1 Clown. Very strangely, they say.
Hamlet. How 'strangely'?   158
1 Clown. Faith, e'en with losing his wits.
Hamlet. Upon what ground?
1 Clown. Why, here in Denmark. I have been sexton
    here, man and boy, thirty years.

138. **Absolute**—Positive.
139. **By the card**—According to the chart, precisely.
139. **Equivocation**—A round-about expression, quibbling.
143. **Kibe**—Chilblain.

Hamlet. How long will a man lie i' th' earth ere he rot?

1 Clown. I' faith, if a' be not rotten before a' die—as we
have many pocky corses now-a-days that will scarce
hold the laying in—a' will last you some eight year or
nine year; a tanner will last you nine year.

Hamlet. Why he more than another?   168

1 Clown. Why, sir, his hide is so tann'd with his trade
that a' will keep out water a great while; and your
water is a sore decayer of your dead body. Here's a
skull now; this skull has lain in the earth three-and-
twenty years.

Hamlet. Whose was it?   174

1 Clown. A mad fellow's it was. Whose do you think
it was?

Hamlet. Nay, I know not.

1 Clown. A pestilence on him for a mad rogue! A'
pour'd a flagon of Rhenish on my head once. This
same skull, sir, was Yorick's skull, the king's jester.

Hamlet. This?

1 Clown. E'en that.   182

Hamlet. Let me see. [*Takes the skull.*] Alas, poor
Yorick! I knew him, Horatio; a fellow of infinite
jest, of most excellent fancy. He hath borne me on
his back a thousand times; and now how abhorred in
my imagination it is! my gorge rises at it. Here hung 187
those lips that I have kiss'd I know not how oft.
Where be your gibes now, your gambols, your songs,

187. **Gorge**—Throat, stomach.

"Alas, poor Yorick!"

Maurice Evans as Hamlet

your flashes of merriment, that were wont to set
the table on a roar? Not one now, to mock your own
grinning? quite chop-fallen? Now, get you to my
lady's chamber, and tell her, let her paint an inch
thick, to this favour she must come: make her laugh
at that! Prithee, Horatio, tell me one thing.   19ʳ

Horatio. What 's that, my lord?

Hamlet. Dost thou think Alexander look'd o' this fashion
i' th' earth?

Horatio. E'en so.

Hamlet. And smelt so? pah!   [*Puts down the skull.*

Horatio. E'en so, my lord.   201

Hamlet. To what base uses we may return, Horatio!
Why may not imagination trace the noble dust of
Alexander till he find it stopping a bung-hole?   204

Horatio. 'T were to consider too curiously, to consider so.

Hamlet. No, faith, not a jot; but to follow him thither
with modesty enough, and likelihood to lead it; as
thus: Alexander died, Alexander was buried, Alexander returneth into dust, the dust is earth, of earth
we make loam, and why of that loam whereto he was
converted might they not stop a beer-barrel?

Imperial Cæsar, dead and turn'd to clay,
Might stop a hole to keep the wind away;
O, that that earth, which kept the world in awe,
Should patch a wall t' expel the winter's flaw!   215

But soft! but soft! Aside! here comes the king,

Enter PRIESTS, *&c., in procession, the corpse of* OPHELIA;
　　LAERTES *and* Mourners *following;* KING, QUEEN, *their*
　　trains, &c.

　　　The queen, the courtiers.　Who is that they follow,
　　　And with such maimed rites?　This doth betoken
　　　The corse they follow did with desperate hand
　　　Fordo it own life.　'T was of some estate.　　　　220
　　　Couch we awhile, and mark.　　[*Retiring with* HORATIO.

Laertes.　What ceremony else?

Hamlet.　That is Laertes, a very noble youth; mark.

Laertes.　What ceremony else?

1 Priest.　Her obsequies have been as far enlarg'd　　225
　　　As we have warrantise.　Her death was doubtful;
　　　And, but that great command o'ersways the order,
　　　She should in ground unsanctified have lodg'd
　　　Till the last trumpet; for charitable prayers,
　　　Shards, flints, and pebbles should be thrown on her. 230
　　　Yet here she is allow'd her virgin crants,
　　　Her maiden strewments, and the bringing home
　　　Of bell and burial.

Laertes.　Must there no more be done?

1 Priest.　　　　　　　　　　No more be done.

　　　We should profane the service of the dead　　　235

218. **Maimed rites**—Shortened services.
225. **Obsequies**—Funeral ceremonies.　226. **Warrantise**—Authority for.
226. **Doubtful**—Whether it is to be considered suicide or accident.
230. **Shards**—Fragments of pottery.
231. **Crants**—Garlands, usually made of white paper and used at the death
　　　of young girls.

To sing a requiem and such rest to her
As to peace-parted souls.

Laertes.   Lay her i' th' earth,
And from her fair and unpolluted flesh
May violets spring! I tell thee, churlish priest,
A minist'ring angel shall my sister be,   240
When thou liest howling.

Hamlet.   What, the fair Ophelia!

Queen. Sweets to the sweet; farewell!

                              [*Scattering flowers.*

I hop'd thou shouldst have been my Hamlet's wife;
I thought thy bride-bed to have deck'd, sweet maid,
And not have strew'd thy grave.

Laertes.   O, treble woe,   245
Fall ten times treble on that cursed head
Whose wicked deed thy most ingenious sense
Depriv'd thee of! Hold off the earth awhile,
Till I have caught her once more in mine arms.

                              [*Leaps into the grave.*

Now pile your dust upon the quick and dead,   250
Till of this flat a mountain you have made
To o'ertop old Pelion, or the skyish head
Of blue Olympus.

Hamlet. [*Advancing*] What is he whose grief
Bears such an emphasis, whose phrase of sorrow
Conjures the wand'ring stars and makes them stand   255
Like wonder-wounded hearers? This is I,

252. **Pelion**—A mountain in Greece.

Hamlet the Dane!   [*Leaps into the grave.*

Laertes. The devil take thy soul!   [*Grappling with him.*

Hamlet.   Thou pray'st not well.

    I prithee, take thy fingers from my throat;

    For, though I am not splenitive and rash,   260

    Yet have I something in me dangerous,

    Which let thy wiseness fear. Hold off thy hand!

King. Pluck them asunder.

Queen.   Hamlet, Hamlet!

All.   Gentlemen,—

Horatio. Good my lord, be quiet.

   [*The* Attendants *part them, and they come out of the grave.*

Hamlet. Why, I will fight with him upon this theme   265

    Until my eyelids will no longer wag.

Queen. O my son, what theme?

Hamlet. I lov'd Ophelia. Forty thousand brothers

    Could not, with all their quantity of love,

    Make up my sum. What wilt thou do for her?   270

King. O, he is mad, Laertes.

Queen. For love of God, forbear him!

Hamlet. 'Swounds, show me what thou 'lt do:

    Woo't weep? woo't fight? woo't fast? woo't tear thy-

      self?

    Woo't drink up eisel? eat a crocodile?   275

    I 'll do 't. Dost thou come here to whine?

    To outface me with leaping in her grave?

    Be buried quick with her, and so will I;

260. **Splenitive**—Quick-tempered. 275. **Eisel**—Probably, vinegar.

And, if thou prate of mountains, let them throw
Millions of acres on us, till our ground,   280
Singeing his pate against the burning zone,
Make Ossa like a wart! Nay, an thou 'lt mouth,
I 'll rant as well as thou.

Queen.   This is mere madness,
And thus a while the fit will work on him.
Anon, as patient as the female dove   285
When that her golden couplets are disclos'd,
His silence will sit drooping.

Hamlet.   Hear you, sir;
What is the reason that you use me thus?
I lov'd you ever. But it is no matter;
Let Hercules himself do what he may,   290
The cat will mew, and dog will have his day.   [*Exit.*

King. I pray you, good Horatio, wait upon him.

                                        [*Exit* Horatio.

[*To* Laertes] Strengthen your patience in our last
    night's speech;
We 'll put the matter to the present push.
Good Gertrude, set some watch over your son.   295
This grave shall have a living monument.
An hour of quiet shortly shall we see;
Till then, in patience our proceeding be.   [*Exeunt.*

282. **Ossa**—A mountain in Greece. 282. **An**—If.
286. **Golden couplets are disclos'd**—Her young are hatched. (The
    dove usually lays two eggs and the baby birds are covered with
    yellow down.)
290. **Hercules**—A hero in Greek mythology, famous for his strength.

Scene II

A hall in the castle. Enter Hamlet *and* Horatio.

Hamlet. So much for this, sir; now shall you see the
other.

You do remember all the circumstance?

Horatio. Remember it, my lord!

Hamlet. Sir, in my heart there was a kind of fighting
That would not let me sleep. Methought I lay   5
Worse than the mutines in the bilboes. Rashly,
And prais'd be rashness for it, let us know,
Our indiscretion sometimes serves us well
When our deep plots do pall; and that should teach us
There 's a divinity that shapes our ends,   10
Rough-hew them how we will.

Horatio.   That is most certain.

Hamlet. Up from my cabin,
My sea-gown scarf'd about me, in the dark
Grop'd I to find out them; had my desire,
Finger'd their packet, and in fine withdrew   15
To mine own room again; making so bold,
My fears forgetting manners, to unseal
Their grand commission; where I found, Horatio—
O royal knavery!—an exact command,
Larded with many several sorts of reasons   20
Importing Denmark's health, and England's too,

6. **Bilboes**—Chains by which mutinous sailors were linked together.

With, ho! such bugs and goblins in my life
That, on the supervise, no leisure bated,
No, not to stay the grinding of the axe,
My head should be struck off.

Horatio.   Is 't possible?   25

Hamlet.   Here 's the commission; read it at more leisure.
But wilt thou hear me how I did proceed?

Horatio.   I beseech you.

Hamlet.   Being thus be-netted round with villainies,—
Ere I could make a prologue to my brains,   30
They had begun the play,—I sat me down;
Devis'd a new commission, wrote it fair.
I once did hold it, as our statists do,
A baseness to write fair, and labour'd much
How to forget that learning; but, sir, now   35
It did me yeoman's service. Wilt thou know
The effect of what I wrote?

Horatio.   Ay, good my lord.

Hamlet.   An earnest conjuration from the king,
As England was his faithful tributary,
As love between them like the palm might flourish,   40
As peace should still her wheaten garland wear,
And stand a comma 'tween their amities,

23. **Supervise**—On the first reading.
30. **Ere I could . . . the play**—Before I could form a plan, my wits had
    made one. (That is, the plan was made on the spur of the moment.)
33. **Statists**—Statesmen.
34. **Baseness**—Fine writing was done by paid secretaries, not by gentle-
    men.
38. **Conjuration**—Solemn appeal.   42. **Comma**—A mark of connection.
42. **Amities**—Friendly relations.

And many such-like 'as'-es of great charge,
That on the view and knowing of these contents,
Without debatement further, more or less,   45
He should the bearers put to sudden death,
Not shriving-time allow'd.

Horatio.   How was this seal'd?

Hamlet. Why, even in that was heaven ordinant.
I had my father's signet in my purse,
Which was the model of that Danish seal;   50
Folded the writ up in form of the other,
Subscrib'd it, gave 't th' impression, plac'd it safely,
The changeling never known. Now, the next day
Was our sea-fight; and what to this was sequent
Thou know'st already.   55

Horatio. So Guildenstern and Rosencrantz go to 't.

Hamlet. Why, man, they did make love to this employ-
          ment;
They are not near my conscience; their defeat
Doth by their own insinuation grow.
'T is dangerous when the baser nature comes   60
Between the pass and fell-incensed points
Of mighty opposites.

Horatio.   Why, what a king is this!

Hamlet. Does it not, think'st thee, stand me now upon—

---

47. **Shriving-time**—Time for confession; any short time.
48. **Ordinant**—Favoring. 54. **Sequent**—Followed.
60. **When the baser nature . . . mighty opposites**—When men of
      lower rank come between the thrusts and sword points of powerful
      opponents.

He that hath kill'd my king, ...
I'opp'd in between th' election and my hopes,   65
Thrown out his angle for my proper life,
And with such cozenage—is 't not perfect conscience
To quit him with his arm? and is 't not to be
    damn'd,
To let this canker of our nature come
In further evil?   70

Horatio. It must be shortly known to him from England
    What is the issue of the business there.

Hamlet. It will be short; the interim is mine,
    And a man's life 's no more than to say 'One.'
    But I am very sorry, good Horatio,   75
    That to Laertes I forgot myself;
    For by the image of my cause I see
    The portraiture of his. I 'll court his favours;
    But, sure, the bravery of his grief did put me
    Into a tow'ring passion.

Horatio.   Peace! who comes here?   80

Enter young Osric.

Osric. Your lordship is right welcome back to Denmark.

Hamlet. I humbly thank you, sir. Dost know this
    waterfly?

Horatio. No, my good lord.   84

---

65. **Election**—Hamlet would have been king, had not his uncle taken the
    throne. 67. **Cozenage**—Deception.
73. **Interim**—Interval. (The ship will return soon. I have until then to
    act.)

Hamlet. Thy state is the more gracious, for 't is a vice
    to know him. He hath much land, and fertile; let
    a beast be lord of beasts, and his crib shall stand at
    the king's mess. 'T is a chough; but, as I say, spacious
    in the possession of dirt.

Osric. Sweet lord, if your lordship were at leisure, I
    should impart a thing to you from his majesty.   91

Hamlet. I will receive it, sir, with all diligence of spirit.
    Put your bonnet to his right use; 't is for the head.

Osiric. I thank your lordship, it is very hot.

Hamlet. No, believe me, 't is very cold; the wind is
    northerly.   96

Osric. It is indifferent cold, my lord, indeed.

Hamlet. But yet methinks it is very sultry and hot for
    my complexion.

Osric. Exceedingly, my lord; it is very sultry—as 't were
    —I cannot tell how. But, my lord, his majesty bade
    me signify to you that he has laid a great wager on
    your head. Sir, this is the matter,—

Hamlet. I beseech you, remember—   104

            [HAMLET *moves him to put on his hat.*

Osric. Nay, in good faith; for mine ease, in good faith.
    Sir, here is newly come to court Laertes; believe me,
    an absolute gentleman, full of most excellent differ-
    ences, of very soft society and great showing: indeed,
    to speak feelingly of him, he is the card or calendar

88. **Chough**—Chattering jackdaw, or perhaps a crude peasant.

of gentry, for you shall find in him the continent of
what part a gentleman would see.   111

Hamlet. Sir, his definement suffers no perdition in you;
   though, I know, to divide him inventorially would
   dizzy the arithmetic of memory, and yet but yaw
   neither, in respect to his quick sail. But, in the verity
   of extolment, I take him to be a soul of great article,
   and his infusion of such dearth and rareness, as,
   to make true diction of him, his semblable is his
   mirror; and who else would trace him, his umbrage,
   nothing more.

Osric. Your lordship speaks most infallibly of him.   121

Hamlet. The concernancy, sir? why do we wrap the gentleman in our more rawer breath?

Osric. Sir?

Horatio. Is 't not possible to understand in another
   tongue? You will do 't, sir, really.   126

Hamlet. What imports the nomination of this gentleman?

Osric. Of Laertes?

Horatio. His purse is empty already; all 's golden words
   are spent.

Hamlet. Of him, sir.   132

110. **Continent**—Sum total of gentlemanly qualities.
112. **Definement . . . umbrage**—A speech purposely expressed in high-
     flown language, meaning apparently—Your description is good
     though it is impossible to tell all his good points. He is a man of
     such fine quality that his likeness may be found only in his mirror,
     and nothing but his shadow can keep up with him.
122. **The concernancy . . . breath**—What is the point of all this talking?

Osric. I know you are not ignorant—

Hamlet. I would you did, sir; yet, in faith, if you did, it would not much approve me. Well, sir?

Osric. You are not ignorant of what excellence Laertes is—   137

Hamlet. I dare not confess that, lest I should compare with him in excellence; but to know a man well, were to know himself.

Osiric. I mean, sir, for his weapon; but, in the imputation laid on him by them, in his meed he's unfellow'd.   143

Hamlet. What's his weapon?

Osric. Rapier and dagger.

Hamlet. That's two of his weapons; but, well.

Osric. The king, sir, hath wager'd with him six Barbary horses, against the which he has impon'd, as I take it, six French rapiers and poniards, with their assigns, as girdle, hanger, and so. Three of the carriages, in faith, are very dear to fancy, very responsive to the hilts, most delicate carriages, and of very liberal conceit.

Hamlet. What call you the carriages?   154

Horatio. I knew you must be edified by the margent ere you had done.

---

142. **In his meed he's unfellow'd**—Has no equal.
152. **Liberal conceit**—Free or charming design.
155. **I knew you . . . had done**—I knew you would have to be instructed by a marginal note. (Old books commonly had explanations in the margin.)

Osric. The carriages, sir, are the hangers.

Hamlet. The phrase would be more germane to the
matter, if we could carry cannon by our sides; I would
it might be hangers till then. But, on: six Barbary
horses against six French swords, their assigns, and
three liberal-conceited carriages; that 's the French
bet against the Danish. Why is this 'impon'd,' as you
call it?   164

Osric. The king, sir, hath laid that in a dozen passes
between yourself and him he shall not exceed you
three hits; he hath laid on twelve for nine; and it
would come to immediate trial, if your lordship
would vouchsafe the answer.

Hamlet. How if I answer 'no'?   170

Osric. I mean, my lord, the opposition of your person in
trial.

Hamlet. Sir, I will walk here in the hall; if it please
his majesty, 't is the breathing time of day with me. 174
Let the foils be brought, the gentleman willing, and
the king hold his purpose, I will win for him if I can;
if not, I 'll gain nothing but my shame and the odd
hits.

Osric. Shall I re-deliver you e'en so?

Hamlet. To this effect, sir; after what flourish your
nature will.   181

Osric. I commend my duty to your lordship.

Hamlet. Yours, yours. [*Exit* Osric.] He does well to

174. **Breathing time**—Time for exercise or relaxation.

commend it himself; there are no tongues else for 's
turn.

Horatio. This lapwing runs away with the shell on his
head.   187

Hamlet. He did comply with his dug before he suck'd
it. Thus has he, and many more of the same bevy
that I know the drossy age dotes on, only got the
tune of the time and outward habit of encounter; a
kind of yesty collection, which carries them through
and through the most fond and winnowed opinions;
and do but blow them to their trial, the bubbles are
out.

Enter a LORD.

Lord. My lord, his majesty commended him to you by
young Osric, who brings back to him, that you attend him in the hall. He sends to know if your
pleasure hold to play with Laertes, or that you will
take longer time.   200

Hamlet. I am constant to my purposes; they follow the
king's pleasure: if his fitness speaks, mine is ready;
now or whensoever, provided I be so able as now.

Lord. The king and queen and all are coming down.

Hamlet. In happy time.   205

Lord. The queen desires you to use some gentle entertainment to Laertes before you fall to play.

186. **Lapwing**—Osric is precocious, as the lapwing runs as soon as hatched.
190. **Drossy age dotes on**—The worthless people of this age are fond of.
192. **Yesty**—Unimportant, frivolous.

Hamlet. She well instructs me.   [*Exit* Lord.

Horatio. You will lose this wager, my lord.   209

Hamlet. I do not think so; since he went into France,
  I have been in continual practice. I shall win at the
  odds. But thou wouldst not think how ill all 's here
  about my heart; but it is no matter.

Horatio. Nay, good my lord,—   214

Hamlet. It is but foolery; but it is such a kind of gain-
  giving as would perhaps trouble a woman.

Horatio. If your mind dislike any thing, obey it. I will
  forestall their repair hither, and say you are not fit. 218

Hamlet. Not a whit; we defy augury. There 's a special
  providence in the fall of a sparrow. If it be now, 't
  is not to come; if it be not to come, it will be now;
  if it be not now, yet it will come; the readiness is all.
  Since no man has aught of what he leaves, what
  is 't to leave betimes? Let be.

Enter King, Queen, Laertes, Lords, Osric, *and other* Attendants *with foils and gauntlets; a table and flagons
  of wine on it.*

King. Come, Hamlet, come, and take his hand from me.
              [King *puts* Laertes' *hand into* Hamlet's.

Hamlet. Give me your pardon, sir: I've done you wrong;
  But pardon 't, as you are a gentleman.
  This presence knows,
  And you must needs have heard, how I am punish'd

With sore distraction. What I have done, 230
That might your nature, honour, and exception
Roughly awake, I here proclaim was madness.
Was 't Hamlet wrong'd Laertes? Never Hamlet!
If Hamlet from himself be ta'en away,
And when he 's not himself does wrong Laertes, 235
Then Hamlet does it not, Hamlet denies it.
Who does it, then? His madness. If 't be so,
Hamlet is of the faction that is wrong'd;
His madness is poor Hamlet's enemy.
Sir, in this audience, 240
Let my disclaiming from a purpos'd evil
Free me so far in your most generous thoughts,
That I have shot mine arrow o'er the house
And hurt my brother.

Laertes. I am satisfied in nature,
Whose motive, in this case, should stir me most 245
To my revenge; but in my terms of honour
I stand aloof, and will no reconcilement
Till by some elder masters of known honour
I have a voice and precedent of peace,
To keep my name ungor'd. But till that time, 250
I do receive your offer'd love like love,
And will not wrong it.

Hamlet. I do embrace it freely,
And will this brother's wager frankly play.

244. **I am satisfied in nature . . . name ungor'd**—Personally, I am satisfied; but honor requires a formal settlement, vouched for by experts.

Give us the foils. Come on.

Laertes.   Come, one for me.

Hamlet. I 'll be your foil, Laertes; in mine ignorance

Your skill shall, like a star i' th' darkest night,   256

Stick fiery off indeed.

Laertes.   You mock me, sir.

Hamlet. No, by this hand.

King. Give them the foils, young Osric. Cousin Hamlet,

You know the wager?

Hamlet.   Very well, my lord;   260

Your grace hath laid the odds o' th' weaker side.

King. I do not fear it; I have seen you both;

But since he is better'd, we have therefore odds.

Laertes. This is too heavy, let me see another.

Hamlet. This likes me well. These foils have all a

length?   [*They prepare to play.*

Osric. Ay, my good lord.   266

King. Set me the stoups of wine upon that table.

If Hamlet give the first or second hit,

Or quit in answer of the third exchange,

Let all the battlements their ordnance fire.   270

The king shall drink to Hamlet's better breath;

And in the cup an union shall he throw,

Richer than that which four successive kings

In Denmark's crown have worn. Give me the cups;

And let the kettle to the trumpet speak,   275

The trumpet to the cannoneer without,

272. **Union**—Pearl. 275. **Kettle**—Kettle-drum.

"My lord, I'll hit him now."

John Gielgud as Hamlet

The cannons to the heavens, the heaven to earth,
'Now the king drinks to Hamlet!' Come, begin;
And you, the judges, bear a wary eye.

Hamlet. Come on, sir.

Laertes.   Come, my lord.   [*They play.*

Hamlet.   One.

Laertes.   No.

Hamlet.   Judgment.

Osric. A hit, a very palpable hit.

Laertes.   Well; again.   281

King. Stay; give me drink. Hamlet, this pearl is thine;
    Here's to thy health.

          [*Trumpets sound, and cannon shot off within.*
              Give him the cup.

Hamlet. I 'll play this bout first; set it by awhile.
    Come. [*They play.*] Another hit; what say you?   285

Laertes. A touch, a touch, I do confess.

King. Our son shall win.

Queen.   He 's fat and scant of breath.
    Here, Hamlet, take my napkin, rub thy brows;
    The queen carouses to thy fortune, Hamlet.

Hamlet. Good madam!

King.   Gertrude, do not drink.   290

Queen. I will, my lord; I pray you, pardon me.

King. [*Aside*] It is the poison'd cup; it is too late.

Hamlet. I dare not drink yet, madam; by and by.

Queen. Come, let me wipe thy face.

Laertes. My lord, I 'll hit him now.

King.   I do not think 't. 295

Laertes. [*Aside*] And yet 't is almost 'gainst my con-
    science.

Hamlet. Come, for the third, Laertes: you but dally;
    I pray you, pass with your best violence;
    I am afeared you make a wanton of me.

Laertes. Say you so? come on.   [*They play.*

Osric. Nothing, neither way.   301

Laertes. Have at you now!

      [LAERTES *wounds* HAMLET; *then, in scuffling, they*
           change rapiers, and HAMLET *wounds* LAERTES.

King.   Part them; they're incens'd.

Hamlet. Nay, come, again.   [*Queen falls.*

Osric.   Look to the queen there, ho!

Horatio. They bleed on both sides. How is 't, my lord?

Osric. How is 't Laertes?
                                   305

Laertes. Why, as a woodcock to mine own springe,
    Osric;
    I am justly kill'd with mine own treachery.

Hamlet. How does the queen?

King.   She swounds to see them bleed.

Queen. No, no, the drink, the drink—O my dear
    Hamlet—
    The drink, the drink! I am poison'd.   [*Dies.*

Hamlet. O villainy! Ho! let the door be lock'd!   311

---

299. **You make a wanton of me**—You are only playing with me.
(Laertes is not doing his best, perhaps because of his conscience, perhaps because he knows the poison will do its work without much ex-
ertion on his part.)

Treachery! seek it out.   [LAERTES *falls.*
Laertes. It is here, Hamlet. Hamlet, thou art slain;
    No medicine in the world can do thee good;
    In thee there is not half an hour of life: 315
    The treacherous instrument is in thy hand,
    Unbated and envenom'd. The foul practice
    Hath turn'd itself on me. Lo, here I lie,
    Never to rise again. Thy mother 's poison'd!
    I can no more. The king, the king's to blame!   320
Hamlet. The point envenom'd too!
    Then, venom, to thy work!   [*Stabs* KING.
All. Treason! treason!
King. O, yet defend me, friends! I am but hurt.
Hamlet. Here, thou incestuous, murd'rous, damned Dane,
    Drink off this potion! Is thy union here?
    Follow my mother!   [KING *dies.*
Laertes.   He is justly serv'd;
    It is a poison temper'd by himself.
    Exchange forgiveness with me, noble Hamlet;
    Mine and my father's death come not upon thee,   330
    Nor thine on me!   [*Dies.*
Hamlet. Heaven make thee free of it! I follow thee.
    I am dead, Horatio. Wretched queen, adieu!
    You that look pale and tremble at this chance,
    That are but mutes or audience to this act,   335
    Had I but time—as this fell sergeant, death,
    Is strict in his arrest—O, I could tell you—
    But let it be. Horatio, I am dead;

Thou liv'st: report me and my cause aright
To the unsatisfied.

Horatio.   Never believe it;   340
I am more an antique Roman than a Dane;
Here's yet some liquor left.

Hamlet.   As thou 'rt a man,
Give me the cup. Let go; by heaven, I 'll have 't.
O good Horatio! what a wounded name,
Things standing thus unknown, shall live behind
    me!   345
If thou didst ever hold me in thy heart,
Absent thee from felicity awhile,
And in this harsh world draw thy breath in pain,
To tell my story.   [*March afar off, and shot within.*
        What warlike noise is this?

Osric. Young Fortinbras, with conquest come from Po-
    land,   350
To th' ambassadors of England gives
This warlike volley.

Hamlet.   O, I die, Horatio;
The potent poison quite o'er-crows my spirit.
I cannot live to hear the news from England;
But I do prophesy th' election lights   355
On Fortinbras; he has my dying voice;
So tell him, with the occurrents, more and less,
Which have solicited—the rest is silence.   [*Dies.*

341. **Antique Roman**—The Romans of old preferred death to disgrace.
357. **Occurrents**—Incidents.
358. **Which have solicited**—Which have made me act as I have.

Horatio. Now cracks a noble heart. Good night, sweet
          prince,
     And flights of angels sing thee to thy rest! [*March within.*
     Why does the drum come hither?   361

Enter Fortinbras, *and the* English Ambassadors, *with drums,*
     colours, and Attendants.

Fortinbras. Where is this sight?
Horatio.   What is it ye would see?
     If aught of woe or wonder, cease your search.
Fortinbras. This quarry cries on havoc. O proud death,
     What feast is toward in thine eternal cell,   365
     That thou so many princes at a shot
     So bloodily hast struck?
1 Ambassador.   The sight is dismal;
     And our affairs from England come too late.
     The ears are senseless that should give us hearing,
     To tell him his commandment is fulfill'd,   370
     That Rosencrantz and Guildenstern are dead.
     Where should we have our thanks?
Horatio.   Not from his mouth,
     Had it th' ability of life to thank you.
     He never gave commandment for their death.
     But since, so jump upon this bloody question,   375
     You from the Polack wars, and you from England,
     Are here arriv'd, give order that these bodies

364. **This quarry cries on havoc**—Perhaps, this heap of dead bodies pro-
     claims indiscriminate slaughter.

High on a stage be placed to the view;
And let me speak to th' yet unknowing world
How these things came about. So shall you hear   380
Of carnal, bloody, and unnatural acts,
Of accidental judgments, casual slaughters,
Of deaths put on by cunning and forc'd cause;
And, in this upshot, purposes mistook
Fall'n on the inventors' heads: all this can I   385
Truly deliver.

Fortinbras.   Let us haste to hear it,
And call the noblest to the audience.
For me, with sorrow I embrace my fortune.
I have some rights of memory in this kingdom,
Which now to claim, my vantage doth invite me.   390

Horatio. Of that I shall have also cause to speak,
And from his mouth whose voice will draw on more;
But let this same be presently perform'd,
Even while men's minds are wild, lest more mis-
    chance,
On plots and errors, happen.

Fortinbras.   Let four captains   395
Bear Hamlet, like a soldier, to the stage;
For he was likely, had he been put on,
To have prov'd most royally; and, for his passage,
The soldiers' music and the rites of war
Speak loudly for him.   400
Take up the bodies. Such a sight as this

"O proud death . . . so bloodily hast struck"
Final scene from the Screen
Production

Becomes the field, but here shows much amiss.
Go, bid the soldiers shoot.

> [*A dead march. Exeunt, bearing off the dead bodies;
> after which a peal of ordnance is shot off.*

ELECTRA

By

Sophocles

FOR A BETTER UNDERSTANDING AND
APPRECIATION OF THE PLAY

Sophocles wrote his *Electra* in stately Greek verse, but even readers with no knowledge of the original may catch some of its beauty in this poetic English version. A Greek drama differs somewhat from a modern play, and even from a play by Shakespeare, for its choral chant and rhythmic dance make an appeal to both eye and ear. To catch its full beauty, as we read we should picture to ourselves the chorus dressed in beautiful flowing costume, now listening sympathetically to the characters, now weaving its pattern on the stage. We should remember, too, that the choral dance usually intensifies the emotional effect of the drama.

In the text, *episodes* correspond to acts and scenes. A Greek play is divided into *prologue,* setting the action in motion; *parodos,* marking the entrance of the chorus; four *episodes,* each followed by a *stasimon* or choral ode and solemn dance; and *exodos,* marking the withdrawal of the chorus and actors.

We will have a better understanding of *Electra* if we know what has happened before the action of the play begins. Agamemnon was the king of Argos and Mycenæ. At the head of his army and accompanied by his brother, Menelaus, he sailed for Troy. When the fleet was detained at Aulis by unfavorable winds, Agamemnon consulted the oracle and learned that only the sacrifice of his daughter Iphigenia upon the altar of Artemis would free his ships. By pretending that he wanted to betroth Iphigenia before he sailed, he persuaded her mother to send the girl to Aulis. Just as the priest was about to sacrifice her, the goddess appeared. Unperceived, she substituted a stag and spirited the maiden away to Tauris to serve as her priestess. Clytemnestra never forgave her husband for deceiving her. When he returned from Troy, she and her paramour Ægisthus slew him at a banquet prepared ostensibly in his honour. Young Orestes might also have been slain as a possible avenger had not his sister Electra contrived to save him, shortly after his father's death, and send him away to be brought up by a friend of the family.

The story of *Electra* is tragic. Electra herself is a high-spirited, unhappy girl who, since early girlhood, has lived in a cloud of tragedy. She suffered a terrible shock when her father, the king, was slain. Her sense of justice and filial piety were further outraged when she learned that her own mother had engineered the plot and then married Ægisthus, the slayer. Reared in the luxury befitting a king's daughter, Electra is now neglected and despised. She is treated like an outcast and is a virtual prisoner in her own home. Frantically she watches her youth slipping away; and with it, all hopes for a happy marriage. She broods over her unhappiness and thinks only of the day when her younger brother, Orestes, now in exile, will return and seek vengeance for their father's death. This desire becomes to her a fearful duty and goads her on to the desperate action revealed in the play.

THE CHARACTERS IN THE PLAY

Aged Servant, *to whose care young Orestes had been entrusted*
Orestes, *son of Agamemnon and Clytemnestra*
Pylades, *cousin and close friend of Orestes*
Electra, *sister of Orestes*
Chrysothemis, *younger sister of Electra*
Clytemnestra, *Queen of Mycenæ and Argos*
Ægisthus, *slayer of Agamemnon and husband of Clytemnestra*
Chorus of Mycenæan Women, *friends of Electra*

Scene: Before the palace of Agamemnon at Mycenæ

Agamemnon—ăg à měm′nŏn.
Orestes—ô rěs′ tēz.
Pylades—pĭl′ à dēz.
Chrysothemis—krĭs ŏth′ ê mĭs.
Clytemnestra—klī těm něs′ trà.
Ægisthus—ê jĭs′ thŭs.
Mycenæan—mī sê nē′ ăn.

Electra

PROLOGUE

Enter AGED SERVANT *with* ORESTES *and* PYLADES.

Aged Servant. O Child of Agamemnon, who sometime
    Was Captain of the host that leaguered Troy,
    'Tis thine at last to view before thee spread
    The scene thy heart was set on. Yonder lies
    Old Argos thou so long hast yearned to see,   5
    Once refuge of the gadfly-driven maid,
    Daughter of Inachus; and, Orestes, here
    The market-place from the Wolf-slayer named;
    There on our left is Hera's far-famed shrine;
    And lo! before us, at our very feet   10
    Thou seest Mycenæ of the golden hoard,
    And there the palace grim of Pelops' line,
    Deep stained with murder. Thence I bore thee once
    Snatched from beside thy father's bleeding corpse

Prologue—For notes on the Prologue and other divisions of a Greek
    play, see page 220.
 1. **Agamemnon**—Leader of the Greeks in the Trojan War.
 7. **Daughter of Inachus (ĭn′á kŭs)**—Refers to Io who was changed
    into a heifer and tortured by a gad-fly sent by jealous Hera. Inachus,
    the river god, was the legendary founder of Argos.
 8. **Wolf-slayer**—Apollo.
 9. **Hera (hē′rȧ)**—Wife of Zeus, chief of the gods.
11. **Mycenæ (mī sē′nē)**—Argos and Mycenæ, neighboring cities, were
    often called by the general name of Argos.
12. **Pelops' line**—The family of Agamemnon were descendants of Pelops.

By kindly hands, thy sister's; rescued thus 15
I fostered thee till thou hadst reached the age
To be the avenger of thy father's blood.
But now, Orestes, and thou, Pylades,
Dearest of friends, the hour for you is ripe
To take resolve and that right speedily. 20
For lo, already the bright beams of day
Waken to melody the pipe of birds,
And black night with her glimmering stars has waned.
So ere a soul be stirring in the streets
Confer together and resolve yourselves. 25
No time for longer pause; now must we act.
Orestes. Dearest of followers, how well thou show'st
The constant service of thy loyalty!
For as the high-bred steed, though he be old,
Pricks up his ears and champs the bit for joy 30
When battle rages, even so dost thou
Both urge us on and follow with the first.
Therefore I will unfold our plans, and thou
Note well my words, and if in aught I seem
To miss the mark, admonish and correct. 35
Know then that when I left thee to consult
The Pythian oracle and learn how best
To execute just vengeance for my sire
On those that slew him, Phœbus answered thus:
Trust not to shields or armed hosts, but steal 40

37. **Pythian oracle**—The famous oracle at Delphi, which the Greeks consulted for advice on all important occasions.
39. **Phœbus**—One of the names of Apollo.

The chance thyself the avenging blow to deal.
Since then the Pythian god hath thus advised,
Go thou and watch thine opportunity
To enter in the palace and observe
What happens there and bring us full report.　　45
And fear not to be recognized; long years
And thy white locks, the blossom of old age,
Have changed thee wholly. Tell some clever tale:
Thou art a Phocian stranger hither sent
By Phanoteus their mightiest ally.　　50
Report, confirming with an oath the tale,
How that Orestes by a fatal chance
Hath perished, from his speeding chariot hurled
(So let thy tale run) at the Pythian games.
And we meanwhile, as the god ordered us,　　55
First having crowned my father's sepulcher
With pure libations and rich offerings
Of new-shorn tresses, will return anon,
An urn of well-wrought brasswork in our hands,
The same we hid in the brushwood, as thou know'st.　60
This will confirm the untrue tale we bring,
That I am dead and to the pyre consigned,
Naught left of me but ashes and gray dust:
Little care I by rumour to be dead,
So I live on to win me deathless fame.　　65
The end, methinks, gives any fraud excuse.
Oft have I heard of men, considered wise,

49. **Phocian**—Native of the ancient Greek state of Phocis (fō'sĭs).

Who spread the rumour of their death, and so
Returning home a heartier welcome found.
Thus by my rumoured death I too aspire   70
To blaze a sudden meteor on my foes.
But O my country and my country's gods,
Give me fair welcome, prosper my emprise!
And greet me too, thou palace of my sires;
A heaven-sent cleanser of thy stain I come.   75
Send me not forth again to banishment,
But O! restore to me its ancient wealth,
May I refound its old prosperity!
Enough of words; go presently, old friend,
Attend thy business; and we two will go,   80
And watch the time, for opportunity
Is the best captain of all enterprise.

Electra. [*Within*] Ah me! unhappy me!

Aged Servant. Hist! from the doors a voice, my son, me-
　　thought,
　　A wailing as of some handmaid within.   85

Orestes. Can it be sad Electra! Shall we stay
　　And overhear her mournful plaint?

Aged Servant. Not so; we first must strive before all else
　　To do as Loxias bade us and thence take
　　Our auspices—with lustral waters bathe   90
　　Thy father's grave, thus shall we surely win

89. **Loxias**—The oracle of Apollo.
90. **Lustral waters bathe**—Pouring out wine for a god was a ceremony to
　　honor the dead.

Vantage at each step, victory in the end.
>   [*Exeunt. Enter* Electra *from the palace.*]
Electra.   O holy light,
>   What sight
Have ye not witnessed in the first gray morn,   95
Beatings of breasts and bosoms madly torn!
>   By night for me is spread
>   No festal banquet in this haunted hall,
>   But my lone pallet bed.
All night I muse upon my father dead,   100
Not in a foreign land at Ares' call,
But here, at home, by my own mother slain;
Her and Ægisthus, . . .
Felled by their axe's bloody stroke,
E'en as the woodman fells an oak.   105
And I, O father, I alone of all
>   Thy house am left forlorn
>   To make my moan, to mourn
>   Thy piteous fall.

Yet never, while these eyes   110
Behold the sun or star-bespangled skies,
Will I restrain my plaint, my bitter cries;
>   But like some nightingale
>   My ravished nest bewail,
And through these halls shall sound my groans 115
>   and sighs.

101. **Ares**—The god of war.

Halls of Persephonè and Death,
Guide of the shades, O Hermes, and O Wraith,
Ye god-sprung Furies dread
Who watch when blood is shed,
Or stained the marriage bed,   120
O aid me to avenge my father slain,
O send my brother back again!
Alone, no more I countervail
Grief that o'erloads the scale.

---

116. **Persephone (pĕr sĕf'ò nè)**—Wife of Pluto who ruled the infernal
regions. Furies and Harpies surrounded the throne.

117. **Hermes**—Messenger god. One of his duties was to conduct the souls
of the dead to Hades.

PARODOS

Enter CHORUS.

Chorus. Child of a mother all unblest,   125
 Electra, how in grief that knows no rest
 Thou witherest;
 Mourning thy father's cruel fate,
 By her betrayed and slaughtered by her mate.
 Black death await   130
 The plotter of that sin,
 If prayer so bold may answer win!

FIRST EPISODE

Electra. Ah, noble friends, ye come, I see,
 To ease my misery;
 Your kind intent, O trust me, I perceive.   135
 Yet can I never leave
 My task, each day, each hour, anew to shed
 Tears o'er my father dead.
 O kindly hearts, so ready to repay
 All friendship owes,   140

Chorus—The Chorus was an essential part of the play. It had these functions: to discuss through its leaders the troubles of the main characters, to serve as the voice of public opinion, to give advice, and to mark the end of each episode with choral hymns and dances.

Leave me, O leave me (this one boon I pray)
To my wild woes.

Chorus. Yet him, thy sire, from Acheron's dark shore
By prayers or cries thou never canst restore,
No, never more;   145
And by excess of grief thou perishest.
If remedy be none, were it not best
From grief to rest?
O rest thee! why
Thus nurse thy fruitless misery?   150

Electra. That child's so heartless who remembers not
His sire's sad lot.
O bird of Zeus, to thine I'll set my note,
Who with full throat
For Itys, Itys griev'st from eve till morn.   155
Ah! Niobe forlorn,
How blest art thou who tombed in stone dost lie
And weep for aye!

Chorus. Not thou alone, hast sorrow; others share
Thy load of care.   160
Think on thy kinsfolk whom afflictions press
Than thine no less,
Iphianassa and Chrysothemis.

143. **Acheron** (ăk'ĕr ŏn)—Swift river in the lower world, which all souls
had to cross. The spirits were ferried across by Charon, the aged
boatman.
153. **Zeus** (Zōōs)—Chief of the Greek gods.
156. **Niobe** (nī'ô bê)—Because she lamented the death of her children, she
was changed into a rock from which water continually gushed.
163. **Iphianassa**—Agamemnon has four daughters, the youngest of whom is
Iphianassa.

Think of thy brother; sorrow now is his,
An exiled youth, yet shortly shall he come   165
By heaven's good guidance home,
And glad Mycenæ shall Orestes own
Heir to his father's throne.

Electra.   Yea, for him long years I wait,
Unwed, childless, desolate,   170
Drenched with tears that ever flow
For my barren load of woe;
And the wrongs whereof he wot,
Or hath heard, are all forgot.
All those messages are vain—   175
How he hopes to come again,
How for home his heart doth yearn!—
Yet he wills not to return.

Chorus. Take heart, my child, Zeus still in heaven is king,
And orders everything;   180
To him commit the wrath that gnaws thy breast,
His will is ever best.
Nurse, as is meet, thy vengeance, but abate
Excess of hate,
For Time can heal, a gentle god and mild.   185
Nor Agamemnon's child
Who long by Crisa's pastoral shore remains,
Nor he who reigns
O'er Acheron will nevermore relent.

173. **Wot**—Knew.
187. **Crisa**—Large town in the ancient Greek state of Phocis.

Electra. Nay but for me is spent   190
  The best of life; I languish in despair.
   Prostrate with care,
  Without a parent's love or husband's aid,
   An orphaned maid.
  Here in the chambers of my sire I wait   195
   In low estate,
  Or like a stranger who in beggar's weeds
   On fragments feeds.
Chorus. Dire was the voice that greeted first
   Thy sire's return, and dire the cry   200
  That from the banquet-chamber burst,
   A wail of agony;
  What time the brazen axe's blow
  Struck him and laid him low,
  'Twas lust begat and craft conceived the deed,   205
  A monstrous offspring of a monstrous seed,
  Whether a god or mortal wrought the woe.

    . . . . . .

Electra. It shames me, friends, that ye should thus set
   down
  To willfulness my too persistent grief.
  But since I yield to hard necessity,   210
  Bear with me. How indeed could any woman
  Of noble blood who sees her father's home
  Plague-stricken, as I see it night and day,
  And each day stricken worse, not do as I?

For me a mother's love has turned to hate;   215
In my own home on sufferance I live
With my sire's murderers, on whose will it rests
To give or to withhold my daily bread.
Think what a life is mine, to see each day
Ægisthus seated on my father's throne,   220
Wearing the royal robes my father wore,
Pouring libations on the hearth, whereat
He slew him, and, to crown his insolence,
Wed my mother—mother shall I call
His paramour? So lost to shame is she   225
That she fears no vengeance. No,
As if exulting in her infamy,
She watches month by month to know the day
Whereon by treachery she slew my sire,
And keeps that day with dance and sacrifice,   230
Each month, of sheep to the protecting gods.
Beholding this I weep and waste within,
And to myself bewail the unhallowed feast
Named of my sire, with silent tears, for e'en
The luxury of wailing is denied me.   235
This woman (saintly is her speech) upbraids
And rates me thus: "Ungodly, hateful girl,
Hast thou alone to bear a father's loss,
Art thou the only mourner? Out upon thee
Destruction seize thee! and in hell may'st thou   240
Find no deliverance from thy present grief!"
So rails she, save at times when rumours run

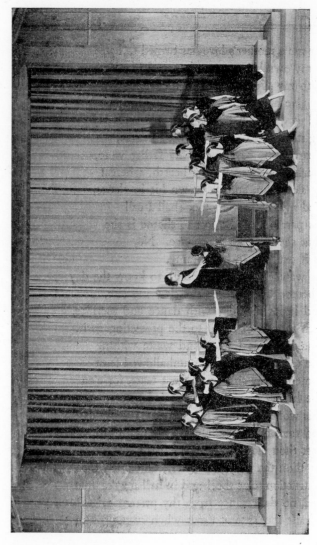

"I wait until Orestes comes to end my woes."

Electra and the Chorus as produced by Bennett Junior College

Orestes is at hand, then wild with rage
She thunders in my ears "This is thy doing;
Was it not thou who from my hands didst steal   245
Orestes and convey him safe away?
Mark my words, thou shalt rue it!" So she screams,
And her partner's there to egg her on,
Her glorious consort who repeats her jeers,
Who fights his battles with a woman's aid.   250
Meanwhile I wait until Orestes comes
To end my woes, and waiting pine away.
By ever dallying he has quite destroyed
The hopes I had and those I might have had.
In such a case what room is there, my friends,   255
For patience, what for piety? In sooth
Those in ill plight are driven to evil ways.

Chorus. Stay, tell me, is Ægisthus nigh at hand,
While thus thou speakest, or is he from home?

Electra. From home, of course! Think you, were he   260
    within,
I should thus venture forth? He is now afield.

Chorus. More freely then may I converse with thee,
If this is so.

Electra.   It is; ask what thou wilt.

Chorus. 'Tis of thy brother I would question thee.   265
Comes he, or tarries yet? I fain would know.

Electra. He says, "I come," but does not what he says.

Chorus. A man thinks twice with some great work in
    hand.

Electra. I thought not twice when I delivered him.

Chorus. Take heart, he is loyal and will not fail his
    friends.   270

Electra. I trust him, else I had not lived so long.

Chorus. No more for this time; at the doors I see
    Chrysothemis, thy sister, of one sire
    Born and one mother; in her hands she bears
    Gifts for the tomb by custom long approved.   275

Enter CHRYSOTHEMIS.

Chrysothemis. Sister, why com'st thou once more to de-
    claim
    In public at the outer gate? Has time
    Not schooled thee to refrain from idle rage?
    I too, my sister, chafe no less than thou
    At our sad fortunes, and had I the power,   280
    Would make it plain how I regard our masters.
    But in the storm 'tis best to reef the sail,
    Nor utter threats we cannot execute.
    I would thou wert likeminded; yet I know
    Justice is on thy side, and I am wrong.   285
    Yet if I am to keep my liberty,
    I needs must bow before the powers that be.

Electra. O shame that thou, the child of such a sire,
    Should'st him forget and take thy mother's part;
    For all these admonitions are not thine,   290
    A lesson thou repeatest, learnt of her.
    Make thine election then, to be unwise,
    Or show thy wisdom by forgetting friends.

Thou saidst, "If but the power were granted me,
I would make plain the hate I feel for them;"   295
And yet when I am straining every nerve
To avenge my sire, thou wilt not aid me; nay,
Dissuadest and wouldst have me hold my hand.
Shall we to all our ills add cowardice?
Tell me—or let me tell thee—what have I   300
To gain by ceasing from my sad complaint?
I still have life? a sorry life, indeed,
But good enough for me; and them I vex,
And vexing them do honour to the dead,
If anything can touch the world of shades.   305
Thou hatest? Nay, thy deeds belie thy words,
While thou dost mingle with the murderers;
So would not I, though they should offer me
The pomp that makes thee proud, the loaded board,
Thy life of ease; no, I would never yield.   310
Enough for me spare diet and a soul
Void of offence; thy state I covet not,
Nor wouldst thou, wert thou wise. Men might have
     called thee
Child of the noblest sire that ever lived;
Be called thy mother's, rightly named as base,   315
Betrayer of thy dead sire and thy kin.
Chorus. No angry words, I pray, for both of you
     There's profit in this talking, if thou
     Wouldst learn of her, and she in turn of thee.
Chrysothemis. I know her moods too well to take offence, 320

Nor had I now approached her, but I learnt
Of new impending peril that is like
To put a finish to her long-drawn woes.
Electra. Say what can be this terror; if 'tis worse
    Than what I now bear, I will call a truce.   325
Chrysothemis. All I have learnt in full I will impart.
    They purpose, if thou wilt not stay thy plaints,
    To send thee where thou shalt not see the sun,
    Far hence, to some dark dungeon, there to spend
    Thy days and nights in prayers of woe.   330
    Therefore reflect, and blame me not too late;
    Take warning and repent while yet 'tis time.
Electra. Have they indeed resolved to treat me thus?
Chrysothemis. The instant that Ægisthus is returned.
Electra. Well, for my part I would he came back soon.   335
Chrysothemis. Foolish girl! What mean'st thou by this
    prayer?
Electra. Would he were here, if this be his intent.
Chrysothemis. That thou mayst suffer—what? Hast thou
    lost thy wits?
Electra. A flight long leagues away from all of you.
Chrysothemis. Art thou indifferent to thy present life?   340
Electra. O 'tis a marvellously happy life!
Chrysothemis. It might have been couldst thou have
    schooled thyself.
Electra. Teach me not basely to betray my friends.
Chrysothemis. Not I; I teach submission to the strong.
Electra. Fawn, if thou wilt; such cringing suits not me.   345

Chrysothemis. Yet not to fall through folly were no blame.

Electra. If needs be, in a father's cause I'll fall.

Chrysothemis. I trust our father pardons us for this.

Electra. Traitors take refuge in like sentiments.

Chrysothemis. Thou wilt not heed then nor be ruled by
    me?   350

Electra. I am not in my dotage, save the mark!

Chrysothemis. Then I will do my errand.

Electra..   Whither away?
For whom art carrying these burnt offerings?

Chrysothemis. My mother bids me crown our father's
    grave.   355

Electra. Her mortal enemy's!   How sayest thou?

Chrysothemis. The husband whom she slew, so thou
    wouldst say.

Electra. Which of her friends advised her? whence this
    whim?

Chrysothemis. A nightly vision warned her, so I think.

Electra. Gods of my fathers, aid me in this pass!   360

Chrysothemis. Dost thou take heart of courage from her
    dread?

Electra. Before I answer let me hear the dream.

Chrysothemis. There is but little that I have to tell.

Electra. Tell it no less. A little word, men say,
    Hath oftentimes determined good or woe.   365

Chrysothemis. 'Tis said that she beheld thy sire and mine
    In bodily presence standing by her side,
    Revisiting the light of day. He took

The scepter of Ægisthus, once his own,
And at the household altar planted it,   370
And from it sprang and spread a fruitful bough,
Till it o'ershadowed all Mycenæ's land.
Such is the tale one told me who was by
When to the Sun-god she declared her dream.
Further I know not, save that in alarm   375
She sent me hither. Hearken then to me.
Sister, I pray thee by our household gods,
Fall not through folly; if thou spurn me now
Too late in sorrow wilt thou seek my aid.

Electra. Nay, let not aught, my sister, touch the tomb,   380
Of all thou bearest. 'Twere a shame, a sin,
To offer on behalf of her, the accursed,
Gifts or libations to our father's ghost.
Scatter them to the winds or bury them
Deep in the dust, where nothing may defile   385
Our father's lone couch; let her find them there,
A buried treasure when she comes to die.
Were she not basest of all womankind,
She ne'er had thought with offerings of hate
To crown her murdered victim's sepulcher.   390
Thinkst thou 'tis likely that her buried lord
Will take these honours kindly at her hands
Who slew him without pity like a foe,

---

374. **To the Sun-god**—Clytemnestra told her dream to the Sun-god because the sun, as the god of light and purity, drives away the darkness.

Mangled his corpse, and for ablution washed
The bloodstains on his head?   Say, is it like   395
These gifts will purge her of blood-guiltiness?
It cannot be.   Fling them away and cut
A tress of thine own locks; and for my share
Give him from me—a poor thing, but my best—
This unkempt lock, this girdle unadorned.   400
Then fall upon thy knees and pray that he
May come, our gracious champion from the dead,
And that the young Orestes yet may live
To trample underfoot his vanquished foes.
So may we some day crown our father's tomb   405
With costlier gifts than these poor offerings.
I can but think, 'tis but a thought, that he
Had part in sending her this ominous dream.
Still, sister, do this service and so aid
Thyself and me, and him the most beloved   410
Of all men, e'en though dead, thy sire and mine.

Chorus. 'Tis piously advised, and thou, my daughter,
       Wilt do her bidding, if thou art discreet.

Chrysothemis. I will. When duty calls, 'twere lack of sense
       For two to wrangle; both should join to act.   415
       Only when I essay this perilous task,

394. **Mangled his corpse**—This was done to prevent the victim from tak-
       ing revenge.
394. **Washed the bloodstains**—The ancients believed that if a murderer
       wiped his weapon upon the head of his victim he would not be pur-
       sued by an avenging spirit.
398. **Tress . . . locks**—Offerings of hair were placed upon a grave as a
       symbol of grief.

Be silent, if you love me, friends, for if
My mother hears of it, I shall have cause
To repent my folly soon or late.

[*Exit* CHRYSOTHEMIS.]

[*End of First Episode*]

FIRST STASIMON

Chorus. Count me a prophet false, a witless wight,   420
    If Justice, who inspires my prophecy,
Comes not, my child, to vindicate the right.
    She comes and that right speedily.
My heart grows bold and nothing fears;
That dream was music in my ears.   425
It tells me that thy sire who led
    The Greeks to victory hath not forgot;
Yea, and that axe with double brazen head
    Still thirsts for blood to wipe away its blot.

So leaping from her ambush, brazen-shod,   430
    Comes the Erinys with an armed host's tread,
For she hath seen a pair who knew not God . . .
Therefore I know that not in vain is sent
    This omen that the fall of guilt foretells,
For, if this vision fails of its intent,   435

431. **Erinys**—Avenging spirit.

Vain is all sooth, all dreams, all oracles.

    O chariot-race of Pelops old,

    The source of sorrows manifold,

    What endless curse hath fallen on us

    Since to his sea-grave Myrtilus   440

    Sank from the golden chariot hurled;

    Woe upon woe, of woes a world.

436. **Oracles**—Places where the Greeks were accustomed to consult their
    gods for advice or prophecy.

437. **Pelops**—See Note, page 223.

441. **Myrtilus**—He was bribed by Pelops to help him win a chariot race and
    a bride. After the race Pelops hurled Myrtilus into the sea for insult-
    ing his wife. As he died, Myrtilus pronounced a curse upon the
    family of Pelops.

SECOND EPISODE

Enter CLYTEMNESTRA.

Clytemnestra. So once again I find thee here at large,
    For he who kept thee close and so restrained
    Thy scandalous tongue, Ægisthus, is away;
    Yet thy complaints, repeated many a time
    To many, censured my tyrannic rule—   5
    The insults that I heaped on thee and thine.
    Was it an insult if I paid in kind
    The sneers and taunts wherewith thou mockest me?
    Thy father, the sole pretext of thy grief,
    Died by my hand, aye mine, I know it well,   10
    'Tis true beyond denial; yet not I,
    Not I alone, but Justice slew him too:
    And thou shouldst side with Justice, wert thou wise.
    This sire of thine for whom thy tears still flow
    Alone of all the Greeks could steel his heart   15
    To yield thy sister as a sacrifice;
    . . . . Tell me now
    Wherefore he offered her, on whose behalf?
    The Greeks, thou sayest. And what right had they
    To kill my child? For Menelaus' sake,   20

16. **Sister . . . sacrifice**—See Story of Agamemnon, page 220.
20. **Kill my child**—Iphigenia was supposed to have died, but she actually was taken away by Artemis, goddess of the hunt.

His brother? Should such pretext stay my hand?
Had not his brother children twain to serve
As victims? Should not they, as born of sire
And mother for whose sake the host embarked,
Have been preferred before my innocent child?   25
Had Death forsooth some craving for my child
Rather than hers? or had the wretch, her sire,
A tender heart for Menelaus' brood,
And for my flesh and blood no tenderness?
That choice was for a father rash and base;   30
So, though I differ from thee, I believe,
And could the dead maid speak, she would agree.
I therefore view the past without remorse,
And if to thee I seem perverted, clear
Thy judgment ere thou makest thyself a judge.   35

Electra. This time thou canst not say that I began
The quarrel or provoked thee. But if thou
Wilt give me leave, I fain would speak the truth
Regarding both my sister and my sire.

Clytemnestra. My leave is given, and, hadst thou always   40
shown
This temper, I had listened without pain.

Electra. Hear then. Thou say'st, "I slew thy father." Who
Could well avow a blacker crime than that?
Justly or not, what matters?   But I'll prove
There was no justice in it; 'twas the lure   45
Of a vile wretch that hurried thee along,—

Thy lover's. Ask the Huntress Artemis
For what offence she prisoned every gust
That blows at Aulis; rather, as from her
Thou mayst not win an answer, I will tell thee.   50
My father once—so have I heard the tale—
Taking his pleasure in her sacred glade
Started an antlered stag with dappled hide,
Shot it, and shooting made some careless boast.
Latona's daughter, wroth thereat, detained   55
The Achæans, that in quittance for her hart
My sire might give his daughter, life for life.
And so it came to pass that she was slain:
The fleet becalmed no other way could win
Homeward or Troyward. For that cause alone   60
Reluctantly, by hard constraint, at last
He slew her, no wise for his brother's sake.
But if, as thou interpretest the deed,
'Twas done to please his brother, even thus
Should he for that have died by hand of thine?   65
What law is this?   In laying down such law
See that against thyself thou lay not up
Dire retribution; for if blood for blood
Be justice, thou wouldst justly die the first.
Look, if thy pleading be not all a lie,   70

47. **Artemis**—The goddess of the hunt, daughter of Zeus and Latona.
    Avoiding the society of men, she devoted herself to hunting. Some-
    times she was accompanied by a group of maidens.
49. **Aulis**—A harbor in Bœotia where the sacrifice of Iphigenia was sup-
    posed to have taken place.

Say, if thou wilt, why thou art living now
A life of shame as partner to
The wretch who aided thee to slay my sire,
Bearing him children, casting out for them
The rightful heirs in rightful wedlock born.   75
Can I approve such acts? Or wilt thou say
This too was vengeance for a daughter's blood?
A shameful plea, if urged, for shame it is
To wed a foeman for a daughter's sake.
But in convincing thee I waste my breath;   80
Thou hast no answer but to scream that I
Revile a mother; and in sooth to us
Thou art mistress more than mother, for I pine
A wretched drudge, by thee and by thy mate
Downtrodden; and that other child who scarce   85
Escaped thy hands, Orestes, wears away
In weary exile his unhappy days.
Oft hast thou charged me that I reared him up
For vengeance; so I willed it, had I power.
Go to, proclaim me out of my own mouth   90
A shrew, a scold, a vixen—what thou wilt.
For if I be accomplished in such arts,
Methinks I show my breed, a trick o' the blood.

Chorus. I see she breathes forth fury and no more
    Heeds if her words with justice harmonize.   95

Clytemnestra. Why then should I heed one who thus
        insults
    A mother, at her ripe age, too? Dost think

That she would stick at any deed of shame?

Electra. Nay, I am shamefaced, though to thee I seem
 Shameless; I know such manners in a maid   100
 Are ill-becoming, in a daughter strange;
 But thy iniquity, thy cruel acts
 Compel me; baseness is from baseness learnt.

Clytemnestra. Thou brazen monster! I, my words, my
  acts,
 Are matter for thy glib speech!   105

Electra. The fault is thine, not mine; for thine the acts,
 And mine are but the words that show them forth.

Clytemnestra. Now, by our lady Artemis, thou shalt rue
 Thy boldness when Ægisthus comes again.

Electra. See, rage distracts thee; first thou grantest me 110
 Free speech, and wilt not listen when I speak.

Clytemnestra. I let thee have thy say, and wilt not thou
 Hush thy wild tongue and let me sacrifice?

Electra. Go, I entreat thee, sacrifice; nor blame
 My voice; henceforth I shall not speak one word. 115

Clytemnestra. Bear this, my maid, this offering of earth's
  fruits,
 That to our King I may uplift my prayers,
 To rid me of the dread that haunts my soul.
 O Phœbus, our Defender, lend an ear
 To my petition; dark and veiled the words 120
 For those who love me not, nor were it meet
 To lay my whole heart bare, while she is by,
 Ready to blab with her poisoned tongue

Through all the town some empty, rash report.
Darkly I pray; to my dark prayer attend!   125
The vision that I yesternight beheld
Of double import, if, Lycean King
It bodes me well, fulfil it; but if ill,
May it upon my enemies recoil!
If there be some who treacherously plot   130
To dispossess me of my wealth and power,
Prevent them, and vouchsafe that I may rule
The house of Atreus in security,
And wield the scepter, sharing prosperous days
With the same friends and with my children—those   135
By malice and deep hatred not estranged.
Grant, O Lycean Phœbus, of thy grace,
To me and mine fulfilment of my prayers.
And for those other things my heart desires,
Though unexpressed, thou as a god, dost know them;   140
For naught is hidden from the sons of Zeus.

Aged Servant. Good ladies, might a stranger crave to learn
    If this indeed be King Ægisthus' house?

Chorus. It is, Sir; thou thyself hast guessed aright.

Aged Servant. And am I right in supposing that I see   145
    His royal consort here?   She looks a queen.

Chorus. Indeed thou art in presence of the queen.

Aged Servant. I greet thee, Madam, and I bear to thee
    Fair news, and to Ægisthus, from a friend.

---

133. **House of Atreus**—Atreus was the father of Agamemnon.

Clytemnestra. I welcome thy fair words, but first would   150
    know
   Who sends thee.
Aged Servant.   Phanoteus, the Phocian,
   On a grave mission.
Clytemnestra.   Tell me, stranger, what.
   It must be friendly coming from a friend.   155
Aged Servant. Orestes' death, to sum in brief my tale.
Electra. Me miserable! Now am I undone.
Clytemnestra. What say'st thou, man, what say'st thou?
    Heed not her.
Aged Servant. I say again, Orestes is no more.
Electra. Ah me, I'm lost, ah wretched me, undone!   160
Clytemnestra. Attend to thine own business. [*To* Aged
    Servant.]
        Tell me, Sir,
   The circumstance and manner of his death.
Aged Servant. That was my errand, and I'll tell thee all.
   To the great festival of Greece he went,   165
   The Delphic Games, and when the herald's voice
   Announced the opening trial, the foot race,
   He stepped into the lists, a radiant form,
   The admired of all beholders. Like a shaft
   He sped from starting point to goal and back,   170
   And bore the crown of glorious victory.
   To speak in brief where there is much to tell,

150. **Fair words**—Clytemnestra has just prayed to Phœbus (Apollo), and
    now good news is brought to her. She accepts it as an omen that her
    prayer will find favor with the gods.

Margaret Anglin as Electra

I never heard of prowess like to his.
This much I'll add, the judges of the games
Announced no single contest wherein he   175
Was not the victor, and each time glad shouts
Hailed the award—"An Argive wins, Orestes,
The son of Agamemnon, King of men,
Who led the hosts of Hellas." So he sped.
But when some angry godhead intervenes   180
The mightiest man is foiled. Another day,
When at sunsetting, chariots vied in speed,
He entered; many were the charioteers.
From Sparta one, and one Achæan, two
From Libya, skilled to guide the yokèd team;   185
The fifth in rank, with mares of Thessaly,
Orestes came, and an Æolian sixth,
With chestnut fillies, a Megarian seventh,
The eighth, with milk-white steeds, an Ænian,
The ninth from Athens, city built by gods;   190
Last a Bœotian made the field of ten.
Then, as the appointed umpires signed to each
By lot his place, they ranged their chariots,
And at the trumpet's brazen signal all
Started, all shook the reins and urged their steeds   195
With shouts; the whole plain echoed with a din
Of rattling cars and the dust rose to heaven.
They drove together, all in narrow space,

177. **Argive (är'jĭve)**—A person from Argos or the surrounding district.
184. **Sparta . . . Bœotian**—This list of proper names gives the districts or cities from which the different chariot racers came.

And plied their whips, each keen to leave behind
The press of whirling wheels and snorting steeds,   200
For each man saw his car beflecked with foam
Or felt the coursers' hot breath at his back.
Orestes, as he rounded either goal,
Steered close and shaved the pillar with his nave,
Urging his offside trace-horse, while he checked   205
The nearer. For a while they all sped on
Unharmed, but soon the Ænian's hard-mouthed steeds
Bolted, and 'twixt the sixth and seventh round
'Gainst the Barcæan chariot headlong dashed.
Then on that first mishap there followed close   210
Shock upon shock, crash upon crash, that strewed
With wrack of cars all the Crisæan plain.
This the shrewd charioteer of Athens marked,
Slackened and drew aside, letting go by
The surge of chariots running in mid course.   215
Last came Orestes who had curbed his team
(He trusted to the finish), but at sight
Of the Athenian, his one rival left,
With a shrill halloa in his horses' ears
He followed; and the two abreast raced on,   220
Now one, and now the other a head in front.
Thus far Orestes, ill-starred youth, had steered
Steadfast at every lap his steadfast team,

204. **Nave**—The hub of the wheel.
209. **Barcæan chariot**—Chariot from the city of Barca, an ancient African
     city no longer in existence.
212. **Crisæan plain**—Plain near Crisa, a city in Phocis.

But at the last, in turning, all too soon
He loosed the left-rein, and ere he knew it   225
The axle struck against the pillar's edge.
The axle box was shattered, and himself
Hurled o'er the chariot rail, and in his fall
Caught in the reins' grip he was dragged along,
While his scared team dashed wildly o'er the course.   230
But as the crowd beheld his overthrow,
There rose a wail of pity for the youth—
His daring deeds and his disastrous end—
Now flung to earth, now bounding to the sky
Feet uppermost. At length the charioteers   235
Stayed in their wild career his steeds and freed
The corpse all blood-bestained, disfigured, marred
Past recognition by his nearest friend.
Straightway the Phocians burnt him on a pyre,
And envoys now are on their way to bring   240
That mighty frame shut in a little urn,
And lay his ashes in his fatherland.
Such is my tale, right piteous to tell;
But for all those who saw it with their eyes,
As I, there never was a sadder sight.   245

Chorus. Alas, alas! our ancient masters' line,
   So it appears, hath perished root and branch.

Clytemnestra. Are these glad tidings? Rather would I say
   Sad, but of profit. Ah how hard my lot
   When I must look for safety to my losses.   250

Aged Servant. Why, lady, why downhearted at my news?

Clytemnestra. Strange is the force of motherhood; a
      mother,
  Whate'er her wrongs, can ne'er forget her child.
Aged Servant. So it would seem our coming was in vain.
Clytemnestra. Nay, not in vain. How canst thou say "in 255
      vain,"
  If of his death thou bringst convincing proof,
  Who from my life drew life, and yet, estranged,
  Forgot the hands that tended him, forgot
  A mother's tender nurture, fled his home,
  And since that day has never seen me more, 260
  Slandered me as the murderer of his sire
  And breathed forth vengeance?—Neither night nor
      day
  Kind slumber closed these eyes, and brooding dread
  Of death each minute stretched me on the rack.
  But now on this glad day, of terror rid 265
  From him and her, a deadlier plague than he,
  That vampire who was housed with me to drain
  My very life blood—now, despite her threats
  Methinks that I shall pass my days in peace.
Electra. Ah woe is me! now verily may I mourn 270
  Thy fate, Orestes, when thou farest thus,
  Mocked by thy mother in death!   Is it not well?
Clytemnestra. Not well with thee, but it is well with him.
Electra. Hear her, Avenging Spirit of the dead
  Whose ashes still are warm! 275
Clytemnestra. .   The Avenger heard

When it pleased her, and hath ruled it well.
Electra. Mock on; this is thine hour of victory.
Clytemnestra. That hour Orestes shall not end, nor thou.
Electra. End it! 'Tis we are ended and undone.   280
Clytemnestra. Thy coming, Sir, would merit large reward,
    If thou indeed hast stopped her wagging tongue.
Aged Servant. Then I may take my leave, if all is well.
Clytemnestra. Not so; such entertainment would reflect
    On me and on thy master, my ally.   285
    Be pleased to enter; leave this girl without
    To wail her friends' misfortune and her own.

[*Exeunt* CLYTEMNESTRA *and* AGED SERVANT.]

Electra. Seemed she to you a mother woe-begone,
    Weeping and wailing for a son thus slain,
    This miserable woman? No, she left us   290
    With mocking laughter. Dearest brother mine,
    Thy death was my death warrant. Woe is me!
    With thee has gone my last fond hope, that thou
    Wast living yet and wouldst return some day
    To avenge my sire and me, unhappy me.   295
    Now whither shall I turn, alone, bereft
    Of thee and of my sire? Henceforth again
    Must I be slave to those I most abhor,
    My father's murderers. Is it not well with me?
    No, never will I cross their threshold more,   300
    But at these gates will lay me down to die,
    There pine away. If any in the house

Think me an eyesore, let him slay me; life
To me were misery and death a boon.

Chorus. Where, O Zeus, are thy bolts, O Sun-god, where 305
  is thy ray,
  If with thy lightning, thy light, these things be not
   shown to the day?

Electra. Ah me! Ah me!

Chorus. Daughter, why weepest thou?

Electra. Woe!

Chorus. Hush! No rash cry! 310

Electra. Thou'lt be my death.

Chorus. What meanest thou?

Electra. If ye would whisper hope
  That they we know for dead may be alive;
  Ye trample on a bleeding heart. 315

Chorus. Nay, I bethink me how
  The Argive seer was swallowed up,
  Snared by a woman for a golden chain,
  And now in the nether world—

Electra. Ah me! 320

Chorus. A living soul he reigns.

Electra. Ah woe!

Chorus. Aye woe! for the murderess—

Electra. Was slain.

Chorus. Aye, slain. 325

---

317. **Argive seer**—Amphiaraus (ăm fĭ á rā′ŭs) was a famous soothsayer of
  Argos. His wife, bribed by a golden necklace, betrayed him to his
  enemies. His son (like Orestes) avenged his father's death.

Electra. I know, I know. A champion was raised up
    To avenge the mourning ghost.
    No champion for me,
    The one yet left is taken, torn away.

Chorus. A weary, weary lot is thine.   330

Electra. I know it well, too well,
    When life, month in month out,
    Like a dark torrent flows,
    Horror on horror, pain on pain.

Chorus. We have watched its tearful course.   335

Electra. Cease then to turn it where—

Chorus. What wouldst thou say?

Electra. No comfort's left of hope
    From him of royal blood,
    Sprung from one stock with me.   340

Chorus. Death is the common lot.

Electra. To die as he died, hapless youth,
    Entangled in the reins
    Beneath the tramp of coursers' hoofs!

Chorus. Torture indescribable!   345

Electra. Yea, in a strange land far away—

Chorus. Alas!

Electra. To lie untended by my hands,
    Unwept, ungraced with burial by me!

          Enter CHRYSOTHEMIS.

Chrysothemis. Joy, dearest sister, sped me hitherward,   350
    And haply with unseemly haste I ran
    To bring the joyful tidings and relief

From all thy woes and weary sufferings.

Electra. And where canst *thou* have found a remedy
    For irremediable woes like mine?   355

Chrysothemis. Orestes—hear it from my lips—is here,
    In bodily presence, as thou see'st me now.

Electra. Art mad, poor sister, making mockery
    Of thine own misery and mine withal?

Chrysothemis. I mock not, by our father's hearth I swear 360
    it;
    In very truth we have him here again.

Electra. O misery! And, prithee, from whose mouth
    Hadst thou this tale so blindly credited?

Chrysothemis. I trusted to none other than myself,
    The clearest proof and evidence of my eyes.   365

Electra. What proof, what evidence! What sight, poor
    girl,
    Lit this illusion in thy fevered brain?

Chrysothemis. O, as thou lov'st me, listen, then decide,
    My story told, if I am mad or sane.

Electra. Well, if it pleases thee to speak, speak on.   370

Chrysothemis. I will, and tell thee all that I have seen.
    As I approached our sire's ancestral tomb,
    I noted that the sepulcher still was wet
    With streams of milk, and round the monument
    Garlands were wreathed of every flower that blows.   375
    I marvelled much and peered around in dread
    Of someone watching me; but when I found
    That nothing stirred, nearer the tomb I crept;

And there upon the grave's edge lay a lock
Of hair fresh-severed; at the sight there flashed 380
A dear familiar image on my soul,
Orestes; 'twas a token and a sign
From him whom most of all the world I love.
I took it my hands and not a sound
I uttered but my eyes o'erbrimmed for joy. 385
I knew, I knew it then as now, for sure:
This shining treasure could be none but his.
Who else could set it there save thee or me?
And 'twas not I assuredly, nor thou;
How couldst thou, when thou mayst not leave the 390
    house
Not e'en to sacrifice? Our mother then?
When did our mother's heart that way incline?
Could she have 'scaped our notice, had she done it?
No, from Orestes comes this offering.
Courage, dear sister. Never destiny 395
Ran one unbroken course. On us till now
She frowned; today gives promise of her smiles.
Electra. Alas! I pity thy simplicity,
    Fond sister.
Chrysothemis.   Are not then my tidings glad? 400
Electra. Thou knowst not in what land of dreams thou
    art.
Chrysothemis. Wouldst have me doubt the evidence of my
    eyes?

Electra. He is dead, I tell thee; look not to the dead
    For a deliverer; *that* hope has gone.

Chrysothemis. Ah woe is me! Who told thee of his   405
    death?

Electra. One who was present when he met his fate.

Chrysothemis. Where is the man? 'Tis strange, 'tis pass-
    ing strange.

Electra. Within; our mother's not unwelcome guest.

Chrysothemis. Ah me! Ah me! And whose then can
    have been
    Those wreaths, that milk outpoured upon the grave?   410

Electra. To me it seems most like that they were brought
    A kindly offering to Orestes dead.

Chrysothemis. And I, poor fool, was hurrying in hot haste
    To bring my joyful message, unaware
    Of our ill plight; and now that I have brought it   415
    I find fresh sorrows added to the old.

Electra. So stands the case; but be advised by me
    And lighten this the burden of our woes.

Chrysothemis. Wouldst have me raise the dead to life
    again?

Electra. I meant not that; I am not so demented.   420

Chrysothemis. What wouldst thou then that lies within
    my powers?

Electra. Be bold to execute what I command.

Chrysothemis. If it can profit, I will not refuse.

Electra. Success, remember, is the reward of toil.

Chrysothemis. I know it, and will help thee all I can.   425

Electra. Then listen how I am resolved to act.
From friends, thou knowest now as well as I,
We cannot look for comfort; death hath snatched
All from us and we two are left alone.
While yet my brother lived and tidings came   430
Of his prosperity, I still had hopes
That he would yet appear to avenge his sire;
But now that he is dead, to thee I turn;
From thee a sister craves a sister's aid,
To slay—shrink not—our father's murderer,   435
Ægisthus. There, I plainly tell thee all.
Why hesitate? What faintest ray of hope
Is left to excuse thy waiting, whose lot
Henceforth must be to mourn the ancestral wealth
Whereof thou art defrauded, to lament   440
A youth that withers fast, unloved, unwed.
For dream not wedded bliss can e'er be thine;
Too wary is Ægisthus to permit
That children should be born of thee or me
For his destruction. But, if thou attend   445
My counsel, thou shalt reap large benefits:
First, from our dead sire, and our brother too,
A name for piety; and furthermore,
A free-born woman thou shalt stand revealed;
And worthy offers shall be thine, for worth   450
In women ever captivates all men.
Seest thou not too the honour thou shalt win
Both for thyself and me, if thou consent?

What countryman, what stranger will not greet
Our presence, when he sees us, with acclaim?   455
"Look, friends, upon this sister pair," he'll cry,
"Who raised their father's house, who dared confront
Their foes in power, who jeopardized their lives
In bloody vengeance. Honour to the pair,
Honour and worship! Yea at every feast   460
Let all the people laud their bravery."
So will our fame be sounded far and wide,
Nor shall our glory fail in life or death.
Sweet sister, hear me, take thy father's part,
Side with thy brother, give me, give thyself   465
Relief from sorrow; and remember this,
A life of shame is shame for noble souls.

Chorus. Forethought for those that speak and those that
            hear,
In such grave issues, is most serviceable.

Chrysothemis. Before she spake, were not her mind per-   470
            verse,
She had remembered caution, but she, friends,
Remembers not. [*To* Electra.] What glamor fooled
            thee thus
To take up arms thus boldly and enlist me?
Thou art a woman, see'st thou not? no man,
No match in battle for thine adversaries;   475
Their fortune rises with the flowing tide,
Ours ebbs and leaves us soon a stranded hulk;
Who then could hope to grapple with a foe

So mighty and escape without a fall?
Bethink thee, if thy speech were overheard,   ·480
We are like to change our evil plight for worse.
Small comfort or small benefit to win
Glory and die a very shameful death!
Mere death were easy, but to crave for death
And be denied that last boon—there's the sting.   485
Nay, I entreat, before we wreck ourselves
And perish root and branch, restrain thy rage.
All thou hast said for me shall be unsaid,
An empty breath. O learn at length, though late,
To yield, nor match thy weakness with their strength. 490

Chorus. Hearken! for mortal man there is no gift
    Greater than forethought and sobriety.

Electra. 'Tis as I thought: before thy answer came
    I knew full well thou wouldst refuse thine aid.
    Unaided then and by myself I'll do it,   495
    For done it must be, though I work alone.

Chrysothemis. Ah well-a-way!
    Would thou hadst been so minded on that day
    Our father died! What couldst thou not have done!

Electra. My temper was the same, my mind less ripe.   500

Chrysothemis. Study to keep the same mind all thy days.

Electra. This counsel means refusal of thine aid.

Chrysothemis. Yes, for misfortune dogs such enterprise.

Electra. I praise thy prudence, hate thy cowardice.

Chrysothemis. E'en when thou shalt commend me, I will 505
    bear

Thy commendation no less patiently.

Electra. That trial thou wilt ne'er endure from me.

Chrysothemis. Who lives will see; time yet may prove
    thee wrong.

Electra. Begone! in thee there is no power to aid.

Chrysothemis. Not so; in thee there is no will to learn.   510

Electra. Go to thy mother; tell it all to her.

Chrysothemis. My hatred of thee does not reach so far.

Electra. Thou wouldst dishonour me; that much is sure.

Chrysothemis. Dishonour? No, I seek to save thine hon-
    our.

Electra. Am I to make thy rule of honour mine?   515

Chrysothemis. When thou art wise, then thou shalt guide
    us both.

Electra. Sound words; 'tis sad they are so misapplied.

Chrysothemis. Thou hittest well the blot that is thine own.

Electra. How? dost deny the plea I urge is just?

Chrysothemis. No; but e'en justice sometimes worketh   520
    harm.

Electra. I choose not to conform to such a rule.

Chrysothemis. Well, if thy purpose hold, thou'lt own me
    right.

Electra. It holds; I shall not swerve in awe of thee.

Chrysothemis. Is this thy last word? Wilt not be advised?

Electra. No, naught is worse than ill advice.   525

Chrysothemis. Thou seemest deaf to all that I can urge.

---

522. **If thy purpose . . . right**—After your unsuccessful attempt you will,
   too late, approve of my prudence in refusing to help you.

Electra. My resolution was not born today.

Chrysothemis. Then I will go, for thou canst not be brought
  To approve my words, nor I to approve thy ways.

Electra. Go in then; I shall never follow thee,   530
  E'en shouldst thou beg me: 'tis insane to urge
  A hopeless cause.

Chrysothemis.   Well, if thou art wise
  In thine own eyes, so let it be; later,
  Sore stricken, thou wilt take my words to heart.   535

[*Exit* CHRYSOTHEMIS.]

[*End of Second Episode*]

SECOND STASIMON

Chorus. Wise nature taught the birds of air
  For those who reared them in the nest to care;
  The parent bird is nourished by his brood,
  And shall not we, as they,
  The debt of nature pay,   540
  Shall man not show like gratitude?
  By Zeus who hurls the lightning,
  By Themis throned in heaven,
  There comes a judgment day;   545
  Not long shall punishment delay.
  O voice that echoes to the world below,

544. **Themis**—A wife of Zeus and goddess of laws.

Bear to the dead a wail of woe,
Tell him his house is stricken sore,
Tell him his children now no more
        In love together dwell;   550
Dire strife the twain divides,

Alone Electra bides,
        Alone she braves the surging swell.

Disconsolate doth she her sire bewail,
Like the forlornest nightingale;   555
Reckless of life, could she but quell
The cursed pair, those Furies fell.
Where shall ye find on earth
A maid to match her worth?

No generous soul were fain   560
By a base life his fair repute to stain.
Such baseness thou didst scorn,
Choosing, my child, to mourn with them that mourn.
Wise and of daughters best—
With double honours thou art doubly blest.   565

O may I see thee tower
As high above thy foes in wealth and power
As now they tower o'er thee;
For now thy state is piteous to see.
Yet brightly dost thou shine,   570
For fear of Zeus far-famed and love of laws divine.

"Ashes within this narrow urn we bear, all that remains of him."

Electra as produced at Randolph-Macon Woman's College

THIRD EPISODE

Enter ORESTES AND PYLADES.

Orestes. Pray tell me, ladies, were we guided right,
    And are we close upon our journey's end?

Chorus. What seek'st thou, stranger, and with what in-
      tent?

Orestes. I seek and long have sought Ægisthus' home.

Chorus. 'Tis here; thy guide is not at all to blame.

Orestes. Would one of you announce to those within
    The auspicious arrival of our company?

Chorus. This maiden, as the next of kin, will do it.

Orestes. Go, madam, say that visitors have come
    And seek Ægisthus—certain Phocians.   10

Electra. Ah woe is me! You come not to confirm
    By ocular proof the rumours that we heard?

Orestes. I've heard no "rumours." Agèd Strophius
    Charged me with tidings of Orestes.

Electra.   Ha!   15
    What tidings, stranger? how I quake with dread!

Orestes. Ashes within this narrow urn we bear,
    All that remains of him, as thou mayst see.

Electra. Ah me unhappy! in my very sight
    Lies visible the burden of my woes.   20

13. **Strophius (strō′fĭ ŭs)**—Prince of Phocis, father of Pylades, uncle of
    Orestes.

Orestes. If for Orestes thou art weeping, know
    This brazen urn contains the dust of him.
Electra. O if it hold his ashes, let me, friend,
    O let me, let me take it in my hands.
    Not for this dust alone, but for myself   25
    And all my house withal, I'll weep and wail.
Orestes. Bring it and give it her, who'er she be;
    For not as an ill-wisher, but as friend,
    Or haply near of kin, she asks the boon.
Electra. Last relics of the man I most did love,   30
    Orestes! high in hope I sent thee forth;
    How hast thou dashed all hope in thy return!
    Radiant as day when thou set forth, and now
    I hold a dusty nothing in my hands.
    Would I had died before I rescued thee   35
    From death and sent thee to a foreign land!
    Then hadst thou fallen together with thy sire
    And lain beside him in the ancestral tomb:
    Now in a strange land, exiled, far from home,
    Far from thy sister thou hast died, ah me!   40
    How miserably! I was not by to bathe
    And deck with loving hands thy corpse, and snatch
    Thy charrèd bones from out the flaming pyre.
    Alas! by foreign hands these rites were paid,
    And now thou comest back to me, of dust   45
    A little burden in this little urn.

41. **To bathe and deck thy corpse—**The nearest of kin performed the
    rite of washing the body of the dead.

O for the nursing and the toil, no toil,
I spent on thee an infant, all in vain!
For thou wast ne'er thy mother's babe, but mine;
Thou hadst no nurse in all the house but me,   50
I was *thy sister,* none so called but me.
But now all this hath vanished in a day,
Dead with thy death, a whirlwind that passed by,
And left all desolate; thy father's gone,
And I am dead in thee, and thou art lost;   55
And our foes laugh.   That mother, mother none,
Whose crimes, as oft thou gav'st me secret word,
Thou wouldst thyself full speedily avenge,
Is mad for joy.   But now most evil fate,
Thy fate and mine, hath blasted all and sent me,   60
Instead of that dear form I loved so well,
Cold ashes and an unavailing shade.

      Ah me!   Ah me!
      O piteous corpse!
      Ah woe is me!   65
O woeful coming! I am all undone,
Undone by thee, beloved brother mine!
Take me, O take me to thy last lone home,
A shadow to a shade, that I may dwell
With thee forever in the underworld;   70
For here on earth we shared alike, and now
I fain would die to share with thee thy tomb;
For with the dead there is no mourning, none.

Chorus. Child of a mortal sire, Electra, think,

Orestes too was mortal; calm thy grief.   75
Death is a debt that all of us must pay.

Orestes. Ah me! what shall I say where all words fail?
And yet I can no longer curb my tongue.

Electra. What sudden trouble made thee speak like this?

Orestes. Is this the famed Electra I behold?   80

Electra. 'Tis she, and very wretched is her state.

Orestes. O for the heavy change! Alas, alas!

Electra. Surely thy pity, sir, is not for *me*.

Orestes. O beauty marred by foul and impious spite!

Electra. Yea, sir, this wreck of womanhood am I.   85

Orestes. Alas, how sad a life of singleness!

Electra. Why gaze thus on me, stranger, and lament?

Orestes. Of my own ills how little then I knew!

Electra. Was this revealed by any word of mine?

Orestes. By seeing thee conspicuous in thy woes.   90

Electra. And yet my looks reveal but half my woes.

Orestes. Could there be woes more piteous to behold?

Electra. Yea, to be housemate with the murderers—

Orestes. Whose murderers? at what villainy dost hint?

Electra. My father's; and their slave am I perforce.   95

Orestes. Who is it puts upon thee this constraint?

Electra. My mother, not a mother save in name.

Orestes. By blows or petty tyrannies or how?

Electra. By blows and tyrannies of every kind.

Orestes. And is there none to help or stay her hand?   100

Electra. None; there *was* one, the man whose dust I hold.

Orestes. Poor maid! my pity's stirred at sight of thee.

Electra. Thou art the first who ever pitied me.

Orestes. I am the first to feel a common woe.

Electra. What, canst thou be some kinsman from afar?   105

Orestes. If these are friends who hear us, I would answer.

Electra. Yes, they are friends; thou needst not fear to
    speak.

Orestes. Give back this urn, and then I'll tell thee all.

Electra. Ask not so hard a thing, good sir, I pray.

Orestes. Do as I bid thee; thou shalt not repent it.   110

Electra. O, I entreat thee, rob me not of that
    The most I prize on earth.

Orestes.   It may not be.

Electra. Ah! woe for thee, Orestes, woe is me,
    If I am not to give thee burial.   115

Orestes. Guard well thy lips; thou hast no right to mourn.

Electra. No right to mourn a brother who is dead!

Orestes. To speak of him in this wise is not meet.

Electra. What, am I so dishonoured of the dead?

Orestes. Of none dishonoured: this is not thy part.   120

Electra. Not if Orestes' ashes here I hold?

Orestes. They are not his, though supposed to pass for his.

Electra. Where then is my unhappy brother's grave?

Orestes. There is no grave; we bury not the living.

Electra. What sayst thou, boy?   125

Orestes.   Nothing that is not true.

Electra. He lives?

Orestes.   As surely as I am alive.

Electra. What, art thou he?

Orestes.   Look at this signet ring,   130
    My father's; let it witness if I lie.

Electra. O happy day!

Orestes.   O, happy, happy day!

Electra. Thy voice I greet!

Orestes.   My voice gives greeting back.   135

Electra. My arms embrace thee!

Orestes.   May they clasp me aye!

Electra. My countrywomen, dearest friends, behold
    Orestes who in feigning died, and so
    By feigning is alive again and safe.   140

Chorus. We see him, daughter, and this glad surprise
    Makes our eyes overflow with happy tears.

Electra. Son of my best loved sire,
    Now hast thou come, art here to find, to see
    Thy heart's desire.   145

Orestes. E'en so; but best keep silence for a while.

Electra. What need for silence?

Orestes. 'Twere wise, lest someone from the house should
    hear.

Electra. Nay, by Queen Artemis, the virgin maid,
    Of women-folk I ne'er will be afraid.   150

Orestes. Yet note that in the breasts of women dwells
    The War-god too, as thou methinks hast found.

Electra. Ah me, ah me!
    Thou wak'st a memory
    Enduring, everlasting,   155
    An ache time cannot quell.

Orestes. I know it, too; but when the hour shall strike
 Then it behoves us to recall those deeds.
Electra. All time, each passing hour
  Henceforward I were fain   160
  To tell my griefs, my pain,
 For late and hardly have I won free speech.
Orestes. 'Tis so; then forfeit not this liberty.
Electra. How forfeit it?
Orestes. By speaking out of season overmuch.   165
Electra. But who would barter speech for silence now,
  Who could be dumb,
  Now that beyond all thought and hope
  I've seen thee come?
Orestes. That sight was then vouchsafed thee when the   170
   gods
 First urged me to turn my steps towards home.
Electra. If a god guided thee
  To seek our halls, this boon
  Surpasses all before, I see   175
  The hand of heaven.
Orestes. To check thy gladness I am loth, and yet
 This ecstasy of joy—it makes me fear.
Electra. O after many a weary year
  Restored to glad my eyes,
  Seeing my utter misery, forbear—   180
Orestes. What is thy prayer?
Electra. Forbear to rob me of the light,
 The presence of thy face.

Orestes. If any dared attempt it, I were wrath.

Electra. Dost thou consent?   185

Orestes.   How could I otherwise?

Electra. [*To* CHORUS]   Friends, a voice is in my ear,
                  That I never hoped to hear.
                  At the glad sound how could I
                  Be mute nor raise a joyous cry?   190
                  But I have thee, and the light
                  Of thy countenance so bright
                  Not e'en sorrow can eclipse,
                  Or still the music of those lips.

Orestes. Spare me all superfluity of words—   195
   How vile our mother, how Ægisthus drains
   By waste and luxury our father's house;
   The time admits not such a flood of speech.
   But tell me rather what will best assist
   Our present need—where we must show ourselves,   200
   Or lie in wait, and either way defeat
   The mockery and triumph of our foes.
   And see that when we twain are gone within
   Our mother reads not in thy radiant looks
   Our secret; weep as overwhelmed with grief   205
   At our feigned story; when the victory's won
   We shall have time and liberty to laugh.

Electra. Yea, as it pleaseth thee it pleases me,
   Brother, for all my pleasure is thy gift,
   Not mine; nor would I purchase for myself   210
   The greatest boon that cost thee the least pang:

So should I cross the Providence that guides us.
How it stands with us, doubtless thou hast heard.
Ægisthus, as thou knowest, is away;
Only our mother keeps the house, and fear not   215
That she will see my face lit up with smiles;
My hatred of her is too deep ingrained.
Moreover, since thy coming I have wept,
Wept for pure joy and still must weep to see
The dead alive, on one day dead and living.   220
It works me strangely; if my sire appeared
In bodily presence, I should now believe it
No mocking phantom but his living self.
Thus far no common fate hath guided thee;
So lead me as thou wilt, for left alone   225
I had myself achieved of two things one,
A noble living or a noble death.

Orestes. Hush, hush! I hear a stir within the house
    As if one issued forth.

Electra. [*To* Orestes *and* Pylades] Pass in, good sirs,   230
    Ye are sure of welcome; they within will not
    Reject your gift, though bitter it may prove.

Enter Aged Servant.

Aged Servant. Fool! madmen! are ye weary of your lives,
    Or are your natural wits too dull to see
    That ye are standing, not upon the brink,   235
    But in the midst of mortal jeopardy?
    Nay, had I not kept watch this weary while,

Here at the door, your plot had slipped inside
Ere ye yourselves had entered. As it is,
My watchfulness has prevented this mishap.   240
Now that your wordy eloquence has an end,
And your excessive cries of joy, go in.
'Tis ill delaying in such case, and well
To make an end.

Orestes.   How shall I fare within?   245

Aged Servant. Right well; to start with, thou art known to
        none.

Orestes. Thou hast reported, I presume, my death.

Aged Servant. They'll speak of thee as though thou wert
        a shade.

Orestes. And are they glad thereat, or what say they?

Aged Servant. I'll tell thee when the time is ripe: mean-   250
        while

Whate'er they do, however ill, is well.

Electra. I pray thee, brother, tell me who is this?

Orestes. Dost thou not see?

Electra.   I know not, nor can guess.

Orestes. Not know the man to whom thou gav'st me   255
        once?

Electra. What man? how mean'st thou?

Orestes.   He that stole me hence,
        Through thy forethought, and safe to Phocis bore.

Electra. Can this be he who, when our sire was slain,
        Faithful among the many false I found?   260

Orestes. 'Tis he; let that suffice thee; ask no more.

Electra. O happy day! O sole deliverer
    Of Agamemnon's house, how cam'st thou hither?
    Art thou indeed our saviour who redeemed
    From endless woes my brother and myself?   265
    O hands beloved, O messenger whose feet
    Were bringers of glad tidings, how so long
    Couldst thou be with me and remain unknown,
    Stay me with feignèd fables and conceal
    The truth that gave me life? Hail, father, hail!   270
    For 'tis a father whom I seem to see.
    Verily no man in the self-same day
    Was hated so and so much loved as thou.
Aged Servant. Enough methinks; the tale 'twixt then and
        now—
    Many revolving nights and days as many   275
    Shall serve, Electra, to unfold it all.

       [*To* ORESTES *and* PYLADES]

    Why stand ye here! 'tis time for you to act,
    Now Clytemnestra is alone; no man
    Is now within; but, if ye stay your hand,
    Not only with her servants will ye fight   280
    But with a troop more numerous and more skilled.
Orestes. Our business, Pylades, would seem to crave
    No longer talk; let us instantly
    Enter, but ere we enter first adore
    The gods who keep the threshold of the house.   285
            [ORESTES *and* PYLADES *enter the palace.*

Electra. O King Apollo! lend a gracious ear
    To them and me, to me, too, who so oft
    Laid on thy shrine with humble hands my best.
    And now with vows (I cannot offer more),
    Apollo, Lord Lycean, I beseech,   290
    Implore, beg thee, prosper this our work,
    Defend the right and show to godless men
    How the gods deal with impiety.

[End of Third Episode]

THIRD STASIMON

Chorus. Breathing out blood and vengeance, lo!
    Stalks Ares, sure though slow.   295
    E'en now the hounds are on the trail;
    Within, the sinners at their coming quail.
    A little while and death shall realize
    The vision that now floats before mine eyes.

    For now within the house is led   300
    By stealth the champion of the dead;
    He treads once more the ancestral hall of kings,
    And death new-whetted in his hands he brings.
    Great Maia's son conducts him on his way
    And shrouds him now, permits no more delay.   305

304. **Maia (mā'-yà)**—Mother of Hermes. See Note, page 228.

FOURTH EPISODE

Electra. O dearest women, even as I speak
    The men are at their work; but not a word.
Chorus. What work? what are they at?
Electra.   E'en now she decks
    The urn for burial and the pair stand by.   5
Chorus. Why rush thou forth?
Electra.   To keep a watch for fear
    Ægisthus should forestall us unawares.
Clytemnestra (within). Woe! woe! O woeful house,
    Of friends forsaken, full of murderers!   10
Electra. Listen! a cry within—hear ye not, friends?
Chorus. I heard and shuddered—oh, an awesome cry.
Clytemnestra. Ah woe is me! Ægisthus, where art thou?
Electra. Hark; once again a wail.
Clytemnestra.   O son, my son,   15
    Have pity on thy mother!
Electra.   Thou hadst none
    On him or on the father that begat him.
Chorus. Unhappy realm and house,
    The curse that dogged thee day by day   20
    Is dying, dying fast.
Clytemnestra. I am stricken, ah!
Electra.   Strike, if thou canst, again.
Clytemnestra. Woe, woe is me once more!

Electra. I would that woe 25
   Were for Ægisthus not for thee alone.

Chorus. The curses work; the buried live again,
   And blood for blood, the slayer's blood they drain,
   The ghosts of victims long since slain.

     Enter Orestes *and* Pylades *from the palace.*
   Lo they come forth with gory hands that reek 30
   Of sacrifice to Ares—'twas done well.

Electra. How have ye fared, Orestes?

Orestes. All within
   Is well, if Phœbus' oracle spake well.

Electra. The wretched woman's dead? 35

Orestes. No longer fear
   Thy mother's arrogance will flout thee more.

Chorus. Cease, for I see Ægisthus full in sight.

Electra. Back, youths, back to the house!

Orestes. Where see ye him? 40

Electra. Approaching from the suburb with an air
   Of exultation. He is ours!

Chorus. Quick to the palace doorway! half your work
   Is well done; do no less well what remains.

Orestes. Fear not, we shall. 45

Electra. Then speed thee on thy way.

Orestes. See, I am gone.

Electra. Leave what is here to me.

     [*Exeunt* Orestes *and* Pylades; Ægisthus *approaches.*

Chorus. 'Twere not amiss to breathe some soft words in his
   ear,

That he may blindly rush into the lists of doom.   50

Ægisthus. Could any of you tell me where to find
    The Phocian strangers who, I hear, have brought
    News of Orestes midst the chariots wrecked?
    Thee, thee I question, thee, in former days
    So willful: it concerns thee most, methinks,   55
    And thou, as best informed, canst tell me best.

Electra. I know for sure, else were I unconcerned
    In what has happened to my nearest kin.

Ægisthus. Where then are these newcomers? Tell me
      straight.

Electra. Within; they've won their kindly hostess' heart.   60

Ægisthus. Did they in very truth report his death?

Electra. They did; and more, they showed us the dead man.

Ægisthus. May I, too, view the body to make sure?

Electra. Thou mayst, but 'tis a gruesome spectacle.

Ægisthus. Thou givest me much joy against thy wont.   65

Electra. I wish thee joy, if here is food for joy.

Ægisthus. Silence! attend! throw open wide the gate,
    For all Mycenæ, Argos all, to see.
    If any heretofore was puffed with hopes
    Of this pretender, now he sees him dead,   70
    Let him in time accept my yoke, nor wait
    Wisdom by punishment to learn too late.

Electra. My lesson's learnt already; time hath taught me
    The wisdom of consenting with the strong.

    [*The scene opens showing a shrouded corpse with
      Orestes and Pylades beside it*]

Ægisthus. O Zeus, I look upon this form laid low   75
  By jealousy of Heaven, but if my words
  Seem to thee overbold, be they unsaid.
  Take from the face the face-cloth; I, as kin,
  I too would pay my tribute of lament.

Orestes. Lift it thyself; 'tis not for me but thee   80
  To see and kindly greet what lieth here.

Ægisthus. Well said, so will I. [*To* Electra.] If she be
  within
  Go call me Clytemnestra, I would see her—

Orestes. She is beside thee; look not elsewhere.

     [Ægisthus *lifts the face-cloth.*]

Ægisthus. O horror!   85

Orestes.   Why dost start? is the face strange?

Ægisthus. Who spread the net wherein, O woe is me,
  I lie enmeshed?

Orestes.   Hast thou not learnt ere this
  The dead of whom thou spakest are alive?   90

Ægisthus. Alas! I read thy riddle; 'tis none else
  Than thou, Orestes, whom I now address.

Orestes. A seer so wise, and yet befooled so long!

Ægisthus. O I am spoiled, undone! yet suffer me,
  One little word.   95

Electra.   Brother, in heaven's name
  Let him not speak a word or plead his cause.
  When a poor wretch is in the toils of fate
  What can a brief reprieve avail him? No,

Slay him outright and having slain him give   100
His corpse to such grave-makers as is meet,
Far from our sight; for me no otherwise
Can he wipe out the memory of past wrongs.

Orestes [*to* Ægisthus]. Quick, get thee in; the issue lies
  not now
 In words; the case is tried and thou must die.   105

Ægisthus. Why hale me indoors? if my doom be just,
 What need of darkness? Why not slay me here?

Orestes. 'Tis not for thee to order; go within;
 Where thou didst slay my father thou must die.

Ægisthus. Ah! is there need this palace should behold   110
 All woes of Pelops' line, now and to come?

Orestes. Thine own they shall; thus much I can predict.

Ægisthus. Thy skill as seer derives not from thy sire.

Orestes. Thou bandiest words; our going is delayed.
 Go.   115

Ægisthus. Lead the way.

Orestes.   No, thou must go the first.

Ægisthus. Lest I escape?

Orestes.   Nay, not to let thee choose
 The manner of thy death; thou must be spared   120
 No bitterness of death, and well it were
 If on transgressors swift this sentence fall,
 Slay him; so wickedness should less abound.

[*End of Fourth Episode*]

EXODOS

Chorus. House of Atreus! thou hast passed
  Through the fire and won at last   125
  Freedom, perfected today
  By this glorious essay.

BEYOND THE HORIZON

By

Eugene O'Neill

THE CHARACTERS IN THE PLAY

JAMES MAYO, *a farmer*
KATE MAYO, *his wife*
CAPTAIN DICK SCOTT, *of the bark* Sunda, *her brother*
ANDREW MAYO,
ROBERT MAYO, } *sons of* JAMES MAYO
RUTH ATKINS
MRS. ATKINS, *her widowed mother*
MARY
BEN, *a farm hand*
DOCTOR FAWCETT

Beyond the Horizon

ACT ONE

Scene I

A section of country highway. The road runs diagonally from the left, forward, to the right, rear, and can be seen in the distance winding toward the horizon like a pale ribbon between the low, rolling hills with their freshly-plowed fields clearly divided from each other, checkerboard fashion, by the lines of stone walls and rough snake fences.

The forward triangle cut off by the road is a section of a field from the dark earth of which myriad bright-green blades of fall-sown rye are sprouting. A straggling line of piled rocks, too low to be called a wall, separates this field from the road.

To the rear of the road is a ditch with a sloping, grassy bank on the far side. From the center of this an old, gnarled apple tree, just budding into leaf, strains its twisted branches heavenwards, black against the pallor of distance. A snake-fence sidles from left to right along the top of the bank, passing beneath the apple tree.

The hushed twilight of a day in May is just beginning. The horizon hills are still rimmed by a faint line of flame, and the sky above them glows with the crimson flush of the sunset. This fades gradually as the action of the scene progresses.

At the rise of the curtain, ROBERT MAYO *is discovered sitting
on the fence. He is a tall, slender young man of twenty-three.
There is a touch of the poet about him expressed in his high
forehead and wide, dark eyes. His features are delicate and
refined, leaning to weakness in the mouth and chin. He is
dressed in gray corduroy trousers pushed into high laced boots,
and a blue flannel shirt with a bright colored tie. He is reading a book by the fading sunset light. He shuts this, keeping
a finger in to mark the place, and turns his head toward the
horizon, gazing out over the fields and hills. His lips move as
if he were reciting something to himself.*

His brother ANDREW *comes along the road from the right,
returning from his work in the fields. He is twenty-seven
years old, an opposite type to* ROBERT—*husky, sun-bronzed,
handsome in a large-featured, manly fashion—a son of the soil,
intelligent in a shrewd way, but with nothing of the intellectual about him. He wears overalls, leather boots, a gray flannel shirt open at the neck, and a soft, mud-stained hat pushed
back on his head. He stops to talk to* ROBERT, *leaning on the
hoe he carries.*

Andrew. [*Seeing* ROBERT *has not noticed his presence—in
a loud shout*] Hey there! [ROBERT *turns with a start.
Seeing who it is, he smiles.*] Gosh, you do take the prize
for day-dreaming! And I see you've toted one of the old
books along with you. [*He crosses the ditch and sits
on the fence near his brother.*] What is it this time—
poetry, I'll bet. [*He reaches for the book.*] Let me see.

Toted—Carried.

Robert. [*Handing it to him rather reluctantly*] Look out you
   don't get it full of dirt.

Andrew. [*Glancing at his hands*] That isn't dirt—it's good
   clean earth. [*He turns over the pages. His eyes read
   something and he gives an exclamation of disgust.*]
   Humph! [*With a provoking grin at his brother he reads
   aloud in a doleful sing-song voice.*] "I have loved wind
   and light and the bright sea. But holy and most sacred
   night, not as I love and have loved thee." [*He hands the
   book back.*] Here! Take it and bury it. I suppose it's
   that year in college gave you a liking for that kind of stuff.
   I'm darn glad I stopped at High School, or maybe I'd been
   crazy too. [*He grins and slaps* Robert *on the back affectionately.*] Imagine me reading poetry and plowing at
   the same time! The team'd run away, I'll bet.

Robert. [*Laughing*] Or picture me plowing.

Andrew. You should have gone back to college last fall, like
   I know you wanted to. You're fitted for that sort of thing
   —just as I ain't.

Robert. You know why I didn't go back, Andy. Pa didn't
   like the idea, even if he didn't say so; and I know he
   wanted the money to use improving the farm. And besides, I'm not keen on being a student, just because you
   see me reading books all the time. What I want to do
   now is keep on moving so that I won't take root in any
   one place.

Andrew. Well, the trip you're leaving on tomorrow will keep
   you moving all right. [*At this mention of the trip they*

both fall silent. There is a pause. Finally ANDREW *goes on, awkwardly, attempting to speak casually.*] Uncle says you'll be gone three years.

Robert. About that, he figures.

Andrew. [*Moodily*] That's a long time.

Robert. Not so long when you come to consider it. You know the *Sunda* sails around the Horn for Yokohama first, and that's a long voyage on a sailing ship; and if we go to any of the other places Uncle Dick mentions—India, or Australia, or South Africa, or South America—they'll be long voyages too.

Andrew. You can have all those foreign parts for all of me. [*After a pause*] Ma's going to miss you a lot, Rob.

Robert. Yes—and I'll miss her.

Andrew. And Pa ain't feeling none too happy to have you go—though he's been trying not to show it.

Robert. I can see how he feels.

Andrew. And you can bet that I'm not giving any cheers about it. [*He puts one hand on the fence near* ROBERT.]

Robert. [*Putting one hand on top of* ANDREW's *with a gesture almost of shyness.*] I know that, too, Andy.

Andrew. I'll miss you as much as anybody, I guess. You see, you and I ain't like most brothers—always fighting and separated a lot of the time, while we've always been together—just the two of us. It's different with us. That's why it hits so hard, I guess.

Robert. [*With feeling*] It's just as hard for me, Andy—believe that! I hate to leave you and the old folks—but—

I feel I've got to. There's something calling me—— [*He points to the horizon.*] Oh, I can't just explain it to you, Andy.

Andrew. No need to, Rob. [*Angry at himself*] You want to go—that's all there is to it; and I wouldn't have you miss this chance for the world.

Robert. It's fine of you to feel that way, Andy.

Andrew. Huh! I'd be a nice son of a gun if I didn't, wouldn't I? When I know how you need this sea trip to make a new man of you—in the body, I mean—and give you your full health back.

Robert. [*A trifle impatiently*] All of you seem to keep harping on my health. You were so used to seeing me lying around the house in the old days that you never will get over the notion that I'm a chronic invalid. You don't realize how I've bucked up in the past few years. If I had no other excuse for going on Uncle Dick's ship but just my health, I'd stay right here and start in plowing.

Andrew. Can't be done. Farming ain't your nature. There's all the difference shown in just the way us two feel about the farm. You—well, you like the home part of it, I expect; but as a place to work and grow things, you hate it. Ain't that right?

Robert. Yes, I suppose it is. For you it's different. You're a Mayo through and through. You're wedded to the soil. You're as much a product of it as an ear of corn is, or a tree. Father is the same. This farm is his life-work, and he's happy in knowing that another Mayo, inspired by the

same love, will take up the work where he leaves off.
I can understand your attitude, and Pa's; and I think it's
wonderful and sincere. But I—well, I'm not made that
way.

Andrew. No, you ain't; but when it comes to understanding,
I guess I realize that you've got your own angle of looking
at things.

Robert. [*Musingly*] I wonder if you do, really.

Andrew. [*Confidently*] Sure I do. You've seen a bit of the
world, enough to make the farm seem small, and you've
got the itch to see it all.

Robert. It's more than that, Andy.

Andrew. Oh, of course. I know you're going to learn navi-
gation, and all about a ship, so's you can be an officer.
That's natural, too. There's fair pay in it, I expect, when
you consider that you've always got a home and grub
thrown in; and if you're set on traveling, you can go any-
where you're a mind to without paying fare.

Robert. [*With a smile that is half sad*] It's more than that,
Andy.

Andrew. Sure it is. There's always a chance of a good thing
coming your way in some of those foreign ports or other.
I've heard there are great opportunities for a young fellow
with his eyes open in some of those new countries that
are just being opened up. [*Jovially*] I'll bet that's what
you've been turning over in your mind under all your
quietness! [*He slaps his brother on the back with a
laugh.*] Well, if you get to be a millionaire all of a sud

den, call 'round once in a while and I'll pass the plate to you. We could use a lot of money right here on the farm without hurting it any.

Robert. [*Forced to laugh*] I've never considered that practical side of it for a minute, Andy.

Andrew. Well, you ought to.

Robert. No, I oughtn't. [*Pointing to the horizon—dreamily*] Supposing I was to tell you that it's just Beauty that's calling me, the beauty of the far off and unknown, the mystery and spell of the East which lures me in the books I've read, the need of the freedom of great wide spaces, the joy of wandering on and on—in quest of the secret which is hidden over there, beyond the horizon? Suppose I told you that was the one and only reason for my going?

Andrew. I should say you were nutty.

Robert. [*Frowning*] Don't, Andy. I'm serious.

Andrew. Then you might as well stay here, because we've got all you're looking for right on this farm. There's wide space enough, Lord knows; and you can have all the sea you want by walking a mile down to the beach; and there's plenty of horizon to look at, and beauty enough for anyone, except in the winter. [*He grins.*] As for the mystery and spell, I haven't met 'em yet, but they're probably lying around somewhere. I'll have you understand this is a first class farm with all the fixings. [*He laughs.*]

Robert. [*Joining in the laughter in spite of himself*] It's no use talking to you, you chump!

Andrew. You'd better not say anything to Uncle Dick about spells and things when you're on the ship. He'll likely chuck you overboard for a Jonah. [*He jumps down from fence.*] I'd better run along. I've got to wash up some as long as Ruth's Ma is coming over for supper.

Robert. [*Pointedly—almost bitterly*] And Ruth.

Andrew. [*Confused—looking everywhere except at* ROBERT— *trying to appear unconcerned*] Yes, Ruth'll be staying too. Well, I better hustle, I guess, and—— [*He steps over the ditch to the road while he is talking.*]

Robert. [*Who appears to be fighting some strong inward emotion—impulsively*] Wait a minute, Andy! [*He jumps down from the fence.*] There is something I want to—— [*He stops abruptly, biting his lips, his face coloring.*]

Andrew. [*Facing him; half-defiantly*] Yes?

Robert. [*Confusedly*] No—never mind—it doesn't matter, it was nothing.

Andrew. [*After a pause, during which he stares fixedly at* ROBERT'S *averted face*] Maybe I can guess—what you were going to say—but I guess you're right not to talk about it. [*He pulls* ROBERT'S *hand from his side and grips it tensely; the two brothers stand looking into each other's eyes for a minute.*] We can't help those things, Rob. [*He turns away, suddenly releasing* ROBERT'S *hand.*] You'll be coming along shortly, won't you?

Robert. [*Dully*] Yes.

Andrew. See you later, then. [*He walks off down the road*

to the left. ROBERT *stares after him for a moment; then
climbs to the fence rail again, and looks out over the hills
an expression of deep grief on his face. After a moment
or so,* RUTH *enters hurriedly from the left. She is a
healthy, blonde, out-of-door girl of twenty, with a graceful, slender figure. Her face, though inclined to round-
ness, is undeniably pretty, her large eyes of a deep blue set
off strikingly by the sun-bronzed complexion. Her small,
regular features are marked by a certain strength—an
underlying, stubborn fixity of purpose hidden in the
frankly-appealing charm of her fresh youthfulness. She
wears a simple white dress but no hat.*]

Ruth. [*Seeing him*] Hello, Rob!

Robert. [*Startled*] Hello, Ruth!

Ruth. [*Jumps the ditch and perches on the fence beside him*]
   I was looking for you.

Robert. [*Pointedly*] Andy just left here.

Ruth. I know. I met him on the road a second ago. He told
   me you were here. [*Tenderly playful*] I wasn't looking
   for Andy, Smarty, if that's what you mean. I was looking for *you*.

Robert. Because I'm going away tomorrow?

Ruth. Because your mother was anxious to have you come
   home and asked me to look for you. I just wheeled Ma
   over to your house.

Robert. [*Perfunctorily*] How is your mother?

Ruth. [*A shadow coming over her face*] She's about the
   same. She never seems to get any better or any worse.

Oh, Rob, I do wish she'd try to make the best of things that can't be helped.

Robert. Has she been nagging at you again?

Ruth. [*Nods her head, and then breaks forth rebelliously*] She never stops nagging. No matter what I do for her she finds fault. If only Pa was still living—— [*She stops as if ashamed of her outburst.*] I suppose I shouldn't complain this way. [*She sighs.*] Poor Ma, Lord knows it's hard enough for her. I suppose it's natural to be cross when you're not able ever to walk a step. Oh, I'd like to be going away some place—like you!

Robert. It's hard to stay—and equally hard to go, sometimes.

Ruth. There! If I'm not the stupid body. I swore I wasn't going to speak about your trip—until after you'd gone; and there I go, first thing!

Robert. Why didn't you want to speak of it?

Ruth. Because I didn't want to spoil this last night you're here. Oh, Rob, I'm going to—we're all going to miss you so awfully. Your mother is going around looking as if she'd burst out crying any minute. You ought to know how I feel. Andy and you and I—why it seems as if we'd always been together.

Robert. [*With a wry attempt at a smile*] You and Andy will still have each other. It'll be harder for me without anyone.

Ruth. But you'll have new sights and new people to take your mind off; while we'll be here with the old, familiar place to remind us every minute of the day. It's a shame

you're going—just at this time, in spring, when everything
is getting so nice. [*With a sigh*] I oughtn't to talk that
way when I know going's the best thing for you. You're
bound to find all sorts of opportunities to get on, your
father says.

Robert. [*Heatedly*] I don't give a darn about that! I
wouldn't take a voyage across the road for the best opportunity in the world of the kind Pa thinks of. [*He
smiles at his own irritation.*] Excuse me, Ruth, for getting worked up over it; but Andy gave me an overdose
of the practical considerations.

Ruth. [*Slowly, puzzled*] Well, then, if it isn't— [*With sudden intensity*] Oh, Rob, why *do* you want to go?

Robert. [*Turning to her quickly, in surprise—slowly*] Why
do you ask that, Ruth?

Ruth. [*Dropping her eyes before his searching glance*] Because— [*Lamely*] It seems such a shame.

Robert. [*Insistently*] Why?

Ruth. Oh, because—everything.

Robert. I could hardly back out now, even if I wanted to.
And I'll be forgotten before you know it.

Ruth. [*Indignantly*] You won't! I'll never forget—— [*She
stops and turns away to hide her confusion.*]

Robert. [*Softly*] Will you promise me that?

Ruth. [*Evasively*] Of course. It's mean of you to think that
any of us would forget so easily.

Robert. [*Disappointedly*] Oh!

Ruth. [*With an attempt at lightness*] But you haven't told me your reason for leaving yet.

Robert. [*Moodily*] I doubt if you'll understand. It's difficult to explain, even to myself. Either you feel it, or you don't. I can remember being conscious of it first when I was only a kid—you haven't forgotten what a sickly specimen I was then, in those days, have you?

Ruth. [*With a shudder*] Let's not think about them.

Robert. You'll have to, to understand. Well, in those days, when Ma was fixing meals, she used to get me out of the way by pushing my chair to the west window and telling me to look out and be quiet. That wasn't hard. I guess I was always quiet.

Ruth. [*Compassionately*] Yes, you always were—and you suffering so much, too!

Robert. [*Musingly*] So I used to stare out over the fields to the hills, out there—[*He points to the horizon.*] and somehow after a time I'd forget any pain I was in, and start dreaming. I knew the sea was over beyond those hills,— the folks had told me—and I used to wonder what the sea was like, and try to form a picture of it in my mind. [*With a smile*] There was all the mystery in the world to me then about that—far-off sea—and there still is! It called to me then just as it does now. [*After a slight pause*] And other times my eyes would follow this road, winding off into the distance, toward the hills, as if it, too, was searching for the sea. And I'd promise myself that when I grew up and was strong, I'd follow that road, and

"I'd promise myself that when I grew up . . . I'd follow that road . . . beyond the horizon."

Robert Mayo as played by Robert Keith

it and I would find the sea together. [*With a smile*] You see, my making this trip is only keeping that promise of long ago.

Ruth. [*Charmed by his low musical voice telling the dreams of his childhood*] Yes, I see.

Robert. Those were the only happy moments of my life then, dreaming there at the window. I liked to be all alone—those times. I got to know all the different kinds of sunsets by heart. And all those sunsets took place over there—[*He points.*] beyond the horizon. So gradually I came to believe that all the wonders of the world happened on the other side of those hills. There was the home of the good fairies who performed beautiful miracles. I believed in fairies then. [*With a smile*] Perhaps I still do believe in them. Anyway, in those days they were real enough, and sometimes I could actually hear them calling to me to come out and play with them, dance with them down the road in the dusk in a game of hide-and-seek to find out where the sun was hiding himself. They sang their little songs to me, songs that told of all the wonderful things they had in their home on the other side of the hills; and they promised to show me all of them, if I'd only come, come! But I couldn't come then, and I used to cry sometimes and Ma would think I was in pain. [*He breaks off suddenly with a laugh.*] That's why I'm going now, I suppose. For I can still hear them calling. But the horizon is as far away and as luring as ever. [*He turns to her—softly.*]

Do you understand now, Ruth?

Ruth. [*Spellbound, in a whisper*] Yes.

Robert. You feel it then?

Ruth. Yes, yes, I do! [*Unconsciously she snuggles close against his side. His arm steals about her as if he were not aware of the action.*] Oh, Rob, how could I help feeling it? You tell things so beautifully!

Robert. [*Suddenly realizing that his arm is around her, and that her head is resting on his shoulder, gently takes his arm away.* Ruth, *brought back to herself, is overcome with confusion.*] So now you know why I'm going. It's for that reason—that and one other.

Ruth. You've another? Then you must tell me that, too.

Robert. [*Looking at her searchingly. She drops her eyes before his gaze.*] I wonder if I ought to! You'll promise not to be angry—whatever it is?

Ruth. [*Softly, her face still averted*] Yes, I promise.

Robert. [*Simply*] I love you. That's the other reason.

Ruth. [*Hiding her face in her hands*] Oh, Rob!

Robert. I wasn't going to tell you, but I feel I have to. It can't matter now that I'm going so far away, and for so long—perhaps forever. I've loved you all these years, but the realization never came 'til I agreed to go away with Uncle Dick. Then I thought of leaving you, and the pain of that thought revealed to me in a flash—that I loved you, had loved you as long as I could remember. [*He gently pulls one of* Ruth's *hands away from her face.*] You mustn't mind my telling you this, Ruth. I realize how impossible it all is—and I understand; for the revelation of my own love seemed to open my eyes to the love of others. I saw Andy's love for you—and I knew that you must love him.

Ruth. [*Breaking out stormily*] I don't! I don't love Andy! I don't! [Robert *stares at her in stupid astonishment.* Ruth *weeps hysterically.*] Whatever—put such a fool notion into—into your head? [*She suddenly throws her arms about his neck and hides her head on his shoulder.*] Oh, Rob! Don't go away! Please! You mustn't, now! You can't! I won't let you! It'd break my—my heart!

Robert. [*The expression of stupid bewilderment giving way to one of overwhelming joy. He presses her close to him—slowly and tenderly.*] Do you mean that—that you love me?

Ruth. [*Sobbing*] Yes, yes—of course I do—what d'you s'pose? [*She lifts up her head and looks into his eyes with a tremulous smile.*] You stupid thing! [*He kisses her.*] I've loved you right along.

Robert. [*Mystified*] But you and Andy were always together!

Ruth. Because you never seemed to want to go any place with me. You were always reading an old book, and not paying any attention to me. I was too proud to let you see I cared because I thought the year you had away to college had made you stuck-up, and you thought yourself too educated to waste any time on me.

Robert. [*Kissing her*] And I was thinking—— [*With a laugh*] What fools we've both been!

Ruth. [*Overcome by a sudden fear*] You won't go away on the trip, will you, Rob? You'll tell them you can't go on account of me, won't you? You can't go now! You can't!

Robert. [*Bewildered*] Perhaps—you can come too.

Ruth. Oh, Rob, don't be so foolish. You know I can't. Who'd take care of Ma? Don't you see I couldn't go— on her account? [*She clings to him imploringly.*] Please don't go—not now. Tell them you've decided not to. They won't mind. I know your mother and father'll be glad. They'll all be. They don't want you to go so far away from them. Please, Rob! We'll be so happy here together where it's natural and we know things. Please tell me you won't go!

Robert. [*Face to face with a definite, final decision, betrays the conflict going on within him*] But—Ruth—I—Uncle Dick——

Ruth. He won't mind when he knows it's for your happiness to stay. How could he? [*As* Robert *remains silent, she bursts into sobs again.*] Oh, Rob! And you said—you loved me!

Robert. [*Conquered by this appeal—an irrevocable decision in his voice*] I won't go, Ruth. I promise you. There! Don't cry! [*He presses her to him, stroking her hair tenderly. After a pause he speaks with happy hopefulness.*] Perhaps after all Andy was right—righter than he knew—when he said I could find all the things I was seeking for here, at home on the farm. I think love must have been the secret—the secret that called to me from over the world's rim—the secret beyond every horizon; and when I did not come, it came to me. [*He clasps* RUTH *to him fiercely.*] Oh, Ruth, our love is sweeter than any distant dream! [*He kisses her passionately and steps to the ground, lifting* RUTH *in his arms and carrying her to the road where he puts her down.*]

Ruth. [*With a happy laugh*] My, but you're strong!

Robert. Come! We'll go and tell them at once.

Ruth. [*Dismayed*] Oh, no, don't, Rob, not 'til after I've gone. There'd be bound to be such a scene with them all together.

Robert. [*Kissing her—gayly*] As you like—little Miss Common Sense!

Ruth. Let's go then. [*She takes his hand, and they start to go off left.* ROBERT *suddenly stops and turns as though for a last look at the hills and the dying sunset flush.*]

Robert. [*Looking upward and pointing*] See! The first star. [*He bends down and kisses her tenderly.*] Our star!

Ruth. [*In a soft murmur*] Yes. Our very own star. [*They stand for a moment looking up at it, their arms around each other. Then* RUTH *takes his hand again and starts to lead him away.*] Come, Rob, let's go. [*His eyes are fixed again on the horizon as he half turns to follow her.* RUTH *urges.*] We'll be late for supper, Rob.

Robert. [*Shakes his head impatiently, as though he were*

throwing off some disturbing thought—with a laugh]
All right. We'll run then. Come on! [*They run off
laughing as*

[*The Curtain Falls*]

Scene II

*The sitting room of the Mayo farmhouse about nine o'clock
the same night. On the left, two windows looking out on the
fields. Against the wall between the windows, an old-
fashioned walnut desk. In the left corner, rear, a sideboard
with a mirror. In the rear wall to the right of the sideboard,
a window looking out on the road. Next to the window a
door leading out into the yard. Further right, a black horse-
hair sofa, and another door opening on a bedroom. In the
corner, a straight-backed chair. In the right wall, near the
middle, an open doorway leading to the kitchen. Farther
forward a double-heater stove with coal scuttle, etc. In the
center of the newly-carpeted floor, an oak dining-room table
with a red cover. In the center of the table, a large oil reading lamp. Four chairs, three rockers with crocheted tidies on
their backs, and one straight-backed, are placed about the
table. The walls are papered a dark red with a scrolly-
figured pattern.*

*Everything in the room is clean, well-kept, and in its exact
place, yet there is no suggestion of primness about the whole.
Rather the atmosphere is one of the orderly comfort of a*

*simple, hard-earned prosperity, enjoyed and maintained by the
family as a unit.*

James Mayo, *his wife, her brother,* Captain Dick Scott,
and Andrew *are discovered.* Mayo *is his son* Andrew *over
again in body and face—an* Andrew *sixty-five years old with
a short, square, white beard.* Mrs. Mayo *is a slight, round-
faced, rather prim-looking woman of fifty-five who had once
been a school teacher. The labors of a farmer's wife have
bent but not broken her, and she retains a certain refinement
of movement and expression foreign to the* Mayo *part of the
family. Whatever of resemblance* Robert *has to his parents
may be traced to her. Her brother, the* Captain, *is short and
stocky, with a weather-beaten, jovial face and a white mustache—a typical old salt, loud of voice and given to gesture.
He is fifty-eight years old.*

James Mayo *sits in front of the table. He wears spectacles,
and a farm journal which he has been reading lies in his lap.*
The Captain *leans forward from a chair in the rear, his hands
on the table in front of him.* Andrew *is tilted back on the
straight-backed chair to the left, his chin sunk forward on his
chest, staring at the carpet, preoccupied and frowning.*

As the Curtain rises, the Captain *is just finishing the rela-
tion of some sea episode. The others are pretending an interest which is belied by the absent-minded expressions on their
faces.*

The Captain. [*Chuckling*] And that mission woman, she
    hails me on the dock as I was acomin' ashore, and she
    says—with her silly face all screwed up serious as judg-

ment—"Captain," she says, "would you be so kind to tell me where the sea-gulls sleeps at night?" Blow me, if them warn't her exact words! [*He slaps the table with the palm of his hands and laughs loudly. The others force smiles.*] Ain't that just like a fool woman's question? And I looks at her serious as I could, "Ma'm," says I, "I couldn't right answer that question. I ain't never seed a sea-gull in his bunk yet. The next time I hears one snorin'," I says, "I'll make a note of where he's turned in, and write you a letter 'bout it." And then she calls me a fool real spiteful and tacks away from me quick. [*He laughs again uproariously.*] So I got rid of her that way. [*The others smile but immediately relapse into expressions of gloom again.*]

Mrs. Mayo. [*Absent-mindedly—feeling that she has to say something*] But when it comes to that, where *do* sea-gulls sleep, Dick?

Scott. [*Slapping the table*] Ho! Ho! Listen to her, James. 'Nother one! Well, if that don't beat all hell—'scuse me for cussin', Kate.

Mayo. [*With a twinkle in his eyes*] They unhitch their wings, Katey, and spreads 'em out on a wave for a bed.

Scott. And then they tells the fish to whistle to 'em when it's time to turn out. Ho! Ho!

Mrs. Mayo. [*With a forced smile*] You men folks are too smart to live, aren't you? [*She resumes her knitting. Mayo pretends to read his paper; Andrew stares at the floor.*]

Scott. [*Looks from one to the other of them with a puzzled air. Finally he is unable to bear the thick silence a minute longer, and blurts out.*] You folks look as if you was settin' up with a corpse. [*With exaggerated concern*] There ain't anyone dead, be there?

Mayo. [*Sharply*] Don't play the dunce, Dick! You know as well as we do there ain't no great cause to be feelin' chipper.

Scott. [*Argumentatively*] And there ain't no cause to be wearin' mourning, either, as far as I can make out.

Mrs. Mayo. [*Indignantly*] How can you talk that way, Dick Scott, when you're taking our Robbie away from us, in the middle of the night, you might say, just to get on that old boat of yours on time! I think you might wait until morning when he's had his breakfast.

Scott. [*Appealing to the others hopelessly*] Ain't that a woman's way o' seein' things for you? Kate, I can't give orders to the tide that it's got to be high just when it suits me to have it. I ain't gettin' no fun out o' missin' sleep and leavin' here at six bells myself. [*Protestingly*] And the *Sunda* ain't an old ship—leastways, not very old —and she's good's she ever was.

Mrs. Mayo. [*Her lips trembling*] I wish Robbie weren't going.

Mayo. [*Looking at her over his glasses—consolingly*] There, Katey!

Six bells—On shipboard, time is marked by the striking of bells from one to eight, every half hour of each four-hour watch. Six bells would be three or seven or eleven. Evidently they are leaving at three in the morning.

Mrs. Mayo. [*Rebelliously*] Well, I *do* wish he wasn't!

Scott. You shouldn't be taking it so hard, 's far as I kin see. This vige'll make a man of him. I'll see to it he learns how to navigate, 'n' study for a mate's c'tificate right off—and it'll give him a trade for the rest of his life, if he wants to travel.

Mrs. Mayo. But I don't want him to travel all his life. You've got to see he comes home when this trip is over. Then he'll be all well, and he'll want to—to marry—[ANDREW *sits forward in his chair with an abrupt movement.*]—and settle down right here. [*She stares down at the knitting in her lap—after a pause.*] I never realized how hard it was going to be for me to have Robbie go—or I wouldn't have considered it a minute.

Scott. It ain't no good goin' on that way, Kate, now it's all settled.

Mrs. Mayo. [*On the verge of tears*] It's all right for *you* to talk. You've never had any children. You don't know what it means to be parted from them—and Robbie my youngest, too. [ANDREW *frowns and fidgets in his chair.*]

Andrew. [*Suddenly turning to them*] There's one thing none of you seem to take into consideration—that Rob wants to go. He's dead set on it. He's been dreaming over this trip ever since it was first talked about. It wouldn't be fair to him not to have him go. [*A sudden uneasiness seems to strike him.*] At least, not if he still

Vige'll—Voyage will.

feels the same way about it he did when he was talking to me this evening.

Mayo. [*With an air of decision*] Andy's right, Katey. That ends all argyment, you can see that. [*Looking at his big silver watch*] Wonder what's happened to Robert? He's been gone long enough to wheel the widder to home, certain. He can't be out dreamin' at the stars his last night.

Mrs. Mayo. [*A bit reproachfully*] Why didn't you wheel Mrs. Atkins back tonight, Andy? You usually do when she and Ruth come over.

Andrew. [*Avoiding her eyes*] I thought maybe Robert wanted to tonight. He offered to go right away when they were leaving.

Mrs. Mayo. He only wanted to be polite.

Andrew. [*Gets to his feet*] Well, he'll be right back, I guess. [*He turns to his father.*] Guess I'll go take a look at the black cow, Pa—see if she's ailing any.

Mayo. Yes—better had, son. [ANDREW *goes into the kitchen on the right.*]

Scott. [*As he goes out—in a low tone*] There's the boy that would make a good, strong sea-farin' man—if he'd a mind to.

Mayo. [*Sharply*] Don't you put no such fool notions in Andy's head, Dick—or you 'n me's goin' to fall out. [*Then he smiles.*] You couldn't tempt him, no ways. Andy's a Mayo bred in the bone, and he's a born farmer, and a very good one, too. He'll live and die right here

on this farm, like I expect to. [*With proud confidence*]
And he'll make this one of the slickest, best-payin' farms
in the state, too, afore he gits through!

Scott.   Seems to me it's a pretty slick place right now.

Mayo.   [*Shaking his head*] It's too small. We need more
land to make it amount to much, and we ain't got the
capital to buy it. [ANDREW *enters from the kitchen. His
hat is on, and he carries a lighted lantern in his hand.
He goes to the door in the rear leading out.*]

Andrew.   [*Opens the door and pauses*] Anything else you
can think of to be done, Pa?

Mayo.   No, nothin' I know of. [ANDREW *goes out, shutting
the door.*]

Mrs. Mayo.   [*After a pause*] What's come over Andy to-
night, I wonder? He acts so strange.

Mayo.   He does seem sort o' glum and out of sorts. It's
'count o' Robert leavin', I s'pose. [*To* SCOTT] Dick, you
wouldn't believe how them boys o' mine sticks together.
They ain't like most brothers. They've been thick as
thieves all their lives, with nary a quarrel I kin remember.

Scott.   No need to tell me that. I can see how they take to
each other.

Mrs. Mayo.   [*Pursuing her train of thought*] Did you notice, James, how queer everyone was at supper? Robert
seemed stirred up about something; and Ruth was so
flustered and giggly; and Andy sat there dumb, looking
as if he'd lost his best friend; and all of them only nibbled
at their food.

Mayo. Guess they was all thinkin' about tomorrow, same as us.

Mrs. Mayo. [*Shaking her head*] No. I'm afraid somethin's happened—somethin' else.

Mayo. You mean—'bout Ruth?

Mrs. Mayo. Yes.

Mayo. [*After a pause—frowning*] I hope her and Andy ain't had a serious fallin'-out. I always sorter hoped they'd hitch up together sooner or later. What d'you say, Dick? Don't you think them two'd pair up well?

Scott. [*Nodding his head approvingly*] A sweet, wholesome couple they'd make.

Mayo. It'd be a good thing for Andy in more ways than one. I ain't what you'd call calculatin' generally, and I b'lieve in lettin' young folks run their affairs to suit themselves; but there's advantages for both o' them in this match you can't overlook in reason. The Atkins farm is right next to ourn. Jined together they'd make a jim-dandy of a place, with plenty o' room to work in. And bein' a widder with only a daughter, and laid up all the time to boot, Mrs. Atkins can't do nothin' with the place as it ought to be done. She needs a man, a first-class farmer, to take hold o' things; and Andy's just the one.

Mrs. Mayo. [*Abruptly*] I don't think Ruth loves Andy.

Mayo. You don't? Well, maybe a woman's eyes is sharper in such things, but—they're always together. And if she don't love him now, she'll likely come around to it in time.

[*As* Mrs. Mayo *shakes her head*] You seem mighty fixed
in your opinion, Katey. How d'you know?

Mrs. Mayo. It's just—what I feel.

Mayo. [*A light breaking over him*] You don't mean to say
—[Mrs. Mayo *nods.* Mayo *chuckles scornfully.*] Shucks!
I'm losin' my respect for your eyesight, Katey. Why,
Robert ain't got no time for Ruth, 'cept as a friend!

Mrs. Mayo. [*Warningly*] Sss-h-h! [*The door from the yard
opens, and* Robert *enters. He is smiling happily, and hum-
ming a song to himself, but as he comes into the room an
undercurrent of nervous uneasiness manifests itself in his
bearing.*]

Mayo. So here you be at last! [Robert *comes forward and
sits on* Andy's *chair.* Mayo *smiles slyly at his wife.*]
What have you been doin' all this time—countin' the stars
to see if they all come out right and proper?

Robert. There's only one I'll ever look for any more, Pa.

Mayo. [*Reproachfully*] You might've even not wasted time
lookin' for that one—your last night.

Mrs. Mayo. [*As if she were speaking to a child*] You ought
to have worn your coat a sharp night like this, Robbie.

Scott. [*Disgustedly*] Kate, you treat Robert as if he was one
year old!

Mrs. Mayo. [*Notices* Robert's *nervous uneasiness*] You look
all worked up over something, Robbie. What is it?

Robert. [*Swallowing hard, looks quickly from one to the
other of them—then begins determinedly*] Yes, there *is*
something—something I must tell you—all of you. [*As he*

"Ruth told me this evening that—she loved me."

Richard Bennett in the role of Robert

begins to talk, ANDREW *enters quietly from the rear, closing
the door behind him, and setting the lighted lantern on
the floor. He remains standing by the door, his arms
folded, listening to* ROBERT *with a repressed expression of
pain on his face.* ROBERT *is so much taken up with what
he is going to say that he does not notice* ANDREW's *presence.*] Something I discovered only this evening—very
beautiful and wonderful—something I did not take into
consideration previously because I hadn't dared to hope
that such happiness could ever come to me. [*Appealingly*]
You must all remember that fact, won't you?

Mayo. [*Frowning*] Let's get to the point, son.

Robert. [*With a trace of defiance*] Well, the point is this,
Pa: I'm not going—I mean—I can't go tomorrow with
Uncle Dick—or at any future time, either.

Mrs. Mayo. [*With a sharp sigh of joyful relief*] Oh, Robbie,
I'm so glad!

Mayo. [*Astounded*] You ain't serious, be you, Robert?
[*Severely*] Seems to me it's a pretty late hour in the day
for you to be upsettin' all your plans so sudden!

Robert. I asked you to remember that until this evening I
didn't know myself. I had never dared to dream——

Mayo. [*Irritably*] What is this foolishness you're talkin' of?

Robert. [*Flushing*] Ruth told me this evening that—she
loved me. It was after I'd confessed I loved her. I told
her I hadn't been conscious of my love until after the trip
had been arranged, and I realized it would mean—leaving
her. That was the truth. I *didn't* know until then. [*As*

if justifying himself to the others] I hadn't intended telling her anything but—suddenly—I felt I must. I didn't think it would matter, because I was going away. And I thought she loved—someone else. [*Slowly—his eyes shining*] And then she cried and said it was I she'd loved all the time, but I hadn't seen it.

Mrs. Mayo. [*Rushes over and throws her arms about him*] I knew it! I was just telling your father when you came in—and, Oh, Robbie, I'm so happy you're not going!

Robert. [*Kissing her*] I knew you'd be glad, Ma.

Mayo. [*Bewilderedly*] Well, I'll be darned! You do beat all for gettin' folks' minds all tangled up, Robert. And Ruth too! Whatever got into her of a sudden? Why, I was thinkin'——

Mrs. Mayo. [*Hurriedly—in a tone of warning*] Never mind what you were thinking, James. It wouldn't be any use telling us that now. [*Meaningly*] And what you were hoping for turns out just the same almost, doesn't it?

Mayo. [*Thoughtfully—beginning to see this side of the argument*] Yes; I suppose you're right, Katey. [*Scratching his head in puzzlement*] But how it ever come about! It do beat anything ever I heard. [*Finally he gets up with a sheepish grin and walks over to* ROBERT.] We're glad you ain't goin', your Ma and I, for we'd have missed you terrible, that's certain and sure; and we're glad you've found happiness. Ruth's a fine girl and'll make a good wife to you.

Robert. [*Much moved*]   Thank you, Pa.   [*He grips his
father's hand in his.*]

Andrew. [*His face tense and drawn comes forward and holds
out his hand, forcing a smile*]   I guess it's my turn to offer
congratulations, isn't it?

Robert. [*With a startled cry when his brother appears before
him so suddenly*]   Andy!   [*Confused*]   Why—I—I didn't
see you.   Were you here when——

Andrew.   I heard everything you said; and here's wishing you
every happiness, you and Ruth.   You both deserve the best
there is.

Robert. [*Taking his hand*]   Thanks, Andy, it's fine of you
to——   [*His voice dies away as he sees the pain in Andrew's eyes.*]

Andrew. [*Giving his brother's hand a final grip*]   Good luck
to you both!   [*He turns away and goes back to the rear
where he bends over the lantern, fumbling with it to hide
his emotion from the others.*]

Mrs. Mayo. [*To the* Captain, *who has been too flabber-
gasted by* Robert's *decision to say a word*].   What's the
matter, Dick?   Aren't you going to congratulate Robbie?

Scott. [*Embarrassed*]   Of course I be!   [*He gets to his feet
and shakes* Robert's *hand, muttering a vague*]   Luck to
you, boy.   [*He stands beside* Robert *as if he wanted to
say something more but doesn't know how to go about it.*]

Robert.   Thanks, Uncle Dick.

Scott.   So you're not acomin' on the *Sunda* with me?   [*His
voice indicates disbelief.*]

Robert. I can't, Uncle—not now. I wouldn't miss it for any' thing else in the world under any other circumstances. [*He sighs unconsciously.*] But you see I've found—a big' ger dream. [*Then with joyous high spirits*] I want you all to understand one thing—I'm not going to be a loafer on your hands any longer. This means the beginning of a new life for me in every way. I'm going to settle right down and take a real interest in the farm, and do my share. I'll prove to you, Pa, that I'm as good a Mayo as you are—or Andy, when I want to be.

Mayo. [*Kindly but skeptically*] That's the right spirit, Rob- ert. Ain't none of us doubts your willin'ness, but you ain't never learned——

Robert. Then I'm going to start learning right away, and you'll teach me, won't you?

Mayo. [*Mollifyingly*] Of course I will, boy, and be glad to, only you'd best go easy at first.

Scott. [*Who has listened to this conversation in mingled consternation and amazement*] You don't mean to tell me you're goin' to let him stay, do you, James?

Mayo. Why, things bein' as they be, Robert's free to do as he's a mind to.

Mrs. Mayo. *Let him!* The very idea!

Scott. [*More and more ruffled*] Then all I got to say is, you're a soft, weak-willed critter to be permittin' a boy— and women, too—to be layin' your course for you wher- ever they pleases.

Mayo. [*Slyly amused*] It's just the same with me as 'twas with you, Dick.   You can't order the tides on the seas to suit you, and I ain't pretendin' I can reg'late love for young folks.

Scott. [*Scornfully*] *Love!* They ain't old enough to know love when they sight it! Love! I'm ashamed of you, Robert, to go lettin' a little huggin' and kissin' in the dark spile your chances to make a man out o' yourself. It ain't common sense—no siree, it ain't—not by a hell of a sight! [*He pounds the table with his fists in exasperation.*]

Mrs. Mayo. [*Laughing provokingly at her brother*] A fine one you are to be talking about love, Dick—an old cranky bachelor like you. Goodness' sakes!

Scott. [*Exasperated by their joking*] I've never been a darn fool like most, if that's what you're steerin' at.

Mrs. Mayo. [*Tauntingly*] Sour grapes, aren't they, Dick? [*She laughs.* Robert *and his father chuckle.* Scott *sputters with annoyance.*] Good gracious, Dick, you do act silly, flying into a temper over nothing.

Scott. [*Indignantly*] Nothin'! You talk as if I wasn't concerned nohow in this here business. Seems to me I've got a right to have my say. Ain't I made all arrangements with the owners and stocked up with some special grub all on Robert's account?

Robert. You've been fine, Uncle Dick; and I appreciate it. Truly.

Mayo. 'Course; we all does, Dick.

Scott. [*Unplacated*] I've been countin' sure on havin' Robert for company on this vige—to sorta talk to and show things

to, and teach, kinda, and I got my mind so set on havin'
him I'm goin' to be double lonesome this vige. [*He
pounds on the table, attempting to cover up this confession of weakness.*] Darn all this silly lovin' business, anyway. [*Irritably*] But all this talk ain't tellin' me what
I'm to do with that sta'b'd cabin I fixed up. It's all painted
white, an' a bran-new mattress on the bunk, 'n' new sheets
'n' blankets 'n' things. And Chips built in a book-case so's
Robert could take his books along—with a slidin' bar fixed
across't it, mind, so's they couldn't fall out no matter how
she rolled. [*With excited consternation*] What d'you
suppose my officers is goin' to think when there's no one
comes aboard to occupy that sta'b'd cabin? And the men
what did the work on it—what'll *they* think? [*He shakes
his finger indignantly.*] They're liable as not to suspicion
it was a *woman* I'd planned to ship along, and that she
gave me the go-by at the last moment! [*He wipes his
perspiring brow in anguish at this thought.*] They're
only lookin' to have the laugh on me for something like
that. They're liable to b'lieve anything, those fellers is!

Mayo. [*With a wink*] Then there's nothing to it but for
you to get right out and hunt up a wife somewheres for
that spick 'n' span cabin. She'll have to be a pretty one,
too, to match it. [*He looks at his watch with exaggerated
concern.*] You ain't got much time to find her, Dick.

Sta'b'd—Starboard, the right side of a ship. The larboard, or port, is
the left side.
Chips—The ship's carpenter.

Scott. [*As the others smile—sulkily*] You kin go to thunder, Jim Mayo!

Andrew. [*Comes forward from where he has been standing by the door, rear, brooding. His face is set in a look of grim determination.*] You needn't worry about that spare cabin, Uncle Dick, if you've a mind to take me in Robert's place.

Robert. [*Turning to him quickly*] Andy! [*He sees at once the fixed resolve in his brother's eyes, and realizes immediately the reason for it—in consternation.*] Andy, you mustn't!

Andrew. You've made your decision, Rob, and now I've made mine. You're out of this, remember.

Robert. [*Hurt by his brother's tone*] But Andy——

Andrew. Don't interfere, Rob—that's all I ask. [*Turning to his uncle*] You haven't answered my question, Uncle Dick.

Scott. [*Clearing his throat, with an uneasy side glance at* JAMES MAYO *who is staring at his elder son as if he thought he had suddenly gone mad*] Of course, I'd be glad to have you, Andy.

Andrew. It's settled then. I can pack the little I want to take in a few minutes.

Mrs. Mayo. Don't be a fool, Dick. Andy's only joking you.

Scott. [*Disgruntedly*] It's hard to tell who's jokin' and who's not in this house.

Andrew. [*Firmly*] I'm not joking, Uncle Dick [*As* SCOTT

looks at him uncertainly] You needn't be afraid I'll go back on my word.

Robert. [*Hurt by the insinuation he feels in* ANDREW's *tone*] Andy! That isn't fair!

Mayo. [*Frowning*] Seems to me this ain't no subject to joke over—not for Andy.

Andrew. [*Facing his father*] I agree with you, Pa, and I tell you again, once and for all, that I've made up my mind to go.

Mayo. [*Dumbfounded—unable to doubt the determination in* ANDREW's *voice—helplessly*] But why, son? Why?

Andrew. [*Evasively*] I've always wanted to go.

Robert. Andy!

Andrew. [*Half angrily*] You shut up, Rob! [*Turning to his father again*] I didn't ever mention it because as long as Rob was going I knew it was no use; but now Rob's staying on here, there isn't any reason for me not to go.

Mayo. [*Breathing hard*] No reason? Can you stand there and say that to me, Andrew?

Mrs. Mayo. [*Hastily—seeing the gathering storm*] He doesn't mean a word of it, James.

Mayo. [*Making a gesture to her to keep silence*] Let me talk, Katey. [*In a more kindly tone*] What's come over you so sudden, Andy? You know's well as I do that it wouldn't be fair o' you to run off at a moment's notice right now when we're up to our necks in hard work.

Andrew. [*Avoiding his eyes*] Rob'll hold his end up as soon as he learns.

Mayo.   Robert was never cut out for a farmer, and you was.

Andrew.   You can easily get a man to do my work.

Mayo.   [*Restraining his anger with an effort*] It sounds strange to hear you, Andy, that I always thought had good sense, talkin' crazy like that. [*Scornfully*] Get a man to take your place! You ain't been workin' here for no hire, Andy, that you kin give me your notice to quit like you've done. The farm is your'n as well as mine. You've always worked on it with that understanding; and what you're sayin' you intend doin' is just skulkin' out o' your rightful responsibility.

Andrew.   [*Looking at the floor—simply*] I'm sorry, Pa. [*After a slight pause*] It's no use talking any more about it.

Mrs. Mayo.   [*In relief*] There! I knew Andy'd come to his senses!

Andrew.   Don't get the wrong idea, Ma. I'm not backing out.

Mayo.   You mean you're goin' in spite of—everythin'?

Andrew.   Yes. I'm going. I've got to. [*He looks at his father defiantly.*] I feel I oughtn't to miss this chance to go out into the world and see things, and—I want to go.

Mayo.   [*With bitter scorn*] So—you want to go out into the world and see thin's! [*His voice raised and quivering with anger*] I never thought I'd live to see the day when a son o' mine 'd look me in the face and tell a bare-faced lie! [*Bursting out*] You're a liar, Andy Mayo, and a mean one to boot!

Mrs. Mayo.   James!

Robert. Pa.

Scott. Steady there, Jim!

Mayo. [*Waving their protests aside*] He is and he knows it.

Andrew. [*His face flushed*] I won't argue with you, Pa. You can think as badly of me as you like.

Mayo. [*Shaking his finger at* Andy, *in a cold rage*] You know I'm speakin' truth—that's why you're afraid to argy! You lie when you say you want to go 'way—and see thin's! You ain't got no likin' in the world to go. I've watched you grow up, and I know your ways, and they're my ways. You're runnin' against your own nature, and you're goin' to be a'mighty sorry for it if you do. 'S if I didn't know your real reason for runnin' away. And runnin' away's the only words to fit it. You're runnin' away 'cause you're put out and riled 'cause your own brother's got Ruth 'stead o' you, and——

Andrew. [*His face crimson—tensely*] Stop, Pa! I won't stand hearing that—not even from you!

Mrs. Mayo. [*Rushing to* Andy *and putting her arms about him protectingly*] Don't mind him, Andy dear. He don't mean a word he's saying! [Robert *stands rigidly, his hands clenched, his face contracted by pain.* Scott *sits dumbfounded and open-mouthed.* Andrew *soothes his mother who is on the verge of tears.*]

Mayo. [*In angry triumph*] It's the truth, Andy Mayo! And you ought to be bowed in shame to think of it!

Robert. [*Protestingly*] Pa!

Mrs. Mayo. [*Coming from* Andrew *to his father; puts her

*hands on his shoulders as though to try and push him
back in the chair from which he has risen*] Won't you
be still, James? Please won't you?

Mayo. [*Looking at* Andrew *over his wife's shoulder—stub-
bornly*] The truth—God's truth!

Mrs. Mayo. Sh-h-h! [*She tries to put a finger across his lips,
but he twists his head away.*]

Andrew. [*Who has regained control over himself*] You're
wrong, Pa, it isn't truth. [*With defiant assertiveness*] I
don't love Ruth. I never loved her, and the thought of
such a thing never entered my head.

Mayo. [*With an angry snort of disbelief*] Humph! You're
pilin' lie on lie!

Andrew. [*Losing his temper—bitterly*] I suppose it'd be
hard for you to explain anyone's wanting to leave this
blessed farm except for some outside reason like that.
But I'm sick and tired of it—whether you want to believe
me or not—and that's why I'm glad to get a chance to
move on.

Robert. Andy! Don't! You're only making it worse.

Andrew. [*Sulkily*] I don't care. I've done my share of
work here. I've earned my right to quit when I want to.
[*Suddenly overcome with anger and grief; with rising intensity*] I'm sick and tired of the whole darn business.
I hate the farm and every inch of ground in it. I'm sick
of digging in the dirt and sweating in the sun like a slave
without getting a word of thanks for it. [*Tears of rage
starting to his eyes—hoarsely*] I'm through, through for

good and all; and if Uncle Dick won't take me on his ship, I'll find another. I'll get away somewhere, somehow.

Mrs. Mayo. [*In a frightened voice*] Don't you answer him, James. He doesn't know what he's saying. Don't say a word to him 'til he's in his right senses again. Please, James, don't——

Mayo. [*Pushes her away from him; his face is drawn and pale with the violence of his passion. He glares at* AN-DREW *as if he hated him.*] You dare to—you dare to speak like that to me? You talk like that 'bout this farm —the Mayo farm—where you was born—you—you—— [*He clenches his fist above his head and advances threateningly on* ANDREW.] You little whelp!

Mrs. Mayo. [*With a shriek*] James! [*She covers her face with her hands and sinks weakly into* MAYO'S *chair.* AN-DREW *remains standing motionless, his face pale and set.*]

Scott. [*Starting to his feet and stretching his arms across the table toward* MAYO] Easy there, Jim!

Robert. [*Throwing himself between father and brother*] Stop! Are you mad?

Mayo. [*Grabs* ROBERT'S *arm and pushes him aside—then stands for a moment gasping for breath before* ANDREW. *He points to the door with a shaking finger.*] Yes—go!— go!—You're no son o' mine—no son o' mine! You can go to hell if you want to! Don't let me find you here—in the mornin'—or—or—I'll *throw* you out!

Robert. Pa! For God's sake! [Mrs. Mayo *bursts into noisy sobbing.*]

Mayo. [*He gulps convulsively and glares at* Andrew.] You go—tomorrow mornin'—and don't come back—don't dare come back—not while I'm livin'—or I'll—I'll—— [*He shakes over his muttered threat and strides toward the door rear, right.*]

Mrs. Mayo. [*Rising and throwing her arms around him—hysterically*] James! James! Where are you going?

Mayo. [*Incoherently*] I'm goin'—to bed, Katey. It's late, Katey—it's late. [*He goes out.*]

Mrs. Mayo. [*Following him, pleading hysterically*] James! Take back what you've said to Andy. James! [*She follows him out.* Robert *and the* Captain *stare after them with horrified eyes.* Andrew *stands rigidly looking straight in front of him, his fists clenched at his sides.*]

Scott. [*The first to find his voice—with an explosive sigh*] Well, if he ain't the devil himself when he's roused! You oughtn't to have talked to him that way, Andy, 'bout the darn farm, knowin' how touchy he is about it. [*With another sigh*] Well, you won't mind what he's said in anger. He'll be sorry for it when he's calmed down a bit.

Andrew. [*In a dead voice*] You don't know him. [*Defiantly*] What's said is said and can't be unsaid; and I've chosen.

Robert. [*With violent protest*] Andy! You can't go! This is all so stupid—and terrible!

Andrew. [*Coldly*] I'll talk to you in a minute, Rob.

[*Crushed by his brother's attitude,* Robert *sinks down into a chair, holding his head in his hands.*]

Scott. [*Comes and slaps* Andrew *on the back*] .I'm darned glad you're shippin' on, Andy. I like your spirit, and the way you spoke up to him. [*Lowering his voice to a cautious whisper*] The sea's the place for a young feller like you that isn't half dead 'n' alive. [*He gives* Andy *a final approving slap.*] You 'n' me 'll get along like twins, see if we don't. I'm goin' aloft to turn in. Don't forget to pack your dunnage. And git some sleep, if you kin. We'll want to sneak out extra early b'fore they're up. It'll do away with more argyments. Robert can drive us down to the town, and bring back the team. [*He goes to the door in the rear, left.*] Well, good night.

Andrew. Good night. [Scott *goes out. The two brothers remain silent for a moment. Then* Andrew *comes over to his brother and puts a hand on his back. He speaks in a low voice, full of feeling.*] Buck up, Rob. It ain't any use crying over spilt milk; and it'll all turn out for the best—let's hope. It couldn't be helped—what's happened.

Robert. [*Wildly*] But it's a lie, Andy, a lie!

Andrew. Of course it's a lie. You know it and I know it,—but that's all ought to know it.

Robert. Pa'll never forgive you. Oh, the whole affair is so senseless—and tragic. Why did you think you must go away?

Andrew. You know better than to ask that. You know why. [*Fiercely*] I can wish you and Ruth all the good luck in the world, and I do, and I mean it; but you can't expect me to stay around here and watch you two together, day after day—and me alone. I couldn't stand it—not after all the plans I'd made to happen on this place thinking—— [*His voice breaks*] thinking she cared for me.

Robert. [*Putting a hand on his brother's arm*] It's horrible! I feel so guilty—to think that I should be the cause of your suffering, after we've been such pals all our lives. If I could have foreseen what'd happen, I swear to you I'd have never said a word to Ruth. I swear I wouldn't have, Andy!

Andrew. I know you wouldn't; and that would've been worse, for Ruth would've suffered then. [*He pats his brother's shoulder.*] It's best as it is. It had to be, and I've got to stand the gaff, that's all. Pa'll see how I felt— after a time [*As* ROBERT *shakes his head*]—and if he don't—well, it can't be helped.

Robert. But think of Ma! Andy, you can't go! You can't!

Andrew. [*Fiercely*] I've got to go—to get away! I've got to, I tell you. I'd go crazy here, bein' reminded every second of the day what a fool I'd made of myself. I've got to get away and try and forget, if I can. And I'd hate the farm if I stayed, hate it for bringin' things back. I couldn't take interest in the work any more, work with no purpose in sight. Can't you see what a hell it'd be? You love her too, Rob. Put yourself in my place, and remember I haven't stopped loving her, and couldn't if I was to stay. Would that be fair to you or to her? Put yourself in my place. [*He shakes his brother fiercely by the shoulder.*] What'd you do then? Tell me the truth! You love her. What'd you do?

Robert. [*Chokingly*] I'd—I'd go, Andy! [*He buries his face in his hands with a shuddering sob.*]

Andrew. [*Seeming to relax suddenly all over his body—in a low, steady voice*] Then you know why I got to go; and there's nothing more to be said.

Robert. [*In a frenzy of rebellion*] Why did this have to happen to us? It's damnable! [*He looks about him wildly, as if his vengeance were seeking the responsible fate.*]

Andrew. [*Soothingly—again putting his hands on his brother's shoulder*] It's no use fussing any more, Rob. It's done. [*Forcing a smile*] I guess Ruth's got a right to have who she likes. She made a good choice—and God bless her for it!

Robert. Andy! Oh, I wish I could tell you half I feel of how fine you are!

Andrew. [*Interrupting him quickly*] Shut up! Let's go to bed. I've got to be up long before sun-up. You, too, if you're going to drive us down.

Robert. Yes. Yes.

Andrew. [*Turning down the lamp*] And I've got to pack yet. [*He yawns with utter weariness.*] I'm as tired as if I'd been plowing twenty-four hours at a stretch. [*Dully*] I feel—dead. [Robert *covers his face again with his hands.* Andrew *shakes his head as if to get rid of his thoughts,*

and continues with a poor attempt at cheery briskness.]
I'm going to douse the light. Come on. [*He slaps his
brother on the back.* ROBERT *does not move.* ANDREW
*bends over and blows out the lamp. His voice comes from
the darkness.*] Don't sit there mourning, Rob. It'll all
come out in the wash. Come on and get some sleep.
Everything'll turn out all right in the end. [ROBERT *can
be heard stumbling to his feet, and the dark figures of the
two brothers can be seen groping their way toward the
doorway in the rear as*

[*The Curtain Falls*]

ACT TWO

Scene I

Same as Act One, Scene Two. Sitting room of the farm-house about half past twelve in the afternoon of a hot, sun-baked day in mid-summer, three years later. All the windows are open, but no breeze stirs the soiled white curtains. A patched screen door is in the rear. Through it the yard can be seen, its small stretch of lawn divided by the dirt path leading to the door from the gate in the white picket fence which borders the road.

The room has changed, not so much in its outward appearance as in its general atmosphere. Little significant details give evidence of carelessness, of inefficiency, of an industry gone to seed. The chairs appear shabby from lack of paint; the table cover is spotted and askew; holes show in the curtains; a child's doll, with one arm gone, lies under the table; a hoe stands in a corner; a man's coat is flung on the couch in the rear; the desk is cluttered up with odds and ends; a number of books are piled carelessly on the sideboard. The noon enervation of the sultry, scorching day seems to have penetrated indoors, causing even inanimate objects to wear an aspect of despondent exhaustion.

A place is set at the end of the table, left, for someone's dinner. Through the open door to the kitchen comes the clatter of dishes being washed, interrupted at intervals by a woman's irritated voice and the peevish whining of a child.

At the rise of the curtain Mrs. Mayo *and* Mrs. Atkins *are discovered sitting facing each other,* Mrs. Mayo *to the rear,* Mrs. Atkins *to the right of the table.* Mrs. Mayo's *face has lost all character, disintegrated, become a weak mask wearing a helpless, doleful expression of being constantly on the verge of comfortless tears. She speaks in an uncertain voice, without assertiveness, as if all power of willing had deserted her.* Mrs. Atkins *is in her wheel chair. She is a thin, pale-faced, unintelligent looking woman of about forty-eight, with hard, bright eyes. A victim of partial paralysis for many years, condemned to be pushed from day to day of her life in a wheel chair, she has developed the selfish, irritable nature of the chronic invalid. Both women are dressed in black.* Mrs. Atkins *knits nervously as she talks. A ball of unused yarn, with needles stuck through it, lies on the table before* Mrs. Mayo.

Mrs. Atkins. [*With a disapproving glance at the place set on the table*] Robert's late for his dinner again, as usual. I don't see why Ruth puts up with it, and I've told her so. Many's the time I've said to her, "It's about time you put a stop to his nonsense. Does he suppose you're runnin' a hotel—with no one to help with things?" But she don't pay no attention. She's as bad as he is, a'most—thinks she knows better than an old, sick body like me.

Mrs. Mayo. [*Dully*] Robbie's always late for things. He can't help it, Sarah.

Mrs. Atkins. [*With a snort*] Can't help it! How you do go on, Kate, findin' excuses for him! Anybody can help anything they've a mind to—as long as they've got health, and ain't rendered helpless like me—[*She adds a pious afterthought.*]—through the will of God.

Mrs. Mayo. Robbie can't.

Mrs. Atkins. Can't! It do make me mad, Kate Mayo, to see folks that God gave all the use of their limbs to potterin' round and wastin' time doin' everything the wrong way— and me powerless to help and at their mercy, you might say. And it ain't that I haven't pointed the right way to 'em. I've talked to Robert thousands of times and told him how things ought to be done. You know that, Kate Mayo. But d'you s'pose he takes any notice of what I say? Or Ruth, either—my own daughter? No, they think I'm a crazy, cranky old woman, half dead a'ready, and the sooner I'm in the grave and out o' their way the better it'd suit them.

Mrs. Mayo. You mustn't talk that way, Sarah. They're not as wicked as that. And you've got years and years before you.

Mrs. Atkins. You're like the rest, Kate. You don't know how near the end I am. Well, at least I can go to my eternal rest with a clear conscience. I've done all a body could do to avert ruin from this house. On their heads be it!

Mrs. Mayo. [*With hopeless indifference*] Things might be

worse.   Robert never had any experience in farming.
You can't expect him to learn in a day.

Mrs. Atkins. [*Snappily*] He's had three years to learn, and
he's gettin' worse 'stead of better.   Not on'y your place
but mine too is driftin' to rack and ruin, and I can't do
nothin' to prevent.

Mrs. Mayo. [*With a spark of assertiveness*] You can't say
but Robbie works hard, Sarah.

Mrs. Atkins. What good's workin' hard if it don't accom-
plish anythin', I'd like to know?

Mrs. Mayo. Robbie's had bad luck against him.

Mrs. Atkins. Say what you've a mind to, Kate, the proof of
the puddin's in the eatin'; and you can't deny that
things have been goin' from bad to worse ever since your
husband died two years back.

Mrs. Mayo. [*Wiping tears from her eyes with her handkerchief*] It was God's will that he should be taken.

Mrs. Atkins. [*Triumphantly*] It was God's punishment on
James Mayo for the blasphemin' and denyin' of God he
done all his sinful life! [MRS. MAYO *begins to weep
softly.*] There, Kate, I shouldn't be remindin' you, I
know.   He's at peace, poor man, and forgiven, let's
pray.

Mrs. Mayo. [*Wiping her eyes—simply*] James was a good
man.

Mrs. Atkins. [*Ignoring this remark*] What I was sayin' was
that since Robert's been in charge, things've been goin'

Blasphemin'—Cursing or speaking disrespectfully of sacred things.

down hill steady. You don't know *how* bad they are. Robert don't let on to you what's happenin'; and you'd never see it yourself if 'twas under your nose. But, thank the lord, Ruth still comes to me once in a while for advice when she's worried near out of her senses by his goin's-on. Do you know what she told me last night? But I forgot, she said not to tell you—still I think you've got a right to know, and it's my duty not to let such things go on behind your back.

Mrs. Mayo. [*Wearily*] You can tell me if you want to.

Mrs. Atkins. [*Bending over toward her—in a low voice*] Ruth was almost crazy about it. Robert told her he'd have to mortgage the farm—said he didn't know how he'd pull through 'til harvest without it, and he can't get money any other way. [*She straightens up—indignantly.*] Now what do you think of your Robert?

Mrs. Mayo. [*Resignedly*] If it has to be——

Mrs. Atkins. You don't mean to say you're goin' to sign away your farm, Kate Mayo—after me warnin' you?

Mrs. Mayo. I'll do what Robbie says is needful.

Mrs. Atkins. [*Holding up her hands*] Well, of all the foolishness!—well, it's your farm, not mine, and I've nothin' more to say.

Mrs. Mayo. Maybe Robbie'll manage 'til Andy gets back and sees to things. It can't be long now.

Mrs. Atkins. [*With keen interest*] Ruth says Andy ought to turn up any day. When does Robert figger he'll get here?

Mrs. Mayo. He says he can't calculate exactly on account o' the *Sunda* being a sailboat. Last letter he got was from England, the day they were sailing for home. That was over a month ago, and Robbie thinks they're overdue now.

Mrs. Atkins. We can give praise to God then that he'll be back in the nick o' time. He ought to be tired of travelin' and anxious to get home and settle down to work again.

Mrs. Mayo. Andy *has* been working. He's head officer on Dick's boat, he wrote Robbie. You know that.

Mrs. Atkins. That foolin' on ships is all right for a spell, but he must be right sick of it by this.

Mrs. Mayo. [*Musingly*] I wonder if he's changed much. He used to be so fine-looking and strong. [*With a sigh*] Three years! It seems more like three hundred. [*Her eyes filling—piteously*] Oh, if James could only have lived 'til he came back—and forgiven him!

Mrs. Atkins. He never would have—not James Mayo! Didn't he keep his heart hardened against him till the last in spite of all you and Robert did to soften him?

Mrs. Mayo. [*With a feeble flash of anger*] Don't you dare say that! [*Brokenly*] Oh, I know deep down in his heart he forgave Andy, though he was too stubborn ever to own up to it. It was that brought on his death— breaking his heart just on account of his stubborn pride. [*She wipes her eyes with her handkerchief and sobs.*]

Mrs. Atkins. [*Piously*] It was the will of God. [*The whin-*

ing crying of the child sounds from the kitchen. MRS.
ATKINS *frowns irritably.*] Drat that young one! Seems
as if she cries all the time on purpose to set a body's
nerves on edge.

Mrs. Mayo. [*Wiping her eyes*] It's the heat upsets her. Mary
doesn't feel any too well these days, poor little child!

Mrs. Atkins. She gets it right from her Pa—bein' sickly all
the time. You can't deny Robert was always ailin' as a
child. [*She sighs heavily.*] It was a crazy mistake for
them two to get married. I argyed against it at the time,
but Ruth was so spelled with Robert's wild poetry notions she wouldn't listen to sense. Andy was the one
would have been the match for her.

Mrs. Mayo. I've often thought since it might have been
better the other way. But Ruth and Robbie seem happy
enough together.

Mrs. Atkins. At any rate it was God's work—and His will
be done. [*The two women sit in silence for a moment.*
RUTH *enters from the kitchen, carrying in her arms her
two-year-old daughter,* MARY, *a pretty but sickly and
anemic looking child with a tear-stained face.* RUTH *has
aged appreciably. Her face has lost its youth and fresh-
ness. There is a trace in her expression of something
hard and spiteful. She sits in a rocker in front of the
table and sighs wearily. She wears a gingham dress with a
soiled apron tied around her waist.*]

Ruth. Land sakes, if this isn't a scorcher! That kitchen's like a furnace. Phew! [*She pushes the damp hair back from her forehead.*]

Mrs. Mayo. Why didn't you call me to help with the dishes?

Ruth. [*Shortly*] No. The heat in there'd kill you.

Mary. [*Sees the doll under the table and struggles on her mother's lap*] Dolly, Mama! Dolly!

Ruth. [*Pulling her back*] It's time for your nap. You can't play with Dolly now.

Mary. [*Commencing to cry whiningly*] Dolly!

Mrs. Atkins. [*Irritably*] Can't you keep that child still? Her racket's enough to split a body's ears. Put her down and let her play with the doll if it'll quiet her.

Ruth. [*Lifting* Mary *to the floor*] There! I hope you'll be satisfied and keep still. [Mary *sits down on the floor before the table and plays with the doll in silence.* Ruth *glances at the place set on the table.*] It's a wonder Rob wouldn't try to get to meals on time once in a while.

Mrs. Mayo. [*Dully*] Something must have gone wrong again.

Ruth. [*Wearily*] I s'pose so. Something's always going wrong these days, it looks like.

Mrs. Atkins. [*Snappily*] It wouldn't if you possessed a bit of spunk. The idea of you permittin' him to come in to meals at all hours—and you doin' the work! I never heard of such a thin'. You're too easy goin', that's the trouble.

Ruth. Do stop your nagging at me, Ma! I'm sick of hearing you. I'll do as I please about it; and thank you for not

interfering. [*She wipes her moist forehead—wearily.*]
Phew! It's too hot to argue. Let's talk of something
pleasant. [*Curiously*] Didn't I hear you speaking about
Andy a while ago?

Mrs. Mayo. We were wondering when he'd get home.

Ruth. [*Brightening*] Rob says any day now he's liable to
drop in and surprise us—him and the Captain. It'll cer-
tainly look natural to see him around the farm again.

Mrs. Atkins. Let's hope the farm'll look more natural, too,
when he's had a hand at it. The way thin's are now!

Ruth. [*Irritably*] Will you stop harping on that, Ma? We
all know things aren't as they might be. What's the
good of your complaining all the time?

Mrs. Atkins. There, Kate Mayo! Ain't that just what I
told you? I can't say a word of advice to my own
daughter even, she's that stubborn and self-willed.

Ruth. [*Putting her hands over her ears—in exasperation*]
For goodness' sakes, Ma!

Mrs. Mayo. [*Dully*] Never mind. Andy'll fix everything
when he comes.

Ruth. [*Hopefully*] Oh, yes, I know he will. He always did
know just the right thing ought to be done. [*With
weary vexation*] It's a shame for him to come home and
have to start in with things in such a topsy-turvy.

Mrs. Mayo. Andy'll manage.

Ruth. [*Sighing*] I s'pose it isn't Rob's fault things go
wrong with him.

Mrs. Atkins. [*Scornfully*] Humph! [*She fans herself nerv-*

ously.]   Land o' Goshen, but it's bakin' in here! Let's
go out in under the trees in back where there's a breath
of fresh air. Come, Kate. [Mrs. Mayo *gets up obediently
and starts to wheel the invalid's chair toward the screen
door.*] You better come too, Ruth. It'll do you good.
Learn him a lesson and let him get his own dinner.
Don't be such a fool.

Ruth. [*Going and holding the screen door open for them—
listlessly*] He wouldn't mind. He doesn't eat much.
But I can't go anyway. I've got to put baby to bed.

Mrs. Atkins. Let's go, Kate. I'm boilin' in here. [Mrs.
Mayo *wheels her out and off left.* Ruth *comes back and
sits down in her chair.*]

Ruth. [*Mechanically*] Come and let me take off your shoes
and stockings, Mary, that's a good girl. You've got to
take your nap now. [*The child continues to play as if
she hadn't heard, absorbed in her doll. An eager expression comes over* Ruth's *tired face. She glances toward the
door furtively—then gets up and goes to the desk. Her
movements indicate a guilty fear of discovery. She takes
a letter from a pigeonhole and retreats swiftly to her
chair with it. She opens the envelope and reads the
letter with great interest, a flush of excitement coming
to her cheeks.* Robert *walks up the path and opens the
screen door quietly and comes into the room. He, too,
has aged. His shoulders are stooped as if under too
great a burden. His eyes are dull and lifeless, his face
burned by the sun and unshaven for days. Streaks of*

sweat have smudged the layer of dust on his cheeks. His lips drawn down at the corners, give him a hopeless, resigned expression. The three years have accentuated the weakness of his mouth and chin. He is dressed in overalls, laced boots, and a flannel shirt open at the neck.]

Robert. [*Throwing his hat over on the sofa—with a great sigh of exhaustion*] Phew! The sun's hot today! [RUTH *is startled. At first she makes an instinctive motion as if to hide the letter in her bosom. She immediately thinks better of this and sits with the letter in her hands looking at him with defiant eyes. He bends down and kisses her.*]

Ruth. [*Feeling of her cheek—irritably*] Why don't you shave? You look awful.

Robert. [*Indifferently*] I forgot—and it's too much trouble this weather.

Mary. [*Throwing aside her doll, runs to him with a happy cry*] Dada! Dada!

Robert. [*Swinging her up above his head—lovingly*] And how's this little girl of mine this hot day, eh?

Mary. [*Screeching happily*] Dada! Dada!

Ruth. [*In annoyance*] Don't do that to her! You know it's time for her nap and you'll get her all waked up; then I'll be the one that'll have to sit beside her till she falls asleep.

Robert. [*Sitting down in the chair on the left of table and cuddling* MARY *on his lap*] You needn't bother. I'll put her to bed.

Ruth. [*Shortly*] You've got to get back to your work, I s'pose.

Robert. [*With a sigh*] Yes, I was forgetting. [*He glances at the open letter on* RUTH's *lap.*] Reading Andy's letter again? I should think you'd know it by heart by this time.

Ruth. [*Coloring as if she'd been accused of something— defiantly*] I've got a right to read it, haven't I? He says it's meant for all of us.

Robert. [*With a trace of irritation*] Right? Don't be so silly. There's no question of right. I was only saying that you must know all that's in it after so many readings.

Ruth. Well, I don't. [*She puts the letter on the table and gets wearily to her feet.*] I s'pose you'll be wanting your dinner now.

Robert. [*Listlessly*] I don't care. I'm not hungry.

Ruth. And here I been keeping it hot for you!

Robert. [*Irritably*] Oh, all right then. Bring it in and I'll try to eat.

Ruth. I've got to get her to bed first. [*She goes to lift* MARY *off his lap.*] Come, dear. It's after time and you can hardly keep your eyes open now.

Mary. [*Crying*] No, no! [*Appealing to her father*] Dada! No!

Ruth. [*Accusingly to* ROBERT] There! Now see what you've done! I told you not to——

Robert. [*Shortly*] Let her alone, then. She's all right where she is. She'll fall asleep on my lap in a minute if you'll stop bothering her.

Ruth. [*Hotly*] She'll not do any such thing! She's got to learn to mind me! [*Shaking her finger at* MARY] You naughty child! Will you come with Mama when she tells you for your own good?

Mary. [*Clinging to her father*] No, Dada!

Ruth. [*Losing her temper*] A good spanking's what you need, my young lady—and you'll get one from me if you don't mind better, d'you hear? [MARY *starts to whimper frightenedly.*]

Robert. [*With sudden anger*] Leave her alone! How often have I told you not to threaten her with whipping? I won't have it. [*Soothing the wailing* MARY] There! There, little girl! Baby mustn't cry. Dada won't like you if you do. Dada'll hold you and you must promise to go to sleep like a good little girl. Will you when Dada asks you?

Mary. [*Cuddling up to him*] Yes, Dada.

Ruth. [*Looking at them, her pale face set and drawn*] A fine one you are to be telling folks how to do things! [*She bites her lips. Husband and wife look into each other's eyes with something akin to hatred in their expressions; then* RUTH *turns away with a shrug of affected indifference.*] All right, take care of her then, if you think it's so easy. [*She walks away into the kitchen.*]

Robert. [*Smoothing* MARY'S *hair—tenderly*] We'll show Mama you're a good little girl, won't we?

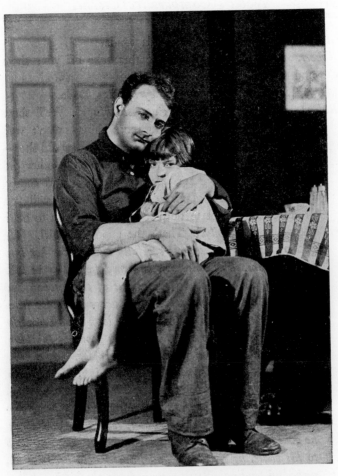

"You must promise to go to sleep like a good little girl."
Robert Keith in the role of Robert

Mary. [*Crooning drowsily*] Dada, Dada.

Robert. Let's see: Does your mother take off your shoes
and stockings before your nap?

Mary. [*Nodding with half-shut eyes*] Yes, Dada.

Robert. [*Taking off her shoes and stockings*] We'll show
Mama we know how to do those things, won't we?
There's one old shoe off—and there's the other old shoe—
and here's one old stocking—and there's the other old
stocking. There we are, all nice and cool and comfy.
[*He bends down and kisses her.*] And now will you
promise to go right to sleep if Dada takes you to bed?
[MARY *nods sleepily.*] That's the good little girl. [*He
gathers her up in his arms carefully and carries her into
the bedroom. His voice can be heard faintly as he lulls
the child to sleep. RUTH comes out of the kitchen and
gets the plate from the table. She hears the voice from
the room and tiptoes to the door to look in. Then she
starts for the kitchen but stands for a moment thinking,
a look of ill-concealed jealousy on her face. At a noise
from inside she hurriedly disappears into the kitchen.
A moment later* ROBERT *re-enters. He comes forward
and picks up the shoes and stockings which he shoves
carelessly under the table. Then, seeing no one about,
he goes to the sideboard and selects a book. Coming back
to his chair, he sits down and immediately becomes absorbed in reading. RUTH returns from the kitchen bringing his plate heaped with food, and a cup of tea. She
sets those before him and sits down in her former place.*

ROBERT *continues to read, oblivious to the food on the table.*]

Ruth. [*After watching him irritably for a moment*] For heaven's sakes, put down that old book! Don't you see your dinner's getting cold?

Robert. [*Closing his book*] Excuse me, Ruth. I didn't notice. [*He picks up his knife and fork and begins to eat gingerly, without appetite.*]

Ruth. I should think you might have some feeling for me, Rob, and not always be late for meals. If you think it's fun sweltering in that oven of a kitchen to keep things warm for you, you're mistaken.

Robert. I'm sorry, Ruth, really I am. Something crops up every day to delay me. I mean to be here on time.

Ruth. [*With a sigh*] Mean-tos don't count.

Robert. [*With a conciliating smile*] Then punish me, Ruth. Let the food get cold and don't bother about me.

Ruth. I'd have to wait just the same to wash up after you.

Robert. But I can wash up.

Ruth. A nice mess there'd be then!

Robert. [*With an attempt at lightness*] The food is lucky to be able to get cold this weather. [*As* RUTH *doesn't answer or smile, he opens his book and resumes his reading, forcing himself to take a mouthful of food every now and then.* RUTH *stares at him in annoyance.*]

Ruth. And besides, you've got your own work that's got to be done.

Robert. [*Absent-mindedly, without taking his eyes from the book*] Yes, of course.

Ruth. [*Spitefully*] Work you'll never get done by reading books all the time.

Robert. [*Shutting the book with a snap*] Why do you persist in nagging at me for getting pleasure out of reading? It is because—— [*He checks himself abruptly.*]

Ruth. [*Coloring*] Because I'm too stupid to understand them, I s'pose you were going to say.

Robert. [*Shamefacedly*] No—no. [*In exasperation*] Why do you goad me into saying things I don't mean? Haven't I got my share of troubles trying to work this cursed farm without your adding to them? You know how hard I've tried to keep things going in spite of bad luck——

Ruth. [*Scornfully*] Bad luck!

Robert. And my own very apparent unfitness for the job, I was going to add; but you can't deny there's been bad luck to it, too. Why don't you take things into consideration? Why can't we pull together? We used to. I know it's hard on you also. Then why can't we help each other instead of hindering?

Ruth. [*Sullenly*] I do the best I know how.

Robert. [*Gets up and puts his hand on her shoulder*] I know you do. But let's both of us try to do better. We can both improve. Say a word of encouragement once in a while when things go wrong, even if it is my fault.

Goad—Drive, nag.

You know the odds I've been up against since Pa died.
I'm not a farmer. I've never claimed to be one. But
there's nothing else I can do under the circumstances,
and I've got to pull things through somehow. With your
help, I can do it. With you against me—— [*He shrugs
his shoulders. There is a pause. Then he bends down
and kisses her hair—with an attempt at cheerfulness.*] So
you promise that; and I'll promise to be here when the
clock strikes—and anything else you tell me to. Is it
a bargain?

Ruth. [*Dully*] I s'pose so. [*They are interrupted by the
sound of a loud knock at the kitchen door.*] There's
someone at the kitchen door. [*She hurries out. A moment later she reappears.*] It's Ben.

Robert. [*Frowning*] What's the trouble now, I wonder?
[*In a loud voice*] Come on in here, Ben. [BEN *slouches
in from the kitchen. He is a hulking, awkward young
fellow with a heavy, stupid face and shifty, cunning
eyes. He is dressed in overalls, boots, etc., and wears
a broad-brimmed hat of coarse straw pushed back on his
head.*] Well, Ben, what's the matter?

Ben. [*Drawlingly*] The mowin' machine's bust.

Robert. Why, that can't be. The man fixed it only last
week.

Ben. It's bust just the same.

Robert. And can't you fix it?

Ben. No. Don't know what's the matter with the goll-
darned thing. 'Twon't work, anyhow.

Robert. [*Getting up and going for his hat*] Wait a minute and I'll go look it over. There can't be much the matter with it.

Ben. [*Impudently*] Don't make no diff'rence t' me whether there be or not. I'm quittin'.

Robert. [*Anxiously*] You don't mean you're throwing up your job here?

Ben. That's what! My month's up today and I want what's owin' t' me.

Robert. But why are you quitting now, Ben, when you know I've so much work on hand? I'll have a hard time getting another man at such short notice.

Ben. That's for you to figger. I'm quittin'.

Robert. But what's your reason? You haven't any complaint to make about the way you've been treated, have you?

Ben. No. 'Tain't that. [*Shaking his finger*] Look-a-here. I'm sick o' being made fun at, that's what; an' I got a job up to Timms' place; an' I'm quittin' here.

Robert. Being made fun of? I don't understand you. Who's making fun of you?

Ben. They all do. When I drive down with the milk in the mornin', they all laughs and jokes at me—that boy up to Harris' and the new feller up to Slocum's, and Bill Evans down to Meade's, and all the rest on 'em.

Robert. That's a queer reason for leaving me flat. Won't they laugh at you just the same when you're working for Timms?

Ben. They wouldn't dare to. Timms is the best farm hereabouts. They was laughin' at me for workin' for *you*, that's what! "How're things up to the Mayo place?" they hollers every mornin'. "What's Robert doin' now— pasturin' the cattle in the cornlot? Is he seasonin' his hay with rain this year, same as last?" they shouts. "Or is he inventin' some 'lectrical milkin' engine to fool them dry cows o' his into givin' hard cider?" [*Very much ruffled*] That's like they talks; and I ain't goin' to put up with it no longer. Everyone's always knowed me as a first-class hand hereabouts, and I ain't wantin' 'em to get no different notion. So I'm quittin' you. And I wants what's comin' to me.

Robert. [*Coldly*] Oh, if that's the case, you can go to the devil. You'll get your money tomorrow when I get back from town—not before!

Ben. [*Turning to doorway to kitchen*] That suits me. [*As he goes out he speaks back over his shoulder.*] And see that I do get it, or there'll be trouble. [*He disappears and the slamming of the kitchen door is heard.*]

Robert. [*As* Ruth *comes from where she has been standing by the doorway and sits down dejectedly in her old place*] The stupid darn fool! And now what about the haying? That's an example of what I'm up against. No one can say I'm responsible for that.

Ruth. He wouldn't dare act that way with anyone else! [*Spitefully, with a glance at* Andrew's *letter on the table.*] It's lucky Andy's coming back.

Robert. [*Without resentment*] Yes, Andy'll see the right thing to do in a jiffy. [*With an affectionate smile*] I wonder if the old chump's changed much? He doesn't seem to from his letters, does he? [*Shaking his head*] But just the same I doubt if he'll want to settle down to a hum-drum farm life, after all he's been through.

Ruth. [*Resentfully*] Andy's not like you. He likes the farm.

Robert. [*Immersed in his own thoughts—enthusiastically*] Gad, the things he's seen and experienced! Think of the places he's been! All the wonderful far places I used to dream about! How I envy him! What a trip! [*He springs to his feet and instinctively goes to the window and stares out at the horizon.*]

Ruth. [*Bitterly*] I s'pose you're sorry now you didn't go?

Robert. [*Too occupied with his own thoughts to hear her— vindictively*] Oh, those cursed hills out there that I used to think promised me so much! How I've grown to hate the sight of them! They're like the walls of a narrow prison yard shutting me in from the freedom and wonder of life! [*He turns back to the room with a gesture of loathing.*] Sometimes I think if it wasn't for you, Ruth, and—[*His voice softening*]—little Mary, I'd chuck everything and walk down the road with just one desire in my heart—to put the whole rim of the world between me and those hills, and be able to breathe freely once more! [*He sinks down into his chair and smiles with bitter self-scorn.*] There I go dreaming again—my old fool dreams.

Ruth. [*In a low, repressed voice—her eyes smoldering*] You're not the only one!

Robert. [*Buried in his own thoughts—bitterly*] And Andy, who's had the chance—what has he got out of it? His letters read like the diary of a—of a farmer! "We're in Singapore now. It's a dirty hole of a place, and hotter than hell. Two of the crew are down with fever and we're short-handed on the work. I'll be darn glad when we sail again, although tacking back and forth in these blistering seas is a rotten job too!" [*Scornfully*] That's about the way he summed up his impressions of the East.

Ruth. [*Her repressed voice trembling*] You needn't make fun of Andy.

Robert. When I think—but what's the use? You know I wasn't making fun of Andy personally, but his attitude toward things is——

Ruth. [*Her eyes flashing—bursting into uncontrollable rage*] You was too making fun of him! And I ain't going to stand for it! You ought to be ashamed of yourself! [Robert *stares at her in amazement. She continues furiously.*] A fine one to talk about anyone else—after the way you've ruined everything with your lazy loafing! —and the stupid way you do things!

Robert. [*Angrily*] Stop that kind of talk, do you hear?

Ruth. You findin' fault—with your own brother who's ten

times the man you ever was or ever will be! You're jealous, that's what! Jealous because he's made a man of himself, while you're nothing but a—but a—— [*She stutters incoherently, overcome by rage.*]

Robert. Ruth! Ruth! You'll be sorry for talking like that.

Ruth. I won't! I won't never be sorry! I'm only saying what I've been thinking for years.

Robert. [*Aghast*] Ruth! You can't mean that!

Ruth. What do you think—living with a man like you— having to suffer all the time because you've never been man enough to work and do things like other people. But no! You never own up to that. You think you're so much better than other folks, with your college education, where you never learned a thing, and always reading your stupid books instead of working. I s'pose you think I ought to be *proud* to be your wife—a poor, ignorant thing like me! [*Fiercely*] But I'm not. I hate it. I hate the sight of you. Oh, if I'd only known! If I hadn't been such a fool to listen to your cheap, silly, poetry talk that you learned out of books! If I could have seen how you were in your true self—like you are now—I'd have killed myself before I'd have married you! I was sorry for it before we'd been together a month. I knew what you were really like—when it was too late.

Robert. [*His voice raised loudly*] And now—I'm finding out what you're really like—what a—a creature I've been living with. [*With a harsh laugh*] It wasn't that I haven't guessed how mean and small you are—but I've

kept on telling myself that I must be wrong—like a fool!
—like a darned fool!

Ruth. You were saying you'd go out on the road if it wasn't
for me. Well, you can go, and the sooner the better!
I don't care! I'll be glad to get rid of you! The farm'll
be better off too. There's been a curse on it ever since you
took hold. So go! Go and be a tramp like you've
always wanted. It's all you're good for. I can get along
without you, don't you worry. [*Exulting fiercely*] Andy's
coming back, don't forget that! He'll attend to things
like they should be. He'll show what a man can do!
I don't need you. Andy's coming!

Robert. [*They are both standing.* Robert *grabs her by the
shoulders and glares into her eyes.*] What do you mean?
[*He shakes her violently.*] What are you thinking of?
What's in your evil mind, you—you—— [*His voice is a
harsh shout.*]

Ruth. [*In a defiant scream*] Yes, I do mean it! I'd say it
if you was to kill me! I do love Andy. I do! I do! I
always loved him. [*Exultantly*] And he loves me! He
loves me! I know he does. He always did! And you
know he did, too! So go! Go if you want to!

Robert. [*Throwing her away from him. She staggers back
against the table—thickly.*] You—you slut! [*He stands
glaring at her as she leans back, supporting herself by the
table, gasping for breath. A loud frightened whimper
sounds from the awakened child in the bedroom. It
continues. The man and woman stand looking at one*

another in horror, the extent of their terrible quarrel suddenly brought home to them. A pause. The noise of a horse and carriage comes from the road before the house. The two, suddenly struck by the same premonition, listen to it breathlessly, as to a sound heard in a dream. It stops. They hear ANDY'S *voice from the road shouting a long hail—"Ahoy there!"*]

Ruth. [*With a strangled cry of joy*] Andy! Andy! [*She rushes and grabs the knob of the screen door, about to fling it open.*]

Robert. [*In a voice of command that forces obedience*] Stop! [*He goes to the door and gently pushes the trembling* RUTH *away from it. The child's crying rises to a louder pitch.*] I'll meet Andy. You better go in to Mary, Ruth. [*She looks at him defiantly for a moment, but there is something in his eyes that makes her turn and walk slowly into the bedroom.*]

Andy's voice. [*In a louder shout*] Ahoy there, Rob!

Robert. [*In an answering shout of forced cheeriness*] Hello, Andy! [*He opens the door and walks out as*

[*The Curtain Falls*]

SCENE II

The top of a hill on the farm. It is about eleven o'clock the next morning. The day is hot and cloudless. In the distance the sea can be seen.

The top of the hill slopes downward slightly toward the left. A big boulder stands in the center toward the rear. Further right, a large oak tree. The faint trace of a path leading upward to it from the left foreground can be detected through the bleached, sun-scorched grass.

Robert *is discovered sitting on the boulder, his chin resting on his hands, staring out toward the horizon seaward. His face is pale and haggard, his expression one of utter despondency.* Mary *is sitting on the grass near him in the shade, playing with her doll, singing happily to herself. Presently she casts a curious glance at her father, and, propping her doll up against the tree, comes over and clambers to his side.*

Mary. [*Pulling at his hand—solicitously*] Dada sick?

Robert. [*Looking at her with a forced smile*] No, dear. Why?

Mary. Play wif Mary.

Robert. [*Gently*] No, dear, not today. Dada doesn't feel like playing today.

Mary. [*Protestingly*] Yes, Dada!

Robert. No, dear. Dada does feel sick—a little. He's got a bad headache.

Mary. Mary see. [*He bends his head. She pats his hair.*] Bad head.

Robert. [*Kissing her—with a smile*] There! It's better now, dear, thank you. [*She cuddles up close against him. There is a pause during which each of them looks out seaward. Finally* Robert *turns to her tenderly.*] Would you like Dada to go away?—far, far away?

Mary. [*Tearfully*] No! No! No, Dada, no!

Robert. Don't you like Uncle Andy—the man that came yesterday—not the old man with the white mustache— the other?

Mary. Mary loves Dada.

Robert. [*With fierce determination*] He won't go away, baby. He was only joking. He couldn't leave his little Mary. [*He presses the child in his arms.*]

Mary. [*With an exclamation of pain*] Oh! Hurt!

Robert. I'm sorry, little girl. [*He lifts her down to the grass.*] Go play with Dolly, that's a good girl; and be careful to keep in the shade. [*She reluctantly leaves him and takes up her doll again. A moment later she points down the hill to the left.*]

Mary. Mans, Dada.

Robert. [*Looking that way*] It's your Uncle Andy. [*A moment later* ANDREW *comes up from the left, whistling cheerfully. He has changed but little in appearance, except for the fact that his face has been deeply bronzed by his years in the tropics; but there is a decided change in his manner. The old easy-going good-nature seems to have been partly lost in a breezy, business-like briskness of voice and gesture. There is an authoritative note in his speech as though he were accustomed to give orders and have them obeyed as a matter of course. He is dressed in the simple blue uniform and cap of a merchant ship's officer.*]

Andrew. Here you are, eh?

Robert.   Hello, Andy.

Andrew. [*Going over to* Mary] And who's this young lady
I find you all alone with, eh? Who's this pretty young
lady? [*He tickles the laughing, squirming* Mary*, then
lifts her up at arm's length over his head.*] Upsy—daisy!
[*He sets her down on the ground again.*] And there you
are! [*He walks over and sits down on the boulder beside* Robert *who moves to one side to make room for
him.*] Ruth told me I'd probably find you up top-side
here; but I'd have guessed it, anyway. [*He digs his
brother in the ribs affectionately.*] Still up to your old
tricks, you old beggar! I can remember how you used
to come up here to mope and dream in the old days.

Robert. [*With a smile*] I come up here now because it's the
coolest place on the farm. I've given up dreaming.

Andrew. [*Grinning*] I don't believe it. You can't have
changed that much. [*After a pause—with boyish enthusiasm*] Say, it sure brings back old times to be up here
with you having a chin all by our lonesomes again. I
feel great being back home.

Robert.   It's great for us to have you back.

Andrew. [*After a pause—meaningly*] I've been looking over
the old place with Ruth. Things don't seem to be——

Robert. [*His face flushing—interrupts his brother shortly*]
Never mind the fool farm! Let's talk about something
interesting. This is the first chance I've had to have a
word with you alone. Tell me about your trip.

Andrew. Why, I thought I told you everything in my letters.

Robert. [*Smiling*] Your letters were—sketchy, to say the least.

Andrew. Oh, I know I'm no author. You needn't be afraid of hurting my feelings. I'd rather go through a typhoon again than write a letter.

Robert. [*With eager interest*] Then you were through a typhoon?

Andrew. Yes—in the China Sea. Had to run before it under bare poles for two days. I thought we were bound down for Davy Jones, sure. Never dreamed waves could get so big or the wind blow so hard. If it hadn't been for Uncle Dick being such a good skipper we'd have gone to the sharks, all of us. As it was we came out minus a main top-mast and had to beat back to Hong Kong for repairs. But I must have written you all this.

Robert. You never mentioned it.

Andrew. Well, there was so much dirty work getting things ship-shape again I must have forgotten about it.

Robert. [*Looking at* ANDREW—*marveling*] Forget a typhoon? [*With a trace of scorn*] You're a strange combination, Andy. And is what you've told me all you remember about it?

Andrew. Oh, I could give you your bellyful of details if I wanted to turn loose on you. It was all-wool-and-a-yard-wide-Hell, I'll tell you. You ought to have been there. I remember thinking about you at the worst of it, and saying to myself: "This'd cure Rob of them ideas of his about the beautiful sea, if he could see it." And it would have too, you bet! [*He nods emphatically.*]

Robert. [*Dryly*] The sea doesn't seem to have impressed you very favorably.

Andrew. I should say it didn't. I'll never set foot on a ship again if I can help it—except to carry me some place I can't get to by train.

Robert. But you studied to become an officer!

Andrew. Had to do something or I'd gone mad. The days were like years. [*He laughs.*] And as for the East you used to rave about—well, you ought to see it, and *smell* it! One walk down one of their filthy narrow streets with the tropic sun beating on it would sicken you for life with the "wonder and mystery" you used to dream of.

Robert. [*Shrinking from his brother with a glance of aversion*] So all you found in the East was a stench?

Andrew. *A* stench! Ten thousand of them!

Robert. But you did like some of the places, judging from your letters—Sydney, Buenos Aires——

Andrew. Yes, Sydney's a good town. [*Enthusiastically*] But Buenos Aires—there's the place for you. Argentine's a country where a fellow has a chance to make good. You're right I like it. And I'll tell you, Rob, that's right where I'm going just as soon as I've seen you folks a while and can get a ship. I can get a berth as second officer, and I'll jump the ship when I get there. I'll need every cent of the wages Uncle's paid me to get a start at something in B. A.

Robert. [*Staring at his brother—slowly*] So you're not going to stay on the farm?

Andrew. Why sure not! Did you think I was? There wouldn't be any sense. One of us is enough to run this little place.

Robert. I suppose it does seem small to you now.

Andrew. [*Not noticing the sarcasm in* ROBERT'S *tone*] You've no idea, Rob, what a splendid place Argentine is. I had a letter from a marine insurance chap that I'd made friends with in Hong Kong to his brother, who's in the grain business in Buenos Aires. He took quite a fancy to me, and what's more important, he offered me a job if I'd come back there. I'd have taken it on the spot, only I couldn't leave Uncle Dick in the lurch, and I'd promised you folks to come home. But I'm going back there, you bet, and then you watch me get on! [*He slaps* ROBERT *on the back.*] But don't you think it's a big chance, Rob?

Robert. It's fine—for you, Andy.

Andrew. We call this a farm—but you ought to hear about the farms down there—ten square miles where we've got an acre. It's a new country where big things are opening up—and I want to get in on something big before I die. I'm no fool when it comes to farming, and I know something about grain. I've been reading up a lot on it too, lately. [*He notices* ROBERT'S *absent-minded expression and laughs.*] Wake up, you old poetry bookworm, you! I know my talking about business makes you want to choke me, doesn't it?

Robert. [*With an embarrassed smile*] No, Andy, I—I just
happened to think of something else. [*Frowning*]
There've been lots of times lately that I've wished I had
some of your faculty for business.

Andrew. [*Soberly*] There's something I want to talk about,
Rob,—the farm. You don't mind, do you?

Robert. No.

Andrew. I walked over it this morning with Ruth—and she
told me about things—— [*Evasively*] I could see the place
had run down; but you mustn't blame yourself. When
luck's against anyone——

Robert. Don't, Andy! It *is* my fault. You know it as well
as I do. The best I've ever done was to make ends meet.

Andrew. [*After a pause*] I've got over a thousand saved, and
you can have that.

Robert. [*Firmly*] No. You need that for your start in
Buenos Aires.

Andrew. I don't. I can——

Robert. [*Determinedly*] No, Andy! Once and for all, no!
I won't hear of it!

Andrew. [*Protestingly*] You obstinate old son of a gun!

Robert. Oh, everything'll be on a sound footing after harvest.
Don't worry about it.

Andrew. [*Doubtfully*] Maybe. [*After a pause*] It's too bad
Pa couldn't have lived to see things through. [*With feeling*] It cut me up a lot—hearing he was dead. He never
—softened up, did he—about me, I mean?

Robert. He never understood, that's a kinder way of putting it. He does now.

Andrew. [*After a pause*] You've forgotten all about what—caused me to go, haven't you, Rob? [ROBERT *nods but keeps his face averted.*] I was a slushier darn fool in those days than you were. But it was an act of Providence I did go. It opened my eyes to how I'd been fooling myself. Why, I'd forgotten all about—that—before I'd been at sea six months.

Robert. [*Turns and looks into* ANDREW's *eyes searchingly*] You're speaking of—Ruth?

Andrew. [*Confused*] Yes. I didn't want you to get false notions in your head, or I wouldn't say anything. [*Looking* ROBERT *squarely in the eyes*] I'm telling you the truth when I say I'd forgotten long ago. It don't sound well for me, getting over things so easy, but I guess it never really amounted to more than a kid idea I was letting rule me. I'm certain now I never was in love—I was getting fun out of thinking I was—and being a hero to myself. [*He heaves a great sigh of relief.*] There! Gosh, I'm glad that's off my chest. I've been feeling sort of awkward ever since I've been home, thinking of what you two might think. [*A trace of appeal in his voice*] You've got it all straight now, haven't you, Rob?

Robert. [*In a low voice*] Yes, Andy.

Andrew. And I'll tell Ruth, too, if I can get up the nerve. She must feel kind of funny having me around—after what used to be—and not knowing how I feel about it.

Robert. [*Slowly*] Perhaps—for her sake—you'd better not tell her.

Andrew. For her sake? Oh, you mean she wouldn't want to be reminded of my foolishness? Still, I think it'd be worse if——

Robert. [*Breaking out—in an agonized voice*] Do as you please, Andy; but let's not talk about it! [*There is a pause.* ANDREW *stares at* ROBERT *in hurt stupefaction.* ROBERT *continues after a moment in a voice which he vainly attempts to keep calm.*] Excuse me, Andy. This rotten headache has my nerves shot to pieces.

Andrew. [*Mumbling*] It's all right, Rob—long as you're not sore at me.

Robert. Where did Uncle Dick disappear to this morning?

Andrew. He went down to the port to see to things on the *Sunda.* He said he didn't know exactly when he'd be back. I'll have to go down and tend to the ship when he comes. That's why I dressed up in these togs.

Mary. [*Pointing down to the hill to the left*] See! Mama! Mama! [*She struggles to her feet.* RUTH *appears at left. She is dressed in white, shows she has been fixing up. She looks pretty, flushed and full of life.*]

Mary. [*Running to her mother*] Mama!

Ruth. [*Kissing her*] Hello, dear! [*She walks toward the rock and addresses* ROBERT *coldly.*] Jake wants to see you about something. He finished working where he was. He's waiting for you at the road.

Robert. [*Getting up—wearily*] I'll go down right away.

[*As he looks at* RUTH, *noting her changed appearance, his face darkens with pain.*]

Ruth. And take Mary with you, please. [*To* MARY] Go with Dada, that's a good girl. Grandma has your dinner most ready for you.

Robert. [*Shortly*] Come, Mary!

Mary. [*Taking his hand and dancing happily beside him*] Dada! Dada! [*They go down the hill to the left.* RUTH *looks after them for a moment, frowning—then turns to* ANDY *with a smile.*] I'm going to sit down. Come on, Andy. It'll be like old times. [*She jumps lightly to the top of the rock and sits down.*] It's so fine and cool up here after the house.

Andrew. [*Half-sitting on the side of the boulder.*] Yes. It's great.

Ruth. I've taken a holiday in honor of your arrival. [*Laughing excitedly*] I feel so free I'd like to have wings and fly over the sea. You're a man. You can't know how awful and stupid it is—cooking and washing dishes all the time.

Andrew. [*Making a wry face*] I can guess.

Ruth. Besides, your mother just insisted on getting your first dinner to home, she's that happy at having you back. You'd think I was planning to poison you the flurried way she shooed me out of the kitchen.

Andrew. That's just like Ma, bless her!

Ruth. She's missed you terrible. We all have. And you can't deny the farm has, after what I showed you and told you when we was looking over the place this morning.

Andrew. [*With a frown*] Things are run down, that's a fact! It's too darn hard on poor old Rob.

Ruth. [*Scornfully*] It's his own fault. He never takes any interest in things.

Andrew. [*Reprovingly*] You can't blame him. He wasn't born for it; but I know he's done his best for your sake and the old folks and the little girl.

Ruth. [*Indifferently*] Yes, I suppose he has. [*Gayly*] But thank the Lord, all those days are over now. The "hard luck" Rob's always blaming won't last long when you take hold, Andy. All the farm's ever needed was someone with the knack of looking ahead and preparing for what's going to happen.

Andrew. Yes, Rob hasn't got that. He's frank to own up to that himself. I'm going to try and hire a good man for him—an experienced farmer—to work the place on a salary and percentage. That'll take it off of Rob's hands, and he needn't be worrying himself to death any more. He looks all worn out, Ruth. He ought to be careful.

Ruth. [*Absent-mindedly*] Yes, I s'pose. [*Her mind is filled with premonitions by the first part of his statement.*] Why do you want to hire a man to oversee things? Seems as if now that you're back it wouldn't be needful.

Andrew. Oh, of course I'll attend to everything while I'm here. I mean after I'm gone.

Ruth. [*As if she couldn't believe her ears*] Gone!

Andrew. Yes. When I leave for the Argentine again.

Ruth. [*Aghast*] You're going away to sea!

Andrew. Not to sea, no; I'm through with the sea for good
as a job. I'm going down to Buenos Aires to get in the
grain business.

Ruth. But—that's far off—isn't it?

Andrew. [*Easily*] Six thousand miles more or less. It's
quite a trip. [*With enthusiasm*] I've got a peach of a
chance down there, Ruth. Ask Rob if I haven't. I've just
been telling him all about it.

Ruth. [*A flush of anger coming over her face*] And didn't
he try to stop you from going?

Andrew. [*In surprise*] No, of course not. Why?

Ruth. [*Slowly and vindictively*] That's just like him—not to.

Andrew. [*Resentfully*] Rob's too good a chum to try and
stop me when he knows I'm set on a thing. And he could
see just as soon's I told him what a good chance it was.

Ruth. [*Dazedly*] And you're bound on going?

Andrew. Sure thing. Oh, I don't mean right off. I'll have
to wait for a ship sailing there for quite a while, likely.
Anyway, I want to stay to home and visit with you folks
a spell before I go.

Ruth. [*Dumbly*] I s'pose. [*With sudden anguish*] Oh,
Andy, you can't go! You can't. Why we've all thought
—we've all been hoping and praying you was coming
home to stay, to settle down on the farm and see to
things. You mustn't go! Think of how your Ma'll take

on if you go—and how the farm'll be ruined if you leave
it to Rob to look after. You can see that.

Andrew. [*Frowning*] Rob hasn't done so bad. When I get
a man to direct things, the farm'll be safe enough.

Ruth. [*Insistently*] But your Ma—think of her.

Andrew. She's used to me being away. She won't object
when she knows it's best for her and all of us for me to
go. You ask Rob. In a couple of years down there I'll
make my pile, see if I don't; and then I'll come back and
settle down and turn this farm into the crackiest place in
the whole state. In the meantime, I can help you both
from down there. [*Earnestly*] I tell you, Ruth, I'm going
to make good right from the minute I land, if working
hard and a determination to get on can do it; and I *know*
they can! [*Excitedly—in a rather boastful tone*] I tell
you, I feel ripe for bigger things than settling down here.
The trip did that for me, anyway. It showed me the
world is a larger proposition than ever I thought it was
in the old days. I couldn't be content any more stuck
here like a fly in molasses. It all seems trifling, somehow.
You ought to be able to understand what I feel.

Ruth. [*Dully*] Yes—I s'pose I ought. [*After a pause—a
sudden suspicion forming in her mind*] What did Rob
tell you—about me?

Andrew. Tell? About you? Why, nothing.

Ruth. [*Staring at him intensely*] Are you telling me the
truth, Andy Mayo? Didn't he say—I—— [*She stops confusedly.*]

Andrew. [*Surprised*] No, he didn't mention you, as I can remember. Why? What made you think he did?

Ruth. [*Wringing her hands*] Oh, I wish I could tell if you're lying or not!

Andrew. [*Indignantly*] What're you talking about? I didn't used to lie to you, did I? And what is there to lie for?

Ruth. [*Still unconvinced*] Are you sure—will you swear—it isn't the reason—— [*She lowers her eyes and half turns away from him.*] The same reason that made you go last time that's driving you away again? 'Cause if it is—I was going to say—you mustn't go—on that account. [*Her voice sinks to a tremulous, tender whisper as she finishes.*]

Andrew. [*Confused—forces a laugh*] Oh, is *that* what you're driving at? Well, you needn't worry about that no more —— [*Soberly*] I don't blame you, Ruth, feeling embarrassed having me around again, after the way I played the dumb fool about going away last time.

Ruth. [*Her hope crushed—with a gasp of pain*] Oh, Andy!

Andrew. [*Misunderstanding*] I know I oughtn't to talk about such foolishness to you. Still I figure it's better to get it out of my system so's we three can be together same's years ago, and not be worried thinking one of us might have the wrong notion.

Ruth. Andy! Please! Don't!

Andrew. Let me finish now that I've started. It'll help clear things up. I don't want you to think once a fool always a fool, and be upset all the time I'm here on my fool account. I want you to believe I put all that silly nonsense back of me a long time ago—and now—it seems—well—as if you'd always been my sister, that's what, Ruth.

Ruth. [*At the end of her endurance—laughing hysterically*] Andy—won't you please stop talking! [*She again hides her face in her hands, her bowed shoulders trembling.*]

Andrew. [*Ruefully*] Seem's if I put my foot in it whenever I open my mouth today. Rob shut me up with almost the same words when I tried speaking to him about it.

Ruth. [*Fiercely*] You told him—what you've told me?

Andrew. [*Astounded*] Why sure! Why not?

Ruth. [*Shuddering*] Oh, my God!

Andrew. [*Alarmed*] Why? Shouldn't I have?

Ruth. [*Hysterically*] Oh, I don't care what you do! I don't care! Leave me alone! [ANDREW *gets up and walks down the hill to the left, embarrassed, hurt, and greatly puzzled by her behavior.*]

Andrew. [*After a pause—pointing down the hill*] Hello! Here they come back—and the Captain's with them. How'd he come to get back so soon, I wonder? That means I've got to hustle down to the port and get on board. Rob's got the baby with him. [*He comes back to the boulder.* RUTH *keeps her face averted from him.*] Gosh, I never saw a father so tied up in a kid as Rob is! He just watches every move she makes. And I don't blame him. You both got a right to feel proud of her. She's surely a little winner. [*He glances at* RUTH *to see if this very obvious attempt to get back in her good graces is having any effect.*] I can see the likeness to Rob standing out all over her, can't you? But there's no denying she's your young one, either. There's something about her eyes——

Ruth. [*Piteously*] Oh, Andy, I've a headache! I don't want to talk! Leave me alone, won't you please?

Andrew. [*Stands staring at her for a moment—then walks away saying in a hurt tone*] Everybody hereabouts seems to be on edge today. I begin to feel as if I'm not wanted around. [*He stands near the path, left, kicking at the grass with the toe of his shoe. A moment later* Captain Dick Scott *enters, followed by* Robert *carrying* Mary. *The* Captain *seems scarcely to have changed at all from the jovial, booming person he was three years before. He wears a uniform similar to* Andrew's. *He is puffing and breathless from his climb and mops wildly at his perspiring countenance.* Robert *casts a quick glance at* Andrew, *noticing the latter's discomfited look, and then turns his eyes on* Ruth *who, at their approach, has moved so her back is toward them, her chin resting on her hands as she stares out seaward.*]

Mary. Mama! Mama! [Robert *puts her down and she runs to her mother.* Ruth *turns and grabs her up in her arms with a sudden fierce tenderness, quickly turning away again from the others. During the following scene she keeps* Mary *in her arms.*]

Scott. [*Wheezily*] Phew! I got great news for you, Andy. Let me get my wind first. Phew! Gosh A'mighty,

mountin' this hill is worser'n goin' aloft to the skys'l yard
in a blow. I got to lay to for a while. [*He sits down on
the grass, mopping his face.*]

Andrew. I didn't look for you this soon, Uncle.

Scott. I didn't figger it, neither; but I run across a bit o' news
down to the Seamen's Home made me 'bout ship and set
all sail back here to find you.

Andrew. [*Eagerly*] What is it, Uncle?

Scott. Passin' by the Home I thought I'd drop in an' let 'em
know I'd be lackin' a mate next trip count o' your leavin'.
Their man in charge o' the shippin' asked after you
'special curious. "Do you think he'd consider a berth as
Second on a steamer, Captain?" he asks. I was goin' to
say no when I thinks o' you wantin' to get back down
south to the Plate agen; so I asks him: "What is she and
where's she bound?" "She's the *El Paso,* a brand new
tramp," he says, "and she's bound for Buenos Aires."

Andrew. [*His eyes lighting up—excitedly*] Gosh, that is
luck! When does she sail?

Scott. Tomorrow mornin'. I didn't know if you'd want to
ship away agen so quick an' I told him so. "Tell him I'll
hold the berth open for him until late this afternoon," he
says. So there you be, an' you can make your own
choice.

Andrew. I'd like to take it. There may not be another ship
for Buenos Aires with a vacancy in months. [*His eyes*

Skys'l yard—The spar or support of the topmost sail.
The Plate—The River Plate on which Buenos Aires is located.

roving from ROBERT *to* RUTH *and back again—uncertainly.*] Still—darn it all—tomorrow morning *is* soon. I wish she wasn't leaving for a week or so. That'd give me a chance—it seems hard to go right away again when I've just got home. And yet it's a chance in a thousand —— [*Appealing to* ROBERT] What do you think, Rob? What would you do?

Robert. [*Forcing a smile*] He who hesitates, you know. [*Frowning*] It's a piece of good luck thrown in your way and—I think you owe it to yourself to jump at it. But don't ask me to decide for you.

Ruth. [*Turning to look at* ANDREW—*in a tone of fierce resentment*] Yes, go, Andy! [*She turns quickly away again. There is a moment of embarrassed silence.*]

Andrew. [*Thoughtfully*] Yes, I guess I will. It'll be the best thing for all of us in the end, don't you think so, Rob? [ROBERT *nods but remains silent.*]

Scott. [*Getting to his feet*] Then, that's settled.

Andrew. [*Now that he has definitely made a decision his voice rings with hopeful strength and energy*] Yes, I'll take the berth. The sooner I go the sooner I'll be back, that's a certainty; and I won't come back with empty hands next time. You bet I won't!

Scott. You ain't got so much time, Andy. To make sure, you'd best leave here soon's you kin. I got to get right back aboard. You'd best come with me.

Andrew. I'll go to the house and repack my bag right away.

Robert. [*Quietly*] You'll both be here for dinner, won't you?

Andrew. [*Worriedly*] I don't know. Will there be time? What time is it now, I wonder?

Robert. [*Reproachfully*] Ma's been getting dinner especially for you, Andy.

Andrew. [*Flushing—shamefacedly*] Gosh! And I was forgetting! Of course I'll stay for dinner if I missed every darned ship in the world. [*He turns to the* Captain— *briskly.*] Come on, Uncle. Walk down with me to the house and you can tell me more about this berth on the way. I've got to pack before dinner. [*He and the* Captain *start down to the left.* Andrew *calls back over his shoulder.*] You're coming soon, aren't you, Rob?

Robert. Yes. I'll be right down. [Andrew *and the* Captain *leave.* Ruth *puts* Mary *on the ground and hides her face in her hands. Her shoulders shake as if she were sobbing.* Robert *stares at her with a grim, somber expression.* Mary *walks backward toward* Robert, *her wondering eyes fixed on her mother.*]

Mary. [*Her voice vaguely frightened, taking her father's hand*] Dada, Mama's cryin', Dada.

Robert. [*Bending down and stroking her hair—in a voice he endeavors to keep from being harsh*] No, she isn't, little girl. The sun hurts her eyes, that's all. Aren't you beginning to feel hungry, Mary?

Mary. [*Decidedly*] Yes, Dada.

Robert. [*Meaningly*] It must be your dinner time now.

Ruth. [*In a muffled voice*]   I'm coming, Mary.   [*She wipes
her eyes quickly and, without looking at* Robert, *comes
and takes* Mary's *hand—in a dead voice.*]   Come on and
I'll get your dinner for you.   [*She walks out left, her
eyes fixed on the ground, the skipping* Mary *tugging at
her hand.*   Robert *waits a moment for them to get ahead
and then slowly follows as*

[*The Curtain Falls*]

ACT THREE

Scene I

Same as Act Two, Scene One—The sitting room of the farmhouse about six o'clock in the morning of a day toward the end of October five years later. It is not yet dawn, but as the action progresses the darkness outside the windows gradually fades to gray.

The room, seen by the light of the shadeless oil lamp with a smoky chimney which stands on the table, presents an appearance of decay, of dissolution. The curtains at the windows are torn and dirty and one of them is missing. The closed desk is gray with accumulated dust as if it had not been used in years. Blotches of dampness disfigure the wall paper. Threadbare trails, leading to the kitchen and outer doors, show in the faded carpet. The top of the coverless table is stained with the imprints of hot dishes and spilt food. The rung of one rocker has been clumsily mended with a piece of plain board. A brown coating of rust covers the unblacked stove. A pile of wood is stacked up carelessly against the wall by the stove.

The whole atmosphere of the room, contrasted with that of former years, is one of an habitual poverty too hopelessly resigned to be any longer ashamed or even conscious of itself.

At the rise of the curtain Ruth *is discovered sitting by the*

stove, with hands outstretched to the warmth as if the air in
the room were damp and cold. A heavy shawl is wrapped
about her shoulders, half-concealing her dress of deep mourning. She has aged horribly. Her pale, deeply lined face has
the stony lack of expression of one to whom nothing more can
ever happen, whose capacity for emotion has been exhausted.
When she speaks her voice is without timbre, low and monotonous. The negligent disorder of her dress, the slovenly arrangement of her hair, now streaked with gray, her muddied
shoes run down at the heel, give full evidence of the apathy
in which she lives.*

*Her mother is asleep in her wheel chair beside the stove to-
ward the rear, wrapped up in a blanket.*

*There is a sound from the open bedroom door in the rear
as if someone were getting out of bed.* RUTH *turns in that
direction with a look of dull annoyance. A moment later*
ROBERT *appears in the doorway, leaning weakly against it for
support. His hair is long and unkempt, his face and body
emaciated. There are bright patches of crimson over his cheek
bones and his eyes are burning with fever. He is dressed in
corduroy pants, a flannel shirt, and wears worn carpet slippers
on his bare feet.*

Ruth. [*Dully*] S-s-s-h-! Ma's asleep.

Robert. [*Speaking with an effort*] I won't wake her. [*He
walks weakly to a rocker by the side of the table and sinks
down in it exhausted.*]

Ruth. [*Staring at the stove*] You better come near the fire
where it's warm.

Robert. No. I'm burning up now.

Ruth. That's the fever. You know the doctor told you not to get up and move round.

Robert. [*Irritably*] That old fossil! He doesn't know anything. Go to bed and stay there—that's his only prescription.

Ruth. [*Indifferently*] How are you feeling now?

Robert. [*Buoyantly*] Better! Much better than I've felt in ages. Really I'm fine now—only very weak. It's the turning point, I guess. From now on I'll pick up so quick I'll surprise you—and no thanks to that old fool of a country quack, either.

Ruth. He's always tended to us.

Robert. Always helped us to die, you mean! He "tended" to Pa and Ma and—[*his voice breaks*]—and to—Mary.

Ruth. [*Dully*] He did the best he knew, I s'pose. [*After a pause*] Well, Andy's bringing a specialist with him when he comes. That ought to suit you.

Robert. [*Bitterly*] Is that why you're waiting up all night?

Ruth. Yes.

Robert. For Andy?

Ruth. [*Without a trace of feeling*] Somebody has got to. It's only right for someone to meet him after he's been gone five years.

Robert. [*With bitter mockery*] Five years! It's a long time.

Ruth. Yes.

Robert. [*Meaningly*] To *wait!*

Ruth. [*Indifferently*] It's past now.

Robert. Yes, it's past. [*After a pause*] Have you got his two
telegrams with you? [Ruth *nods.*] Let me see them, will
you? My head was so full of fever when they came I
couldn't make head or tail to them. [*Hastily*] But I'm
feeling fine now. Let me read them again. [*Ruth takes
them from the bosom of her dress and hands them to
him.*]

Ruth. Here. The first one's on top.

Robert. [*Opening it*] New York. "Just landed from steamer.
Have important business to wind up here. Will be home
as soon as deal is completed." [*He smiles bitterly.*]
"Business first" was always Andy's motto. [*He reads.*]
"Hope you are all well. Andy." [*He repeats ironically.*]
"Hope you are all well!"

Ruth. [*Dully*] He couldn't know you'd been took sick till
I answered that and told him.

Robert. [*Contritely*] Of course he couldn't. I'm a fool. I'm
touchy about nothing lately. Just what did you say in
your reply?

Ruth. [*Inconsequentially*] I had to send it collect.

Robert. [*Irritably*] What did you say was the matter with
me?

Ruth. I wrote you had lung trouble.

Robert. [*Flying into a petty temper*] You *are* a fool. How
often have I explained to you that it's *pleurisy* that is the
matter with me. You can't seem to get it into your head
that the pleura is outside the lungs, not in them!

Ruth. [*Callously*] I only wrote what Doctor Smith told me.

Robert. [*Angrily*] He's a stupid ignoramus!

Ruth. [*Dully*] Makes no difference. I had to tell Andy something, didn't I?

Robert. [*After a pause, opening the other telegram*] He sent this last evening. Let's see. [*He reads.*] "Leave for home on midnight train. Just received your wire. Am bringing specialist to see Rob. Will motor to farm from Port." [*He calculates.*] What time is it now?

Ruth. Round six, must be.

Robert. He ought to be here soon. I'm glad he's bringing a doctor who knows something. A specialist will tell you in a second that there's nothing the matter with my lungs.

Ruth. [*Stolidly*] You've been coughing an awful lot lately.

Robert. [*Irritably*] What nonsense! Haven't you ever had a bad cold yourself? [RUTH *stares at the stove in silence.* ROBERT *fidgets in his chair. There is a pause. Finally* ROBERT'S *eyes are fixed on the sleeping* MRS. ATKINS.] Your mother is lucky to be able to sleep so soundly.

Ruth. Ma's tired. She's been sitting up with me most of the night.

Robert. [*Mockingly*] Is she waiting for Andy, too? [*There is a pause.* ROBERT *sighs.*] I couldn't get to sleep to save my soul. I counted ten million sheep if I counted one. No use! I gave up trying finally and just laid there in the dark thinking. [*He pauses, then continues in a tone of tender sympathy*.] I was thinking about you, Ruth—of how hard these last years must have been for you. [*Appealingly*] I'm sorry, Ruth.

Ruth. [*In a dead voice*] I don't know. They're past now. They were hard on all of us.

Robert. Yes; on all of us but Andy. [*With a flash of sick jealousy*] Andy's made a big success of himself—the kind he wanted. [*Mockingly*] And now he's coming home to let us admire his greatness. [*Frowning—irritably*] What am I talking about? My brain must be sick, too. [*After a pause*] Yes, these years have been terrible for both of us. [*His voice is lowered to a trembling whisper.*] Especially the last eight months since Mary—died. [*He forces back a sob with a convulsive shudder—then breaks out in a passionate agony.*] Our last hope of happiness! I could curse God from the bottom of my soul—if there was a God! [*He is racked by a violent fit of coughing and hurriedly puts his handkerchief to his lips.*]

Ruth. [*Without looking at him*] Mary's better off—being dead.

Robert. [*Gloomily*] We'd all be better off for that matter. [*With a sudden exasperation*] You tell that mother of yours she's got to stop saying that Mary's death was due to a weak constitution inherited from me. [*On the verge of tears of weakness*] It's got to stop, I tell you!

Ruth. [*Sharply*] S-h-h! You'll wake her; and then she'll nag at me—not you.

Robert. [*Coughs and lies back in his chair weakly—a pause*]

It's all because your mother's down on me for not begging
Andy for help.

Ruth. [*Resentfully*] You might have. He's got plenty.

Robert. How can *you* of all people think of taking money
from *him?*

Ruth. [*Dully*] I don't see the harm. He's your own
brother.

Robert. [*Shrugging his shoulders*] What's the use of talking
to you? Well, *I* couldn't. [*Proudly*] And I've managed
to keep things going, thank God. You can't deny that
without help I've succeeded in—— [*He breaks off with a
bitter laugh.*] My God, what am I boasting of? Debts
to this one and that, taxes, interest unpaid! I'm a fool!
[*He lies back in his chair closing his eyes for a moment,
then speaks in a low voice.*] I'll be frank, Ruth. I've been
an utter failure, and I've dragged you with me. I couldn't
blame you in all justice—for hating me.

Ruth. [*Without feeling*] I don't hate you. It's been my
fault too, I s'pose.

Robert. No. You couldn't help loving—Andy.

Ruth. [*Dully*] I don't love anyone.

Robert. [*Waving her remark aside*] You needn't deny it.
It doesn't matter. [*After a pause—with a tender smile*]
Do you know, Ruth, what I've been dreaming back there
in the dark? [*With a short laugh*] I was planning our
future when I get well. [*He looks at her with appealing
eyes as if afraid she will sneer at him. Her expression
does not change. She stares at the stove. His voice takes

on a note of eagerness.] After all, why shouldn't we have
a future? We're young yet. If we can only shake off
the curse of this farm! It's the farm that's ruined our
lives, damn it! And now that Andy's coming back—I'm
going to sink my foolish pride, Ruth! I'll borrow the
money from him to give us a good start in the city. We'll
go where people live instead of stagnating, and start all
over again. [*Confidently*] I won't be the failure there
that I've been here, Ruth. You won't need to be ashamed
of me there. I'll prove to you the reading I've done can
be put to some use. [*Vaguely*] I'll write, or something
of that sort. I've always wanted to write. [*Pleadingly*]
You'll want to do that, won't you, Ruth?

Ruth. [*Dully*] There's Ma.

Robert. She can come with us.

Ruth. She wouldn't.

Robert. [*Angrily*] So that's your answer! [*He trembles with
violent passion. His voice is so strange that* RUTH *turns
to look at him in alarm.*] You're lying, Ruth! Your
mother's just an excuse. You want to stay here. You
think that because Andy's coming back that—— [*He
chokes and has an attack of coughing.*]

Ruth. [*Getting up—in a frightened voice*] What's the matter? [*She goes to him.*] I'll go with you, Rob. Stop that
coughing for goodness' sake! It's awful bad for you.
[*She soothes him in dull tones.*] I'll go with you to the
city—soon's you're well again. Honest I will, Rob, I
promise! [ROB *lies back and closes his eyes. She stands*

looking down at him anxiously.] Do you feel better now?

Robert. Yes. [Ruth *goes back to her chair. After a pause he opens his eyes and sits up in his chair. His face is flushed and happy*.] Then you *will* go, Ruth?

Ruth. Yes.

Robert. [*Excitedly*] We'll make a new start, Ruth—just you and I. Life owes us some happiness after what we've been through. [*Vehemently*] It must! Otherwise our suffering would be meaningless—and that is unthinkable.

Ruth. [*Worried by his excitement*] Yes, yes, of course, Rob, but you mustn't——

Robert. Oh, don't be afraid. I feel completely well, really I do—now that I can hope again. Oh, if you knew how glorious it feels to have something to look forward to! Can't you feel the thrill of it, too—the vision of a new life opening up after all the horrible years?

Ruth. Yes, yes, but do be——

Robert. Nonsense! I won't be careful. I'm getting back all my strength. [*He gets lightly to his feet*.] See! I feel light as a feather. [*He walks to her chair and bends down to kiss her smilingly*.] One kiss—the first in years, isn't it?—to greet the dawn of a new life together.

Ruth. [*Submitting to his kiss—worriedly*] Sit down, Rob, for goodness' sake!

Robert. [*With tender obstinacy—stroking her hair*] I won't sit down. You're silly to worry. [*He rests one hand on the back of her chair*.] Listen. All our suffering has been a test through which we had to pass to prove ourselves worthy of a finer realization. [*Exultingly*] And we did pass through it! It hasn't broken us! And now the dream is to come true! Don't you see?

Ruth. [*Looking at him with frightened eyes as if she thought he had gone mad*] Yes, Rob, I see; but won't you go back to bed now and rest?

Robert. No. I'm going to see the sun rise. It's an augury of good fortune. [*He goes quickly to the window in the rear left, and pushing the curtains aside, stands looking out.* RUTH *springs to her feet and comes quickly to the table, left, where she remains watching* ROBERT *in a tense, expectant attitude. As he peers out, his body seems gradually to sag, to grow limp and tired. His voice is mournful as he speaks.*] No sun yet. It isn't time. All I can see is the black rim of the cursed hills outlined against a creeping grayness. [*He turns around; letting the curtains fall back, stretching a hand out to the wall to support himself. His false strength of a moment has evaporated leaving his face drawn and hollow-eyed. He makes a pitiful attempt to smile.*] That's not a very happy augury, is it? But the sun'll come—soon. [*He sways weakly.*]

Ruth. [*Hurrying to his side and supporting him*] Please go to bed, won't you, Rob? You don't want to be all wore out when the specialist comes, do you?

Robert. [*Quickly*] No. That's right. He mustn't think

Augury—An omen or sign of the future.

I'm sicker than I am. And I feel as if I could sleep now—
[*Cheerfully*]—a good, sound, restful sleep.

Ruth. [*Helping him to the bedroom door*] That's what you
need most. [*They go inside. A moment later she reappears calling back.*] I'll shut this door so's you'll be
quiet. [*She closes the door and goes quickly to her
mother and shakes her by the shoulder.*] Ma! Ma!
Wake up!

Mrs. Atkins. [*Coming out of her sleep with a start*] Glory
be! What's the matter with you?

Ruth. It was Rob. He's just been talking to me out here. I
put him back to bed. [*Now that she is sure her mother
is awake her fear passes and she relapses into dull indifference. She sits down in her chair and stares at the stove—
dully.*] He acted—funny; and his eyes looked so—so wild
like.

Mrs. Atkins. [*With asperity*] And is that all you woke me
out of a sound sleep for, and scared me near out of my
wits?

Ruth. I was afraid. He talked so crazy. I couldn't quiet
him. I didn't want to be alone with him that way. Lord
knows what he might do.

Mrs. Atkins. [*Scornfully*] Humph! A help I'd be to you
and me not able to move a step! Why didn't you run and
get Jake?

Ruth. [*Dully*] Jake isn't here. He quit last night. He
hasn't been paid in three months.

Mrs. Atkins. [*Indignantly*] I can't blame him. What decent person'd want to work on a place like this? [*With sudden exasperation*] Oh, I wish you'd never married that man.

Ruth. [*Wearily*] You oughtn't to talk about him now when he's sick in his bed.

Mrs. Atkins. [*Working herself into a fit of rage*] You know very well, Ruth Mayo, if it wasn't for me helpin' you on the sly out of my savin's, you'd both been in the poor house—and all 'count of his pigheaded pride in not lettin' Andy know the state thin's were in. A nice thin' for me to have to support him out of what I'd saved for my last days—and me an invalid with no one to look to!

Ruth. Andy'll pay you back, Ma. I can tell him so's Rob'll never know.

Mrs. Atkins. [*With a snort*] What'd Rob think you and him was livin' on, I'd like to know?

Ruth. [*Dully*] He didn't think about it, I s'pose. [*After a slight pause*] He said he'd made up his mind to ask Andy for help when he comes. [*As a clock in the kitchen strikes six*] Six o'clock. Andy ought to get here directly.

Mrs. Atkins. D'you think this special doctor'll do Rob any good?

Ruth. [*Hopelessly*] I don't know. [*The two women remain silent for a time staring dejectedly at the stove.*]

Mrs. Atkins. [*Shivering irritably*] For goodness' sake put some wood on that fire. I'm most freezin'!

Ruth. [*Pointing to the door in the rear*] Don't talk so loud. Let him sleep if he can. [*She gets wearily from the*

chair, puts a few pieces of wood into the stove.] This is
the last of the wood. I don't know who'll cut more now
that Jake's left. [*She sighs and walks to the window in
the rear, left, pulls the curtains aside, and looks out.*] It's
getting gray out. [*She comes back to the stove.*] Looks
like it'd be a nice day. [*She stretches out her hands to
warm them.*] Must've been a heavy frost last night.
We're paying for the spell of warm weather we've been
having. [*The throbbing whine of a motor sounds from
the distance outside.*]

Mrs. Atkins. [*Sharply*] S-h-h! Listen! Ain't that an auto I
hear?

Ruth. [*Without interest*] Yes. It's Andy, I s'pose.

Mrs. Atkins. [*With nervous irritation*] Don't sit there like
a silly goose. Look at the state of this room! What'll this
strange doctor think of us? Look at that lamp chimney
all smoke! Gracious sakes, Ruth——

Ruth. [*Indifferently*] I've got a lamp all cleaned up in the
kitchen.

Mrs. Atkins. [*Peremptorily*] Wheel me in there this minute.
I don't want him to see me looking a sight. I'll lay down
in the room at the other side. You don't need me now and
I'm dead for sleep. [RUTH *wheels her mother off right.
The noise of the motor grows louder and finally ceases as
the car stops on the road before the farmhouse.* RUTH
*returns from the kitchen with a lighted lamp in her hand
which she sets on the table beside the other. The sound
of footsteps on the path is heard—then a sharp rap on the*

door. Ruth *goes and opens it.* Andrew *enters, followed by* Doctor Fawcett *carrying a small black bag.* Andrew *has changed greatly. His face seems to have grown high-strung, hardened by the look of decisiveness which comes from being constantly under a strain where judgments on the spur of the moment are compelled to be accurate. His eyes are keener and more alert. There is even a suggestion of ruthless cunning about them. At present, however, his expression is one of tense anxiety.* Doctor Fawcett *is a short, dark, middle-aged man with a Vandyke beard. He wears glasses.*]

Ruth. Hello, Andy! I've been waiting——

Andrew. [*Kissing her hastily*] I got here as soon as I could. [*He throws off his cap and heavy overcoat on the table, introducing* Ruth *and the* Doctor *as he does so. He is dressed in an expensive business suit and appears stouter.*] My sister-in-law, Mrs. Mayo—Doctor Fawcett. [*They bow to each other silently.* Andrew *casts a quick glance about the room.*] Where's Rob?

Ruth. [*Pointing*] In there.

Andrew. I'll take your coat and hat, Doctor. [*As he helps the* Doctor *with his things*] Is he very bad, Ruth?

Ruth. [*Dully*] He's been getting weaker.

Andrew. This way, Doctor. Bring the lamp, Ruth. [*He goes into the bedroom, followed by the* Doctor *and* Ruth *carrying the clean lamp.* Ruth *reappears almost immediately closing the door behind her, and goes slowly to the outside door, which she opens, and stands in the doorway looking out. The sound of* Andrew's *and* Robert's *voices comes from the bedroom. A moment later* Andrew *re-enters, closing the door softly. He comes forward and sinks down in the rocker on the right of table, leaning his head on his hand. His face is drawn in a shocked ex-pression of great grief. He sighs heavily, staring mourn-fully in front of him.* Ruth *turns and stands watching him. Then she shuts the door and returns to her chair by the stove, turning it so she can face him.*]

Andrew. [*Glancing up quickly—in a harsh voice*] How long has this been going on?

Ruth. You mean—how long has he been sick?

Andrew. [*Shortly*] Of course! What else?

Ruth. It was last summer he had a bad spell first, but he's been ailin' ever since Mary died—eight months ago.

Andrew. [*Harshly*] Why didn't you let me know—cable me? Do you want him to die, all of you? I'm darned if it doesn't look that way! [*His voice breaking*] Poor old chap! To be sick in this out-of-the-way hole without anyone to attend to him but a country quack! It's a shame!

Ruth. [*Dully*] I wanted to send you word once, but he only got mad when I told him. He was too proud to ask any-thing, he said.

Andrew. Proud? To ask *me*? [*He jumps to his feet and paces nervously back and forth.*] I can't understand the way you've acted. Didn't you see how sick he was get-ting? Couldn't you realize—why, I nearly dropped in

my tracks when I saw him! He looks—[*He shudders.*]—
terrible! [*With fierce scorn*] I suppose you're so used to
the idea of his being delicate that you took his sickness as
a matter of course. Oh, if I'd only known!

Ruth. [*Without emotion*] A letter takes so long to get
where you were—and we couldn't afford to telegraph.
We owed everyone already, and I couldn't ask Ma. She'd
been giving me money out of her savings till she hadn't
much left. Don't say anything to Rob about it. I never
told him. He'd only be mad at me if he knew. But I had
to, because—God knows how we'd have got on if I hadn't.

Andrew. You mean to say—— [*His eyes seem to take in
the poverty-stricken appearance of the room for the first
time.*] You sent that telegram to me collect. Was it because—— [RUTH *nods silently.* ANDREW *pounds on the
table with his fist.*] Good God! And all this time I've
been—why I've had everything! [*He sits down in his
chair and pulls it close to* RUTH's—*impulsively.*] But—I
can't get it through my head. Why? Why? What has
happened? How did it ever come about? Tell me!

Ruth. [*Dully*] There's nothing much to tell. Things kept
getting worse, that's all—and Rob didn't seem to care. He
never took any interest since way back when your Ma
died. After that he got men to take charge, and they
nearly all cheated him—he couldn't tell—and left one after
another. Then, after Mary died, he didn't pay no heed to
anything any more—just stayed indoors and took to read-

ing books again. So I had to ask Ma if she wouldn't help us some.

Andrew. [*Surprised and horrified*] Why, damn it, this is frightful! Rob must be mad not to have let me know. Too proud to ask help of *me!* [*A sudden, horrible suspicion entering his mind*] Ruth! Tell me the truth. His mind hasn't gone back on him, has it?

Ruth. [*Dully*] I don't know. Mary's dying broke him up terrible—but he's used to her being gone by this time, I s'pose.

Andrew. [*Looking at her queerly*] Do you mean to say *you're* used to it?

Ruth. [*In a dead tone*] There's a time comes—when you don't mind any more—anything.

Andrew. [*Looks at her fixedly for a moment—with great pity*] I'm sorry, Ruth—if I seemed to blame you. I didn't realize—— The sight of Rob lying in bed there, so gone to pieces—it made me furious at everyone. Forgive me, Ruth.

Ruth. There's nothing to forgive. It doesn't matter.

Andrew. [*Springing to his feet again and pacing up and down*] Thank God I came back before it was too late. This doctor will know exactly what to do. That's the first thing to think of. When Rob's on his feet again, we can get the farm working on a sound basis once more. I'll see to that—before I leave.

Ruth. You're going away again?

Andrew. I've got to.

Ruth.   You wrote Rob you was coming back to stay this time.

Andrew.   I expected to—until I got to New York.   Then I learned certain facts that make it necessary.   [*With a short laugh*]   To be candid, Ruth, I'm not the rich man you've probably been led to believe by my letters—not now.   I was when I wrote them.   I made money hand over fist as long as I stuck to legitimate trading; but I wasn't content with that.   I wanted it to come easier, so like all the rest of the idiots, I tried speculation.   Oh, I won all right!   Several times I've been almost a millionaire —on paper—and then come down to earth again with a bump.   Finally the strain was too much.   I got disgusted with myself and made up my mind to get out and come home and forget it and really live again.   [*He gives a harsh laugh.*]   And now comes the funny part.   The day before the steamer sailed I saw what I thought was a chance to become a millionaire again.   [*He snaps his fingers.*]   That easy!   I plunged.   Then, before things broke, I left—I was so confident I couldn't be wrong.   But when I landed in New York—I wired you I had business to wind up, didn't I?   Well, it was the business that wound me up!   [*He smiles grimly, pacing up and down, his hands in his pockets.*]

Ruth.   [*Dully*]   You found—you'd lost everything?

Andrew.   [*Sitting down again*]   Practically.   [*He takes a cigar from his pocket, bites the end off, and lights it.*]   Oh, I don't mean I'm dead broke.   I've saved ten thousand from the wreckage, maybe twenty.   But that's a poor showing for five years' hard work. That's why I'll have to go back. [*Confidently*] I can make it up in a year or so down there—and I don't need but a shoestring to start with.]*A weary expression comes over his face and he sighs heavily.*] I wish I didn't have to. I'm sick of it all.

Ruth. It's too bad—things seem to go wrong so.

Andrew. [*Shaking off his depression—briskly*] They might be much worse. There's enough left to fix the farm O. K. before I go. I won't leave 'til Rob's on his feet again. In the meantime I'll make things fly around here. [*With satisfaction*] I need a rest, and the kind of rest I need is hard work in the open—just like I used to do in the old days. [*Stopping abruptly and lowering his voice cautiously*] Not a word to Rob about my losing money! Remember that, Ruth! You can see why. If he's grown so touchy, he'd never accept a cent if he thought I was hard up; see?

Ruth. Yes, Andy. [*After a pause, during which* ANDREW *puffs at a cigar abstractedly, his mind evidently busy with plans for the future, the bedroom door is opened and* DOCTOR FAWCETT *enters, carrying a bag. He closes the door quietly behind him and comes forward, a grave expression on his face.* ANDREW *springs out of his chair.*]

Andrew. Ah, Doctor! [*He pushes a chair between his own and* RUTH's] Won't you have a chair?

Fawcett. [*Glancing at his watch*] I must catch the nine o'clock back to the city. It's imperative. I have only a moment. [*Sitting down and clearing his throat—in a perfunctory, impersonal voice*] The case of your brother, Mr. Mayo, is—— [*He stops and glances at* Ruth *and says meaningly to* Andrew.] Perhaps it would be better if you and I——

Ruth. [*With dogged resentment*] I know what you mean, Doctor. [*Dully*] Don't be afraid I can't stand it. I'm used to bearing trouble by this time; I can guess what you've found out. [*She hesitates for a moment—then continues in a monotonous voice*.] Rob's going to die.

Andrew. [*Angrily*] Ruth!

Fawcett. [*Raising his hand as if to command silence*] I am afraid my diagnosis of your brother's condition forces me to the same conclusion as Mrs. Mayo's.

Andrew. [*Groaning*] But, Doctor, surely——

Fawcett. [*Calmly*] Your brother hasn't long to live—perhaps a few days, perhaps only a few hours. It's a marvel that he's alive at this moment. My examination revealed that both of his lungs are terribly affected.

Andrew. [*Brokenly*] Good God! [Ruth *keeps her eyes fixed on her lap in a trance-like stare*.]

Fawcett. I am sorry I have to tell you this. If there was anything that could be done——

Andrew. There isn't anything?

Fawcett. [*Shaking his head*] It's too late. Six months ago there might have——

Andrew. [*In anguish*] But if we were to take him to the mountains—or to Arizona—or——

Fawcett. That might have prolonged his life six months ago.

[*Andrew groans.*] But now—— [*He shrugs his shoulders significantly.*]

Andrew. [*Appalled by a sudden thought*] Good heavens, you haven't told him this, have you, Doctor?

Fawcett. No. I lied to him. I said a change of climate—— [*He looks at his watch again nervously.*] I must leave you. [*He gets up.*]

Andrew. [*Getting to his feet—insistently*] But there must still be some chance——

Fawcett. [*As if he were reassuring a child*] There is always that last chance—the miracle. [*He puts on his hat and coat—bowing to* Ruth.] Good-by, Mrs. Mayo.

Ruth. [*Without raising her eyes—dully*] Good-by.

Andrew. [*Mechanically*] I'll walk to the car with you, Doctor. [*They go out of the door.* Ruth *sits motionlessly. The motor is heard starting and the noise gradually recedes into the distance.* Andrew *re-enters and sits down in his chair, holding his head in his hands.*] Ruth! [*She lifts her eyes to his.*] Hadn't we better go in and see him? I'm afraid to! I know he'll read it in my face. [*The bedroom door is noiselessly opened and* Robert *appears in the doorway. His cheeks are flushed with fever, and his eyes appear unusually large and brilliant.* Andrew *continues with a groan.*] It can't be, Ruth. It can't be as hopeless as he said. There's always a fighting chance. We'll take Rob to Arizona. He's *got* to get well. There *must* be a chance!

Robert. [*In a gentle tone*] Why must there, Andy? [RUTH
turns and stares at him with terrified eyes.]

Andrew. [*Whirling around*] Rob! [*Scoldingly*] What are
you doing out of bed? [*He gets up and goes to him.*]
Get right back now and obey the Doc, or you're going to
get a licking from me!

Robert. [*Ignoring these remarks*] Help me over to the chair,
please, Andy.

Andrew. You're going right back to bed, that's where you're
going, and stay there! [*He takes hold of* ROBERT's *arm.*]

Robert. [*Mockingly*] Stay there 'til I die, eh, Andy?
[*Coldly*] Don't behave like a child. I'm sick of lying
down. I'll be more rested sitting up. [*As* ANDREW *hesitates—violently*] I swear I'll get out of bed every time
you put me there. You'll have to sit on my chest, and that
wouldn't help my health any. Come on, Andy. Don't
play the fool. I want to talk to you, and I'm going to.
[*With a grim smile*] A dying man has some rights,
hasn't he?

Andrew. [*With a shudder*] Don't talk that way! I'll only
let you sit down if you'll promise that. Remember. [*He
helps* ROBERT *to the chair between his own and* RUTH's.]
Easy now! There you are! Wait, and I'll get a pillow
for you. [*He goes into the bedroom.* ROBERT *looks at*
RUTH *who shrinks away from him in terror.* ROBERT
smiles bitterly. ANDREW *comes back with the pillow which
he places behind* ROBERT's *back.*] How's that?

Robert. [*With an affectionate smile*] Fine! Thank you!

[*As* Andrew *sits down*] Listen, Andy. You've asked me
not to talk—and I won't after I've made my position clear.
[*Slowly*] In the first place I know I'm dying. [Ruth
*bows her head and covers her face with her hands. She
remains like this all during the scene between the two
brothers.*]

Andrew. Rob! That isn't so!

Robert. [*Wearily*] It *is* so! Don't lie to me. After Ruth
put me to bed before you came, I saw it clearly for the
first time. [*Bitterly*] I'd been making plans for our future—Ruth's and mine—so it came hard at first—the
realization. Then when the doctor examined me, I knew
—although he tried to lie about it. And then to make sure
I listened at the door to what he told you. So don't mock
me with fairy tales about Arizona, or any such rot as that.
Because I'm dying is no reason you should treat me as
an imbecile or a coward. Now that I'm sure what's happening, I can say Kismet to it with all my heart. It was
only the silly uncertainty that hurt. [*There is a pause.
Andrew looks around in impotent anguish, not knowing
what to say. Robert regards him with an affectionate
smile.*]

Andrew. [*Finally blurts out*] It isn't foolish. You *have* got
a chance. If you heard all the Doctor said, that ought to
prove it to you.

Robert. Oh, you mean when he spoke of the miracle?
[*Dryly*] I don't believe in miracles—in my case. Besides,

Kismet—Destiny, fate.

I know more than any doctor on earth *could* know—because I *feel* what's coming. [*Dismissing the subject*] But we've agreed not to talk of it. Tell me about yourself, Andy. That's what I'm interested in. Your letters were too brief and far apart to be illuminating.

Andrew. I meant to write oftener.

Robert. [*With a faint trace of irony*] I judge from them you've accomplished all you set out to do five years ago?

Andrew. That isn't much to boast of.

Robert. [*Surprised*] Have you really, honestly reached that conclusion?

Andrew. Well, it doesn't seem to amount to much now.

Robert. But you're rich, aren't you?

Andrew. [*With a quick glance at* Ruth] Yes, I s'pose so.

Robert. I'm glad. You can do to the farm all I've undone. But what did you do down there? Tell me. You went in the grain business with that friend of yours?

Andrew. Yes. After two years I had a share in it. I sold out last year. [*He is answering* Robert's *questions with great reluctance.*]

Robert. And then?

Andrew. I went in on my own.

Robert. Still in grain?

Andrew. Yes.

Robert. What's the matter? You look as if I were accusing you of something.

Andrew. I'm proud enough of the first four years. It's after that I'm not boasting of. I took to speculating.

Robert. In wheat?

Andrew. Yes.

Robert. And you made money—gambling?

Andrew. Yes.

Robert. [*Thoughtfully*] I've been wondering what the great change was in you. [*After a pause*] You—a farmer—to gamble in a wheat pit with scraps of paper. There's a spiritual significance in that picture, Andy. [*He smiles bitterly.*] I'm a failure, and Ruth's another—but we can both justly lay some of the blame for our stumbling on God. But you're the deepest-dyed failure of the three, Andy. You've spent eight years running away from yourself. Do you see what I mean? You used to be a creator when you loved the farm. You and life were in harmonious partnership. And now—— [*He stops as if seeking vainly for words.*] My brain is muddled. But part of what I mean is that your gambling with the thing you used to love to create proves how far astray—— So you'll be punished. You'll have to suffer to win back—— [*His voice grows weaker and he sighs wearily.*] It's no use. I can't say it. [*He lies back and closes his eyes, breathing pantingly.*]

Andrew. [*Slowly*] I think I know what you're driving at, Rob—and it's true, I guess. [Robert *smiles gratefully and stretches out his hand, which* Andrew *takes in his.*]

Robert. I want you to promise me to do one thing, Andy, after——

Andrew. I'll promise anything, as God is my Judge!

Robert. Remember, Andy, Ruth has suffered double her share. [*His voice faltering with weakness*] Only through contact with suffering, Andy, will you—awaken. Listen. You must marry Ruth—afterwards.

Ruth. [*With a cry*] Rob! [ROBERT *lies back, his eyes closed, gasping heavily for breath.*]

Andrew. [*Making signs to her to humor him—gently*] You're tired out, Rob. You better lie down and rest a while, don't you think? We can talk later on.

Robert. [*With a mocking smile*] Later on! You always were an optimist, Andy! [*He sighs with exhaustion.*] Yes, I'll go and rest a while. [*As* ANDREW *comes to help him*] It must be near sunrise, isn't it?

Andrew. It's after six.

Robert. [*As* ANDREW *helps him into the bedroom*] Shut the door, Andy. I want to be alone. [ANDREW *reappears and shuts the door softly. He comes and sits down on his chair again, supporting his head on his hands. His face is drawn with the intensity of his dry-eyed anguish.*]

Ruth. [*Glancing at him—fearfully*] He's out of his mind now, isn't he?

Andrew. He may be a little delirious. The fever would do that. [*With impotent rage*] What a shame! And there's nothing we can do but sit and—wait! [*He springs from his chair and walks to the stove.*]

Ruth. [*Dully*] He was talking—wild—like he used to— only this time it sounded—unnatural, don't you think?

Andrew. I don't know. The things he said to me had truth

in them—even if he did talk them way up in the air, like he always sees things. Still—— [*He glances down at* Ruth *keenly*.] Why do you suppose he wanted us to promise we'd—— [*Confusedly*] You know what he said.

Ruth. [*Dully*] His mind was wandering, I s'pose.

Andrew. [*With conviction*] No—there was something back of it.

Ruth. He wanted to make sure I'd be all right—after he'd gone, I expect.

Andrew. No, it wasn't that. He knows very well I'd naturally look after you without—anything like that.

Ruth. He might be thinking of—something happened five years back, the time you came home from the trip.

Andrew. What happened? What do you mean?

Ruth. [*Dully*] We had a fight.

Andrew. A fight? What has that to do with me?

Ruth. It was about you—in a way.

Andrew. [*Amazed*] About *me?*

Ruth. Yes, mostly. You see I'd found out I'd made a mistake about Rob soon after we were married—when it was too late.

Andrew. Mistake? [*Slowly*] You mean—you found out you didn't love Rob?

Ruth. Yes.

Andrew. Oh!

Ruth. And then I thought that when Mary came it'd be different, and I'd love him; but it didn't happen that way.

And I couldn't bear with his blundering and book-read-
ing—and I grew to hate him, almost.

Andrew. Ruth!

Ruth. I couldn't help it. No woman could. It had to be
because I loved someone else, I'd found out. [*She sighs
wearily.*] It can't do no harm to tell you now—when it's
all past and gone—and dead. *You* were the one I really
loved—only I didn't come to the knowledge of it 'til too
late.

Andrew. [*Stunned*] Ruth! Do you know what you're
saying?

Ruth. It was true—then. [*With sudden fierceness*] How
could I help it? No woman could.

Andrew. Then—you loved me—that time I came home?

Ruth. [*Doggedly*] I'd known your real reason for leaving
home the first time—everybody knew it—and for three
years I'd been thinking——

Andrew. That I loved you?

Ruth. Yes. Then that day on the hill you laughed about
what a fool you'd been for loving me once—and I knew it
was all over.

Andrew. But I never thought—— [*He stops, shuddering at
his remembrance.*] And did Rob——

Ruth. That was what I'd started to tell. We'd had a fight
just before you came and I got crazy mad—and I told him
all I've told you.

Andrew. [*Gaping at her speechless for a moment*] You told
Rob—you loved me?

Ruth. Yes.

Andrew. [*Shrinking away from her in horror*] You—you—you mad fool, you! How could you do such a thing?

Ruth. I couldn't help it. I'd got to the end of bearing things —without talking.

Andrew. Then Rob must have known every moment I stayed here! And yet he never said or showed—How he must have suffered! Didn't you know how much he loved you?

Ruth. [*Dully*] Yes. I knew he liked me.

Andrew. Liked you! What kind of a woman are you? Couldn't you have kept silent? Did you have to torture him? No wonder he's dying! And you've lived together for five years with this between you?

Ruth. We've lived in the same house.

Andrew. Does he still think——

Ruth. I don't know. We've never spoke a word about it since that day. Maybe, from the way he went on, he s'poses I care for you yet.

Andrew. But you don't. It's outrageous. It's stupid! You don't love me!

Ruth. [*Slowly*] I wouldn't know how to feel love, even if I tried, any more.

Andrew. [*Brutally*] And I don't love you, that's sure! [*He sinks into his chair, his head between his hands.*] It's damnable such a thing should be between Rob and me. Why, I love Rob better'n anybody in the world and always did. There isn't a thing on God's green earth I wouldn't

have done to keep trouble away from him. And I have
to be the very one—it's damnable! How am I going to
face him again? What can I say to him now? [*He
groans with anguished rage. After a pause*] He asked
me to promise—what am I going to do?

Ruth. You can promise—so's it'll ease his mind—and not
mean anything.

Andrew. What? Lie to him now—when he's dying? [*Determinedly*] No! It's *you* who'll have to do the lying,
since it must be done. You've got a chance now to undo
some of all the suffering you've brought on Rob. Go in
to him! Tell him you never loved me—it was all a mistake. Tell him you only said so because you were mad
and didn't know what you were saying! Tell him something, anything, that'll bring him peace!

Ruth. [*Dully*] He wouldn't believe me.

Andrew. [*Furiously*] You've got to make him believe you,
do you hear? You've got to—now—hurry—you never
know when it may be too late. [*As she hesitates—imploringly*] For God's sake, Ruth! Don't you see you owe it
to him? You'll never forgive yourself if you don't.

Ruth. [*Dully*] I'll go. [*She gets wearily to her feet and
walks slowly toward the bedroom.*] But it won't do any
good. [ANDREW's *eyes are fixed on her anxiously. She
opens the door and steps inside the room. She remains
standing there for a minute. Then she calls in a frightened voice.*] Rob! Where are you? [*Then she hurries
back, trembling with fright.*] Andy! Andy! He's gone!

Andrew. [*Misunderstanding her—his face pale with dread*]
    He's not——

Ruth. [*Interrupting him—hysterically*] He's gone! The
    bed's empty. The window's wide open. He must have
    crawled out into the yard!

Andrew. [*Springing to his feet. He rushes into the bedroom
    and returns immediately with an expression of alarmed
    amazement on his face.*] Come! He can't have gone
    far! [*Grabbing his hat, he takes* Ruth's *arm and shoves
    her toward the door.*] Come on! [*Opening the door*]
    Let's hope—— [*The door closes behind them, cutting off
    his words as*

[*The Curtain Falls*]

Scene II

*Same as Act One, Scene One—A section of country high-
way. The sky to the east is already alight with bright color
and a thin, quivering line of flame is spreading slowly along
the horizon rim of the dark hills. The roadside, however, is
still steeped in the grayness of the dawn, shadowy and vague.
The field in the foreground has a wild uncultivated appearance as if it had been allowed to remain fallow the preceding
summer. Parts of the snake fence in the rear have been
broken down. The apple tree is leafless and seems dead.*

Robert *staggers weakly in from the left. He stumbles into
the ditch and lies there for a moment: then crawls with a*

*great effort to the top of the bank where he can see the sun
rise, and collapses weakly.* Ruth *and* Andrew *come hurriedly
along the road from the left.*

Andrew. [*Stopping and looking about him*] There he is!
I knew it! I knew we'd find him here.

Robert. [*Trying to raise himself to a sitting position as they
hasten to his side—with a wan smile*] I thought I'd given
you the slip.

Andrew. [*With kindly bullying*] Well you didn't, you old
scoundrel, and we're going to take you right back where
you belong—in bed. [*He makes a motion to lift* Robert.]

Robert. Don't, Andy. Don't, I tell you!

Andrew. You're in pain?

Robert. [*Simply*] No. I'm dying. [*He falls back weakly.*
Ruth *sinks down besides him with a sob and pillows his
head on her lap.* Andrew *stands looking down at him
helplessly.* Robert *moves his head restlessly on* Ruth's
lap.] I couldn't stand it back there in the room. It
seemed as if all my life—I'd been cooped in a room. So I
thought I'd try to end as I might have—if I'd had the
courage—alone—in a ditch by the open road—watching
the sun rise.

Andrew. Rob! Don't talk. You're wasting your strength.
Rest a while and then we'll carry you——

Robert. Still hoping, Andy? Don't. I know. [*There is a pause
during which he breathes heavily, straining his eyes toward the horizon.*] The sun comes so slowly. [*With an*

ironical smile] The doctor told me to go to the far-off places—and I'd be cured. He was right. That was always the cure for me. It's too late—for this life—but—— [*He has a fit of coughing which racks his body.*]

Andrew. [*With a hoarse sob*] Rob! [*He clenches his fists in an impotent rage against Fate.*] God! God! [Ruth *sobs brokenly and wipes* Robert's *lips with her handkerchief.*]

Robert. [*In a voice which is suddenly ringing with the happiness of hope*] You mustn't feel sorry for me. Don't you see I'm happy at last—free—free!—freed from the farm—free to wander on and on—eternally! [*He raises himself on his elbow, his face radiant, and points to the horizon.*] Look! Isn't it beautiful beyond the hills? I can hear the old voices calling me to come—— [*Exultantly*] And this time I'm going! It isn't the end. It's a free beginning—the start of my voyage! I've won to my trip—the right of release—beyond the horizon! Oh, you ought to be glad—glad—for my sake! [*He collapses weakly.*] Andy! [Andrew *bends down to him.*] Remember Ruth——

Andrew. I'll take care of her, I swear to you, Rob!

Robert. Ruth has suffered—remember, Andy—only through sacrifice—the secret beyond there—— [*He suddenly raises himself with his last remaining strength and points to the horizon where the edge of the sun's disc is rising from the rim of the hills.*] The sun! [*He remains with his eyes fixed on it for a moment. A rattling noise throbs from his throat. He mumbles]* Remember! [*And falls back and is still.* RUTH *gives a cry of horror and springs to her feet, shuddering, her hands over her eyes.* ANDREW *bends on one knee beside the body, placing a hand over* ROBERT'S *heart, then he kisses his brother reverentially on the forehead and stands up.*]

Andrew. [*Facing* RUTH, *the body between them—in a dead voice*] He's dead. [*With a sudden burst of fury*] You never told him!

Ruth. [*Piteously*] He was so happy without my lying to him.

Andrew. [*Pointing to the body—trembling with the violence of his rage*] This is your doing, you coward, you murderess!

Ruth. [*Sobbing*] Don't, Andy! I couldn't help it—and he knew how I'd suffered, too. He told you—to remember.

Andrew. [*Stares at her for a moment, his rage ebbing away, an expression of deep pity gradually coming over his face. Then he glances down at his brother and speaks brokenly in a compassionate voice.*] Forgive me, Ruth—for his sake—and I'll remember—— [RUTH *lets her hands fall from her face and looks at him uncomprehendingly. He lifts his eyes to hers and forces out falteringly.*] I—you—we've both made a mess of things! We must try to help each other—and—in time—we'll come to know what's right—— [*Desperately*] And perhaps we—— [*But* RUTH, *if she is aware of his words, gives no sign. She re-*

mains silent, gazing at him dully with the sad humility
of exhaustion, her mind already sinking back into that
spent calm beyond the further troubling of any hope.]

[*The Curtain Falls*]

AIDS FOR APPRECIATING AND
UNDERSTANDING HAMLET

William Shakespeare

BIOGRAPHICAL NOTES

Shakespeare

If you should ever go to England, of course you would make a pilgrimage out to that pleasant, central county of Warwick, which enshrines the little town of Stratford-on-Avon. So many thousands every year do make that pilgrimage that the thrifty inhabitants have turned the whole place into a veritable Shakespeare museum. All available documents and mementos have been collected in one or another of the spots associated with his life so that as you go from place to place the whole story lies open before you.

The beginning and the end are in Trinity Church, the ancient, familiar building by the river. Here the Parish Register stands open at two important pages. On one, a line of cramped writing, under the date of April 26, 1564, announces in Latin the christening of William, son of John Shakespeare. There is no known record of his birth, but, as children were usually christened when three days old and as, moreover, there is a persistent tradition that he died on his birthday, the date April 23 is commonly accepted. A few pages farther on in the same book, under the date April 25, 1616, appears the burial entry of *Will Shakespeare, Gent.* Between these two records lie the fifty-two years so vital to the history of English literature.

The double house on Henley Street, where the poet was born, is carefully preserved as the most precious of all the museums. The birth chamber is a small, bare, low-ceiled room, the walls of which are closely scribbled with the autographs of the great and the obscure who have done homage there. The living-room has an interesting inglenook from which, through the wide chimney-top, one may catch glimpses of the sky. It is easy to imagine the boy Shakespeare sitting here and thinking "long, long thoughts."

In a small garden behind the house, grow specimens of all the flowers mentioned in the plays. Recalling the many famous flower passages, one realizes the ambitious nature of this project.

The other side of the house is said to have been used by John Shakespeare in his business. Just what that was seems doubtful. He is spoken of as farmer, glover, and wool trader. He appears to have been a merchant of some sort and to have been in prosperous circumstances when his son was born. Various documents on exhibition attest his success and the esteem of his townsmen. He held several offices, among them that of High Bailiff, the equivalent of Mayor. Though there are few records of the poet's mother, Mary Arden, it is known that she came of an old and substantial Warwickshire family and brought her husband considerable landed property.

Not far from Henley Street, the grammar school which Shakespeare attended is still in active service. Between a modern chapel and a picturesque row of old almshouses, through an inconspicuous gateway, one enters an inner courtyard and climbs a staircase to the quaint, oak-timbered classrooms. Here, for perhaps seven years of his life, the boy recited his Latin verbs and acquired what other learning the place had to offer. The bench at which he sat has now been removed to the house on Henley Street; but an inscription, suspiciously near the master's desk, marks the place he occupied. At fourteen he is said to have left school. Perhaps he was needed at home, as documents show that John Shakespeare's affairs were not going well. About this time he was sued for debt, and later he was deprived of his alderman's gown.

The next four years of the young poet's life have left few traces. Of course if you choose to believe the tradition that he was caught stealing deer and was severely reprimanded by the owner, Sir Thomas Lucy, you may make a brief expedition out to Charlecote, the Lucy estate. There you may see the stately house, the park with the deer still placidly feeding, and the tumble-down stile where a fleeing culprit might be caught. But probably deer were not kept in the park in Shakespeare's time, and the whole story rests on such a flimsy foundation that it is better rejected.

You will, however, want to walk across the fields to Shottery, following Shakespeare's footsteps to the thatched roof cottage where lived Anne Hathaway. It is an interesting place, furnished more completely than the Stratford house, with furniture that is of the period if not actually original. Here, perhaps on this very oaken settle by the fire, the young couple carried on their courtship. They were married in 1582 when the youthful bridegroom was only eighteen and his bride twenty-six.

Whether or not this marriage was happy is in dispute. Certain references and the fact that he lived in London without her have been taken as hints that all was not well; but the evidence is inconclusive. There was every reason why he should go to London and should go alone. By the time he was twenty-one he had three children to support, a daughter Susanna and the twins, Judith and Hamnet. There was little gainful occupation for a young man in his small home town, and, if he intended to make his way in the city, it would be far cheaper and easier to provide for his family if they remained in their cottage at home. Ample proof exists that he made frequent trips to Stratford during his London period; and when he had amassed enough money, we know that he returned there to end his days with his wife and children.

Of the most important twenty years in London, Stratford has naturally few direct records; but the results of his stay there are visible in the early editions of his plays preserved in the Henley Street museum. Little indeed is known of the steps by which Shakespeare rose to eminence in the theater. He may have served first in some humble capacity; then gained a place on the stage as actor; later, revised or adapted plays; and finally gained enough experience and skill to produce, in his own right, those marvelous works that have never since been equaled by any writer. He was associated with the theater also in a business way, as, at his death, he owned part interests in both the Blackfriars and the Globe playhouses.

In 1597 he purchased New Place, the finest estate in Stratford, as a final home. Not a vestige of this house remains. Only the site is left and a garden of later date. Even the famous mulberry tree which Shakespeare is said to have planted was cut down by a peevish owner who was troubled by the questions of literary pilgrims. But reports describe it as a beautiful place, and here Shakespeare spent some years before his death. His son, Hamnet, had died years before; and his daughter Susanna had married Dr. John Hall of the town; but Judith and Anne remained; and old friends and associates surrounded him. He died there, April 23, 1616.

We must go back to the village church to see his grave. He is buried within the church, just inside the chancel rail. A plain flat stone guards his resting-place with the warning *Curst be he that moves my bones*. Beside him lie his wife, his daughter Susanna, and her husband, Dr. Hall. On the wall above his grave is a bust in colors, said to be an authentic likeness.

Many contemporary references indicate the place that Shakespeare held in his lifetime. Greene speaks of him with envy, Jonson with affection and admiration. Meres gives a list of his plays. He is mentioned first among the actors who walked in procession at the coronation of James I. He died, prosperous and honored. But probably, for all his wonderful imagination, never in its wildest flights did he dream that, more than three hundred years after his death, his plays would still be acted not only in his own country but in far distant lands, and that every year thousands of visitors from across the sea would walk the streets of his native town, seeking out and treasuring every relic of his sojourn there. Yet so it is. All nations and lands pay tribute to this man, for he spoke a universal language——

"With tears and laughter for all time."

Shakespeare's Plays

The plays, considered chronologically, fall naturally into four main divisions, each marking a distinct advance over the preceding in mastery of technique, in beauty and variety of expression, and in depth of spiritual experience. Professor Dowden has gone so far as to give names to these periods.

He calls the first *In the workshop,* because, as he says, the author was still "learning his trade as a dramatic craftsman." The second he names *In the world,* for it was now that the poet "came to understand the world and the men in it; his plays began to deal in an original and powerful way with the matter of history." *Out of the depths* is the third period when Shakespeare had known sorrow and had begun "to sound with his imagination the depths of the human heart; to inquire into the darkest and saddest parts of human life; to study the great mystery of evil." The last division is *On the heights,* because now the poet had learned the secret of life and had "ascended out of the turmoil to a pure elevation."

His chief plays, with their approximate dates, are as follows:

PERIOD I *(1590-1594)*
Love's Labor Lost
Comedy of Errors
Midsummer Night's Dream
Two Gentlemen of Verona
Richard III
Romeo and Juliet

PERIOD II *(1594-1600)*
King John

Merchant of Venice
Henry IV—Parts I and II
Henry V
Merry Wives of Windsor
Much Ado About Nothing
Taming of the Shrew
As You Like It
Twelfth Night
All's Well That Ends Well

PERIOD III *(1600-1609)*	PERIOD IV *(1609-1612)*
Hamlet	Cymbeline
Julius Cæsar	The Tempest
Measure for Measure	The Winter's Tale
Othello	
Macbeth	*Poetry*
King Lear	Venus and Adonis—*1593*
Antony and Cleopatra	Rape of Lucrece—*1594*
Coriolanus	Sonnets—*1609*

Publication

During Shakespeare's lifetime, there was no authorized edition of his works. Indeed efforts were made to keep them out of print. They were intended to be seen on the stage, not read. If they should appear in book form, rival companies might, because of the lack of copyright laws, produce them and reap the financial reward. Only the actors' prompt books and a few, small, usually pirated copies, called quartos, existed.

But about seven years after the author's death, two of his friends, John Heminge and Henry Condell, made a conscientious effort to present an authorized edition, using the original manuscripts and some of the quartos. This was the famous First Folio of 1623.

Hamlet appeared first in quarto form in 1603. The following year a second quarto was published, differing widely from the first version. Some think, therefore, that the first was a rough draft while the second was polished and perfected. Others believe the first version was taken down in shorthand from the stage presentation and pirated, while the second was authorized. A third quarto in 1605 is a reprint of the second, and later two more appeared. The Folio of 1623 differs somewhat from any previous publication. The standard version of the play is collated from the second quarto and the Folio.

AIDS TO UNDERSTANDING

Sources of the Plot

The story of Hamlet is very old. Traces of it are found in Scandinavian and Irish folk-lore as early as the tenth century. In the thirteenth century, Saxo Grammaticus in his *Historica Danica* tells in Latin the story essentially as we know it today. In this version, Hamlet's father is murdered by his brother who then marries Gerutha, Hamlet's mother. To save his own life and plan revenge, Hamlet feigns madness. The king, suspecting a ruse, sends a beautiful woman to penetrate Hamlet's secret. When that fails, a high official hides behind a curtain to overhear an interview between Hamlet and his mother. Hamlet kills him. Hamlet is then sent to England with two false friends who bear a letter requesting the king to put Hamlet to death. This letter Hamlet contrives to alter, substituting the friends' names for his own. At the English court Hamlet marries the king's daughter and returns to Denmark to take revenge upon his foes and ascend the throne.

In the fourteenth and fifteenth centuries, the story was known in Europe and was finally put into crude verse by Hans Sach. Some think this poem served as a source book for Shakespeare.

Toward the end of the sixteenth century, an English play by the name of *Hamlet* is referred to by Greene and by Henslowe, but no traces of this play have been found. It may have been written by Thomas Kyd or even by Shakespeare himself. Shakespeare's version appeared in the first quarto of 1603. The title page spoke of the play as having been acted "diverse times" both in London and at the two Universities. But the text of this quarto is very corrupt, and it was not until the appearance of the second quarto in 1604 that the play was published essentially in its present form.

If then the story was so well known, why do we speak of it as the work of Shakespeare? The answer to that would be apparent if we could read the earlier crude, brutal, blood-and-horror versions and then compare them with Shakespeare's poetic, beautiful, well-characterized work.

He took the bare bones of the old tragedy, clothed them with flesh, endowed them with wit and wisdom, and out of the Senecan horror evolved this masterpiece. Ophelia in the earlier version, for instance, is merely a character to discover Hamlet's secret, but Shakespeare makes her one of the loveliest, most sensitive, most pathetic of all his creations. Moreover, by adding gay young Laertes and doddering old Polonius to the family group, he has achieved human interest. Hamlet, himself, instead of the clownish boor, running through the streets in his pretended madness, becomes the "mould of fashion and the glass of form," the wise, witty, accomplished philosopher, sorely burdened by a crushing task. Gertrude, Claudius, Horatio, even Rosencrantz and Guildenstern, are brought to life by a touch of the magic wand, and the play stands forth as Shakespeare's very own, a challenge to the mind and a joy to the senses.

Stage Presentations

Hamlet has always been as popular with players as with the public. It would seem that the height of every actor's ambition has been reached when he dons the somber garments of the melancholy Dane and philosophizes on life here and hereafter.

Though his claim has been disputed, Richard Burbage of Shakespeare's own company was probably the first Hamlet. Tradition says that at the same time Shakespeare himself played the ghost.

During the Restoration Period, the great actor Thomas Betterton was the chief representative. It is interesting to note that Mistress

Edwin Booth as Hamlet

Saunderson, who afterwards became Mrs. Betterton, was undoubtedly the first woman to play Ophelia, a part hitherto taken by boy actors.

In the eighteenth century, many famous actors essayed the part of Hamlet, but the greatest interpreter yet seen appeared about the middle of the century in the person of David Garrick. Although he made some seemingly unnecessary and unwarrantable changes in arrangement and presentation, his Hamlet remained supreme until his retirement from the stage. After him came John Philip Kemble, brother of the famous Mrs. Siddons, who played Ophelia to his Hamlet. Later Mrs. Siddons herself tried the part of the Prince, the first woman to do so. Since then other women, notably Sarah Bernhardt, have aspired to pluck out the heart of Hamlet's mystery.

In the nineteenth century, the great tradition was carried on by Edmund Kean, Macready, Edwin Booth, and Henry Irving, among others. The play was popular abroad and was given successfully in France by Mounet-Sully, and in Italy by Salvini and Rossi.

In recent years there have been many fine presentations of Hamlet. The names of Sothern, Barrymore, Hampden, Mansfield, Leslie Howard, John Gielgud and Maurice Evans come at once to mind. Each has added something new to our conception of the many-sided Prince and has revealed new beauty in the familiar phrases. One of the most interesting performances of *Hamlet* was the recent full-length presentation of the play, with Maurice Evans in the title rôle. The curtain rose at six-thirty and the play continued, except for a thirty-minute intermission, for nearly five hours. This was the first time the complete play had ever been given in this country.

"I have been pleasantly terrified by it *(Hamlet)* on several occasions," commented Brooks Atkinson in the *New York Times.* "First, by Forbes-Robertson about twenty-five years ago and most recently by Mr. Evans and his trenchant players. At the close of the opening performance Mr. Evans declared that it had been his intention to present Hamlet as a character in a play and not as 'a case of dyspepsia.' Well, he did. More than any other actor of recent memory, Mr. Evans has lifted Hamlet out of the books into the brisk reality of today. . . . the lucidity and electric pitch of this play come also from the uncut version which rounds out the subordinate characters, improves the dramatic proportions, and clarifies the story. . . . Even in its own day, *Hamlet* was a long play, overcrowded with characters. For Shakespeare loved characters, even more than stories, and he brought them alive by the radiance of his imagination. The uncut version shows how much personal interest he had in their varied ways of living."

After more than three hundred years we find that the play is still beloved by actors and playgoers alike. In the next three hundred years there will probably be little abatement in its popularity, for it has all the elements that appeal to human nature. There is the revenge motif. A sorely wronged hero is pitted against a powerful foe. Danger lurks on every hand. The hero must out-think and outwit his opponents constantly. There is the unhappy love affair; the pretended madness of Hamlet and the real insanity of Ophelia; the ghost; the murders; the play within the play; the fencing bout; and the final catastrophe. It is "good theater" as well as great literature, and, unless tastes change remarkably, there seems no reason why ambitious young actors may not continue to look forward to the rôle of Hamlet as the apex of their careers.

EXPLANATORY NOTES

Act I—Scene 1

Ghost—Elizabethan interest in the supernatural is amply proved, not only by the existence of such books as King James's *Demonology,* but also by Shakespeare's frequent use of ghosts, witches, fairies, and supernatural happenings. Among the examples familiar to readers of Shakespeare are the following: the ghosts and witches in *Macbeth;* supernatural events foretelling the death of Julius Cæsar; fairies in *Midsummer Night's Dream;* sprites and goblins in *The Tempest.*

109. **This portentous figure**—Note that there is no suspicion of a murder to be avenged. Horatio and Bernardo think the appearance of the king's ghost relates to the warlike preparations on foot. Since portents have accompanied great events at other times, it is not strange that the former king returns to his distressed country.

Scene 3

58 ff. **These few precepts**—This famous advice should be carefully studied. Exactly what does Polonius say about general conduct, friendship, quarrels, dress, money matters? What is his final summary? How wise is the advice? How much of it has value today?

Scene 5

31. **Sweep to my revenge**—But Hamlet does not hasten. He delays and almost fails to carry out his revenge. Why?

98. **Table of my memory**—Hamlet here announces the policy which is shown later in his treatment of Ophelia. He is resolved from now on to have but one purpose in life, revenge. He must

give up, therefore, all he has hitherto held dear. How does this explain his later conduct?

170. **How strange or odd**—Here Hamlet foreshadows his pretence of madness. Is it entirely pretence or does he sometimes actually lose command of his wits?

Act II—Scene 2

95. **More matter with less art**—Come to the point without so much rhetoric. The Elizabethans delighted in word-juggling, analytical hair-splitting, long-drawn-out discussions, puns, high-sounding phrases. Shakespeare satirizes this tendency in Polonius' tedious definitions of the obvious, and later in Osric's flowery language.

263. **By my fay, I cannot reason**—At this point Hamlet is depressed and melancholy. With the courtiers he argues lightly but each side is trying to solve the secrets of the other. Hamlet outplays them. He wishes to find out the nature of the crime which he believes was committed but of which he has no evidence. His plans are confused. He does not know what to do; what to think; whether his own mother knows of the murder; or what is the attitude of the court toward him. He distrusts the king and fears for his own safety. He is not considering what he will do with the criminal when he gathers all the evidence. Now he is only searching for that evidence and to obtain it he is acting as one mad. His first move is to tell the two courtiers why they have been sent to him.

331. **Late innovation**—Probably this refers to the license given January 30, 1603, to the Children of the Queen's Revels to play at Blackfriar's Theater. These children became so popular that they may well have driven older companies out of the city and into the provinces. Shakespeare, speaking through Rosencrantz, says this nest of young hawks rant at the top of their

lungs and are loudly applauded. They disturb the regular actors and many men fear what they may say and are almost afraid to attend the play. Hamlet wonders if they are not shortsighted in their actions since they must eventually become regular actors themselves and will then find their profession harmed. It must be remembered that Shakespeare is using an English custom of his own time, not a Danish custom of Hamlet's day.

377. **Hawk from a handsaw**—This is a much-discussed line. Perhaps the best explanation translates *handsaw* as *hernshaw* or *heron*. It may be a figure from falconry. The hawk and the heron looked somewhat alike, and when the birds were flying at certain angles, the falconer could hardly tell whether it was his own bird he saw or a wild heron. When the wind or the flying angle was right, however, he could tell a hawk from a hernshaw.

Act III—Scene 1

143. **I have heard of your paintings**—Shakespeare evidently objected to excessive make-up. At this point in the play Hamlet's treatment of Ophelia is a little severe, and not in harmony with his true nature. It must be remembered that he has decided to act as a madman. He is likely to be watched as a madman would be. If he acted normally towards Ophelia, he might be seen; or she might, by some indiscreet action, disclose his plans. On the other hand, Hamlet does not regard her as a spy, nor does he distrust her. Ophelia does not take his words as a personal slight, but as a general complaint.

Scene 2

1. **Advice to players**—Play producers consider the first fifteen lines of this speech very valuable warning against over-acting. Shakespeare is evidently voicing his own feeling through the

words of Hamlet. He was especially incensed when clowns, in their effort to get a laugh, extemporized lines regardless of the importance of the original lines in the play. He always took pains to see that the clown had something to say to keep the groundlings amused, but he objected to injudicious additions. A certain actor in his company, one Will Kemp, is said to have been a chief offender in this respect. Perhaps Shakespeare had this man in mind when he wrote these lines.

126. **Hobby-horse**—A figure fastened upon the morris dancer in such a way that he seemed to be riding the horse. Ballads refer to the hobby-horse as "forgot," perhaps because it was eventually omitted from the games or because the Puritans were trying to suppress the revels entirely.

128. **Dumb-show**—Often the plot of a play was foreshadowed by being briefly acted in pantomime before the dialogue began. In this case it is hard to see how the king could fail to get the drift of the play long before he did, if the dumb-show had been presented. Some critics think the king and queen may have been whispering together and thus missed the pantomime.

132. **Prologue**—A player announced the theme of the play and sometimes gave explanations, as in *Midsummer Night's Dream,* where the prologue assured the audience that the lion was not real. Occasionally an Epilogue summed up the play, as in *As You Like It.*

Scene 4

68. **You cannot call it love**—How old was Gertrude? Is Hamlet right in supposing she is past the age of loving, or is this simply the arrogant assumption of youth that such emotions are its own sole property?

Act IV—Scene 1

7. **Mad as the sea and wind**—The queen follows Hamlet's instructions, and by reporting him mad, makes this the reason

for the death of Polonius. The resulting situation seems to justify Hamlet's plan of feigning madness to divert suspicion from his course of action in the play.

Scene 5

156. **There's rosemary**—This is one of Shakespeare's famous flower passages. Compare Perdita's speech in *Winter's Tale*. Flowers were popularly associated with certain meanings. Thus rosemary stood for remembrance, pansies for thoughts (French— *penser*), fennel for flattery, columbines for ingratitude, rue for sorrow, the daisy for faithlessness, and violets for faithfulness. It is interesting to note or to conjecture to whom Ophelia gave the different blossoms. Does she need violets?

163. **With a difference**—Perhaps suggesting that she and the queen have different reasons for their sadness.

Scene 6

14. **They have letters for him**—Hamlet probably sent this letter to the king, hoping that the surprise would throw the king off guard, and in his desire to learn all the facts would cause him to send for Hamlet. This would give Hamlet immediate access to the king's person. Notice how the king now becomes the aggressor.

Act V—Scene 1

10. **Here lies the point**—Note the Elizabethan fondness for logical discussion, here reduced to absurdity by the clown's attempt to use words and expressions only partly understood. Puns were also used constantly, even in serious circumstances. Note the play on *fines, lie, quick,* etc.

268. **I lov'd Ophelia**—This is Hamlet's first public avowal.

Can it be substantiated by his conduct? Trace the affair and try to imagine how it might have proceeded under other circumstances.

Scene 2

81. **Enter young Osric**—Shakespeare is here satirizing the foppish, fashionable courtier of his own land and time. Such a one had more money than brains. He adopted the affected speech of the Euphuists, mistaking extravagance for wit and getting "only the tune of the time." As soon as Hamlet, mocking him, uses even more extravagant phrases, Osric is out of his depth and at a loss how to answer. That Shakespeare disliked the type is shown by his treatment of M. Le Beau in *As You Like It* and of Hotspur's "certain lord, perfumed like a milliner" in *Henry IV, Part I*.

302. **They change rapiers**—This has been acted in various ways on the stage. Edwin Booth as Hamlet struck the foil out of Laertes' hand, picked it up, and threw down his own for Laertes to use. In Salvini's version, Laertes dropped his foil which Hamlet immediately covered with his foot, offering his own foil meanwhile to Laertes. A third method is for both to be disarmed, each picking up the sword of the other. In still a fourth arrangement, Laertes, pressing close, seizes Hamlet's rapier by the hilt, whereupon Hamlet, releasing his own, takes his opponent's.

It is a tense moment for spectators as they know of the poisoned point and they see Laertes' reluctance to pick up the weapon which must seal his fate.

STUDY OF CHARACTERS

By citing references to the play, prove that each of the following comments is or is not justified:

Laertes—"The cultured young gentleman of the period. He is accomplished, chivalric, gallant; but the accomplishments are superficial, the chivalry theatrical, the gallantry of a showy kind."
—*Dowden*

Laertes—"An impetuous youth, a man of action, and the greatest possible contrast to Hamlet."

Ophelia—"It is the helplessness of Ophelia, arising merely from her innocence, and pictured without any indication of weakness, which melts us with such profound pity."—*Mrs. Jameson*

Ophelia—"Her insanity is complete, unconscious, and such as, it is said, never ends but with the sufferer's death. There is no method in it: she is like one walking in her sleep; her mind still busy, but its sources of activity all within; literally 'incapable of her own distress.'"—*Hudson*

Rosencrantz and Guildenstern—"What these two persons are and do, it is impossible to represent by one. These soft approaches, this smirking and bowing, this assenting, wheedling, flattering, this whisking agility, this wagging of the tail,—how can they be expressed by a single man?"—*Goethe*

Polonius—"The shrewd, wary, subtle, pompous, garrulous old courtier."—*Mrs. Jameson*

Polonius—"A politician somewhat past his faculties; shrewd, careful, conceited, meddlesome, and pedantic."—*Hudson*

Polonius—"Such a man is positive and confident, because he knows that his mind was once strong, but knows not that it has become weak."—*Dr. Johnson*

Horatio—"A most manly soul, full alike of strength, tenderness, and solidity."—*Hudson*

Horatio—"Perfect calmness of mind and equability of temperament are his chief characteristics. He is nothing in extremes."

—*Purcell and Somers*

Osric—"A representative of the showy and fashionable courtier of Elizabeth's reign, rather than a type of Danish society. He is superficial and shallow, forward and insincere."

—*Purcell and Somers*

The Queen—"Shakespeare exhibits her with such a mixture of good and bad as neither disarms censure nor precludes pity."

—*Hudson*

The King—"No inward virtues adorn the hypocritical 'laughing villain' unless it be that quick perception of his understanding and of his guilty conscience, which makes him attentive to every change and threat, which makes him gather round him with skilful grasp the weakest spies and tools."—*Gervinus*

Hamlet—"To me it is clear that Shakespeare meant to represent the effects of a great action laid upon a soul unfit for the performance of it."—*Goethe*

Hamlet—"As is usually the case with irresolute persons, Hamlet frequently acts from impulse or from blind passion."

—*Purcell and Somers*

Hamlet—"There is no indecision about Hamlet as far as his own sense of duty is concerned; he knows well what he ought to do, and over and over again he makes up his mind to do it."

—*Coleridge*

CAN YOU TELL WHO THEY ARE?

Who is the speaker? About whom is he speaking? Is the comment justified?

1. One may smile, and smile, and be a villain.
2. The courtier's, scholar's, soldier's, eye, tongue, sword;
   Th' expectancy and rose of the fair state,
   The glass of fashion and the mould of form,
   Th' observ'd of all observers.
3. See, what a grace was seated on this brow;
   Hyperion's curls; the front of Jove himself,
   An eye like Mars, to threaten and command;
   A station like the herald Mercury
   New-lighted on a heaven-kissing hill.
4. This water-fly.
5. A king of shreds and patches.
6.   O rose of May!
   Dear maid, kind sister.
7. A man that fortune's buffets and rewards
   Hath ta'en with equal thanks: and blest are those
   Whose blood and judgment are so well commingl'd,
   That they are not a pipe for fortune's finger
   To sound what stop she please.
8. Hath there been such a time—I'd fain know that—
   That I have positively said ' 'Tis so,'
   When it proved otherwise?
9. What's Hecuba to him, or he to Hecuba,
   That he should weep for her?
10. Why man, they did make love to this employment;
    They are not near my conscience; their defeat
    Doth by their own insinuation grow.

ORAL OR WRITTEN COMPOSITION TOPICS

1. Hamlet's Madness.
   (Collect all the evidence that it is pretended. Is there anything to say on the other side?)

2. Ophelia's Madness.
   (Mrs. Jameson says it is "a mind utterly wrecked! past hope, past cure." Do you agree with her?)

3. Account for the long delay of Hamlet although he has promised to sweep to his revenge.

4. Stage Presentations.
   (What have you seen? Which impressed you most? Why?)

5. Hamlet in Modern Dress.
   (Would it be effective? Why?)

6. It has been said that every man sees himself in Hamlet. Is this true?

7. How is Hamlet saved from being merely a Senecan tragedy of blood?

8. Polonius as a Father.

9. Hamlet's Treatment of Ophelia.

10. Hamlet's Scholarship.

11. The Supernatural in the Play. (Compare with *Macbeth*.)

12. Why do great actors like to play the part of Hamlet?

13. Claudius and Gertrude. (Can you find anything good to say about them?)

14. Horatio—the Steadfast Friend.

15. *Hamlet* as a Source Book of Quotations.

437

GAME OF QUOTATIONS

Hamlet is particularly rich in quotations. In reading this play one is often surprised to discover here a source of familiar passages.

A. *See how many of the following quotations you can locate by telling the speaker and the circumstances under which the lines were spoken.*

B. *How many of them have you heard quoted in ordinary conversation? In what connection?*

(If you have difficulty locating the quotations, consult the Key on page 486.)

1. Sweets to the sweet.
2. When sorrows come, they come not single spies,
   But in battalions.
3. A hit, a very palpable hit.
4. To flaming youth let virtue be as wax.
5. 'Twas caviare to the general.
6. Frailty, thy name is woman.
7. Something is rotten in the state of Denmark.
8. For this relief much thanks.
9. A little more than kin, and less than kind.
10. To the noble mind
    Rich gifts wax poor when givers prove unkind.
11. Give me that man
    That is not passion's slave, and I will wear him
    In my heart's core, ay, in my heart of heart.
12. The counterfeit presentment of two brothers.
13. I have shot mine arrow o'er the house
    And hurt my brother.
14. Though this be madness, yet there is method in't.
15. Brevity is the soul of wit.
16. To be, or not to be,—that is the question.
17. There is nothing either good or bad, but thinking makes it so.

18. There's a special providence in the fall of a sparrow.
19.   Rightly to be great
    Is not to stir without great argument,
    But greatly to find quarrel in a straw
    When honour's at the stake.
20. You would pluck out the heart of my mystery.
21. When the wind is southerly, I know a hawk from a handsaw
22. What's Hecuba to him, or he to Hecuba,
    That he should weep for her?
23. Unpack my heart with words.
24. The play's the thing.
25. Angels and ministers of grace defend us!
26. Springes to catch woodcocks.
27. The funeral bak'd-meats
    Did coldly furnish forth the marriage tables.
28. A countenance more in sorrow than in anger.
29. There are more things in heaven and earth, Horatio,
    Than are dreamt of in our philosophy.
30. A king of shreds and patches.
31. 'T is true 't is pity,
    And pity 't is 't is true.
32. The glass of fashion and the mould of form,
    Th' observ'd of all observers.
33. O, my offence is rank, it smells to heaven.
34. But to my mind, though I am native here
    And to the manner born, it is a custom
    More honour'd in the breach than the observance.
35. Thou know'st 'tis common; all that lives must die,
    Passing through nature to eternity.
36. One may smile, and smile, and be a villain.
37. Neither a borrower nor a lender be;
    For loan oft loses both itself and friend,
    And borrowing dulls the edge of husbandry

GENERAL QUESTIONS

Act I—Scene 1

1. What is the setting of the first scene? How does it prepare us for what is to come?
2. How many times has the ghost appeared before this?
3. Why have the soldiers asked Horatio to watch with them?
4. Describe the appearance and actions of the ghost.
5. What was the Elizabethan feeling about such appearances?
6. Why are the soldiers standing guard?
7. Is Horatio any more successful than the soldiers in getting the ghost to speak? Why?

Scene 2

1. What impression does Claudius make by his first speech?
2. Had he consulted the Danish lords before marrying Gertrude?
3. What reasons might they have for approving?
4. What matter of state is before the Council now?
5. What personal matters are taken up?
6. Has Hamlet any special motive in enumerating the usual signs of mourning?
7. What do you think of the comfort offered Hamlet for his father's death?
8. Why does Hamlet contemplate suicide? Does he suspect that his father has been murdered? Would he have objected to his mother's marriage if she had waited longer? What would have been his own status if she had not married?
9. Was there any reason for such haste in the marriage?

10. What is Hamlet's mood in speaking to Horatio about the wedding?
11. How does he receive news of the ghost?

Scene 3

1. Why does Laertes warn Ophelia against Hamlet? How does she take the warning?
2. What seems to be the feeling between brother and sister?
3. Would a modern brother give his sister such advice? How would the sister receive it?
4. Why may not Hamlet choose freely whom he will marry?
5. Would it have been impossible for him to marry Ophelia?
6. Analyze the advice of Polonius to Laertes.
7. What added light does it throw on the character of Polonius?
8. Compare it with the advice a modern father might give his son.
9. Why and how does Polonius supplement Laertes' advice to Ophelia? Is his tone like that of Laertes?
10. What sort of person does Ophelia seem to be? Compare her with a modern girl.

Scene 4

1. What Danish custom does Hamlet object to? Why?
2. Why do Horatio and Marcellus fear to let Hamlet follow the ghost?
3. What is Hamlet's answer to them?

Scene 5

1. What is the ghost's message to Hamlet?
2. What does Hamlet promise?
3. What is the significance of "I'll wipe away all trivial, fond records"?
4. Why does he not tell the others what the ghost has said?

5. Account for Hamlet's apparent joking with the ghost during the swearing scene.
6. What is Hamlet's reason for assuming madness?
7. What is the significance of the concluding lines?

Just what has Act I contributed toward the development of the play?

Is there any dramatic reason for having the ghost seen first by the soldiers, then by Horatio, then by Hamlet?

Why does the audience see only the last two appearances?

Act II—Scene 1

1. What does Polonius want Reynaldo to do? What light does this throw on the character of Polonius?
2. What do you think of the ethics of such spying on his son? Would a modern father be justified in such a scheme?
3. What is the significance of —"By the mass,—"? (Line 50.)
4. Account for Hamlet's visit to Ophelia and his conduct there. (Consider his resolve. How has Ophelia treated him lately? Does Hamlet know the reason?)
5. How much reason has Polonius for thinking Hamlet has gone mad because his love for Ophelia has been spurned?

Scene 2

1. Who are Rosencrantz and Guildenstern? Why have they come to the castle?
2. Why does Shakespeare need two men for this purpose?
3. Where has Voltimand been? What success has he had?
4. What took place between Fortinbras and his uncle?
5. How does Polonius illustrate his own saying that brevity is the soul of wit?
6. What Elizabethan characteristic does he show here?

7. What is Polonius' estimate of himself? How does the king regard him? What is your opinion?

8. What are the successive steps in the madness of Hamlet as Polonius sees them?

9. What is Hamlet's feeling about Polonius?

10. What instances are there of method in his madness?

11. How does Hamlet receive Rosencrantz and Guildenstern? When and why does he begin to suspect them?

12. How does he account for his state of mind?

13. Why are the players traveling instead of staying in the city?

14. Is Shakespeare speaking now of conditions in Denmark at the time of Hamlet or in the England of his own day?

15. What warning does Hamlet give Rosencrantz and Guildenstern?

16. Contrast Hamlet's remarks to Polonius with those to the players. Account for the difference. But why does he forbid the players to mock the old man? (Line 541.)

17. What does Hamlet's reception of the players show about his taste?

18. Who is "my young lady and mistress"?

19. Why did the play Hamlet mentions "please not the million"? Compare with the reasons for the failure of modern plays.

20. Who is the better critic, Hamlet or Polonius? Prove.

21. How important did Hamlet consider players? How important are they now?

22. What light is thrown upon Hamlet by his words, "Look you mock him not"?

23. How does Hamlet compare the player's emotion to his own?

24. Why does he "unpack his heart in words" instead of acting?

25. What use does he hope to make of the players?

Act III—Scene 1

1. What, so far, has been the success of the visit of Rosencrantz and Guildenstern? Do they think Hamlet is mad?
2. What speech of Polonius pricks the conscience of the king?
3. Is this the first time Hamlet has considered suicide? What are his reasons for and against?
4. What are the things he finds that "make calamity of so long life"? What would a modern list include?
5. Account for the abrupt change in Hamlet's manner to Ophelia. Does she deserve it?
6. Why does he advise her to go to a nunnery? What does he really mean?
7. Is he speaking of Ophelia or of all women when he says, "I have heard—"? Can you mention any other play where Shakespeare shows his dislike of make-up?
8. What is the picture Ophelia draws of Hamlet? Is it too favorable?
9. Why is the king not quite convinced that Hamlet is mad because of love?
10. On what pretext is he to be sent to England?

Scene 2

1. Summarize Hamlet's advice to the players. How much would be useful today? What would you substitute?
2. According to Hamlet, what is the purpose of acting? Explain and comment.
3. What is the significance of "And let those that play the clown——?"
4. Give a pen picture of Horatio as Hamlet sees him. Point out parts of the play that seem to justify or fail to justify this picture.

5. Why does Hamlet sit by Ophelia rather than his mother?
6. Explain the use of the dumb show, the prologue.
7. What justification has Hamlet for saying—"As woman's love"?
8. Was the real name of the play *The Mousetrap*?
9. At what point does the king succumb?
10. Why does Guildenstern say, "This courtesy is not of the right breed"?
11. What is the point of Hamlet's comparison of himself to a recorder?
12. Account for the scene in which Hamlet points out the clouds to Polonius.
13. What is Hamlet's intention with regard to his mother?

Scene 3

1. What does Rosencrantz say of a king's responsibility?
2. Why cannot the king pray? Compare with *The Ancient Mariner*.
3. Why will not Hamlet kill the king at prayer?

Scene 4

1. Why does the queen not want to go on with the interview?
2. How and why does Hamlet kill Polonius? Does this seem natural after his long indecision?
3. Why does Hamlet find his mother's second marriage so loathsome?
4. Can you justify her at all?
5. Is Hamlet's feeling that his mother is too old to love characteristic of youth? Is it justified?
6. Had Gertrude known before this that her husband was murdered?
7. How does Hamlet feel about the slaying of Polonius?

8. Has Hamlet as yet formed a definite plan to "delve one yard below their mines"?

What has Act III added to development of the plot?
The turning point should be in this act. Is it? Where? Prove.

Act IV—Scene 1

1. What problem faces the king as a result of Polonius' death?
2. How does he propose to settle it?

Scene 2

1. How has Rosencrantz deserved the epithet "sponge"?
2. What warning does Hamlet give the two courtiers?

Scene 3

1. Why may not the king proceed directly against Hamlet?
2. Is it still true that the multitude "like not in their judgment but their eyes"? Give instances.
3. What pretext does the king give Hamlet for sending him to England? What is his real purpose?

Scene 4

1. How is Hamlet's dull revenge spurred by his talk with the captain?
2. On what other occasions has he lamented his own delay?

Scene 5

1. Why will not Gertrude see Ophelia? What has happened to Ophelia?
2. Why is her insanity pathetic rather than tragic?
3. How does it affect the king and the queen?

4. Is this madness in keeping with Ophelia's temperament and character?
5. Under what circumstances does Laertes arrive?
6. Compare his immediate action with Hamlet's delays. Account for the difference.
7. How does Claudius meet the emergency?
8. What effect has the sight of Ophelia upon Laertes?
9. What effect does this second appearance have upon an audience? Why?
10. Is there any significance in her choice of flowers?
11. Is the scene "good theater"?

Scene 6

1. What has happened to Hamlet meanwhile?
2. It has been suggested that the coming of the pirate was prearranged by Hamlet. Comment on this suggestion.

Scene 7

1. How does the king win Laertes to his side?
2. What plan do they form?
3. Describe Ophelia's death.

What has Act IV added to the development of the plot?

Act V—Scene 1

1. Comment on the introduction of comedy in the midst of tragedy.
2. What is the nature of the humor here?
3. How does the scene grow gradually more serious prior to the entrance of the funeral train?
4. Why are the ceremonies curtailed?

5. Why do Laertes and Hamlet leap into the grave?
6. Is Hamlet speaking the truth when he says he loved Ophelia?

Scene 2

1. How has Hamlet managed to escape the snares laid for him?
2. Why does he not regret the fate to which he has sent his old friends?
3. Has any change taken place in him? Is he likely to delay further?
4. How do Hamlet and Horatio regard Osric?
5. Is Osric typical of Elizabethan England or of Denmark in Hamlet's time?
6. Prove that Shakespeare disliked this foppish, affected type.
7. What premonition had Hamlet about the duel?
8. Why does he nevertheless accept the challenge?
9. Comment on his apology to Laertes. Should he claim madness as an excuse?
10. How did each of following die:—Gertrude, Laertes, the king, Hamlet?
11. Why did not Horatio die also?
12. What glimpse into the future is given at the end?

How does Act V serve as a conclusion to the drama?

AIDS FOR APPRECIATING AND
UNDERSTANDING ELECTRA

Sophocles

BIOGRAPHICAL NOTES

Sophocles

Sophocles, the second of the three great writers of tragedy, seems to have been one of those mortals who are favored by the gods. Talented, handsome, graceful, well-born, and wealthy, he could ask nothing more in personal gifts. Added to this, he was born and spent his boyhood among ideal surroundings in a beautiful little country district just outside of Athens, a district "watered by the silvery Cephissus and rich in flowers and trees among whose leaves the nightingales sang."

But most important of all, his life coincided in time with the golden age of Athenian greatness. Persia had failed in her attacks and Athens, at peace, was building up that brilliant society which has been the wonder of the world. Men like Pericles, Phidias, Thucydides, Herodotus, and Socrates, pre-eminent in politics, art, history, and philosophy, were his contemporaries. Of his two rival dramatists, Æschylus was but twenty-eight years his senior while Euripides was sixteen years his junior.

Sophocles was born in Colonus in 496 B.C. Since his father was a wealthy man, the boy received the finest education the time afforded. At the age of sixteen, he won prizes in music. About the same time, he was also chosen to lead the solemn dance that was held at Salamis to celebrate the final victory over Persia. When he was twenty-eight, he competed against Æschylus and won first prize.

During his long life, he wrote about a hundred plays and won the prize twenty times. Of the majority of these plays only fragments remain. The following seven are complete:

Antigone
Electra

451

Trachinian Maidens
Œdipus the King
Œdipus at Colonus
Ajax
Philoctetes

In the latter part of his life, Sophocles took part in public affairs and remained active until his death in 406 B.C.

It is generally conceded that Sophocles brought Greek drama to the highest point of which it was capable. By his addition of a third actor, he made possible many more dramatic situations and more spirited dialogue, thus bringing to a climax the work begun by Arion and carried on by Thespis and Æschylus. Because of his skill in portraying character, his carefully drawn plots, and his smooth versifying, most critics accord Sophocles first place among the three great writers of tragedy.

In choice of subject and in style, he stands midway between his rivals. Æschylus so loved the sublime that he was sometimes betrayed into unregulated flights of fancy and became vague in idea and grandiose in language. Euripides, on the other hand, in his zeal for the human element often descends to the commonplace and grows prosy. Sophocles, steering a middle course, more nearly reaches the goal of artistic perfection. Though he lacks the grandeur of the one and the wide range of the other, his work is more finished. His plots are coherent; his characters are alive, and most of them are inspired by high motives. Though only seven of the many plays he wrote remain for us to read, they are enough to justify the high esteem in which Sophocles was held by his contemporaries and the reputation which he has successfully maintained throughout the centuries.

AIDS TO UNDERSTANDING

Sources of the Plot

Like other Greek tragedies, *Electra* is based upon a well-known story. Sophocles follows closely the outlines of the familiar tale, but he reverts to Homer's view that the deed of Orestes is laudable. This serves to concentrate the sympathies of the audience against Clytemnestra and Ægisthus. The theatergoers of his time knew what the outcome would be, for the story of Orestes, the avenger, was part of their tradition. So well known was it that both Æschylus and Euripides also wrote tragedies based on the *Electra* theme. Even though the dramatist handled old material, he had ample opportunity to display his skill and ingenuity in presentation, in interpretation of character and motive, and in clever phrasing and the use of picturesque background.

With Sophocles the interest depends mostly on the portrayal of human character. He contrives this by means of ingenious situations that are full of dramatic effect. One of his finest touches is the way in which he shows how Electra has shrunk back from the world about her into an inward life of the imagination. She is so withdrawn that at times she impresses us as being a somewhat unpleasant person, so obsessed by the idea of vengeance that she has lost the softer virtues and has grown shrewish and self-centered. Yet the union of tenderness with strength is expressed in this tragic play in passages of exquisite beauty. Sophocles portrays this strength by showing us a Clytemnestra as she lived and felt in the years that followed the crime. Clytemnestra is strong and wicked. When she meets her daughter in argument, the better cause must win. Thus, Sophocles has purposely refrained from making Clytemnestra a tragic figure, since that would require her punishment, rather than that of Ægisthus, to be the climax of the play.

Sophocles made other changes in the plot. The aged servant tells Clytemnestra of her son's death, and a little later the urn arrives. This is a two-fold device that not only wins belief in Electra's mind, but arouses keen interest in the audience since it has been taken into the secret. And from the belief that her brother is dead springs the resolve that shows Electra at her best; she will avenge her father without help. This resolve of hers, expressed in lyrics of unparalleled beauty, marks the highest point of the play. The deed of vengeance will bring the troubles of the House to a close.

EXPLANATORY NOTES

Greek Customs

The play alludes to many Greek customs. Especially interesting are those ceremonies for the dead. Orestes pours a libation of milk upon his father's grave; he cuts off locks of his hair to place on the grave as a sign of mourning and then strews the tomb with flowers. His own body is reported to have been burned on a pyre and the ashes collected in an urn. Before cremation, the Greeks often placed the body near the threshold of the house for all to see. This is the reason why Ægisthus orders the gates to be opened. He thinks the strangers have brought the body of Orestes and he wants to flaunt his triumph before the city.

Equally interesting is the belief in omens and dreams. Clytemnestra is troubled by her dream and seeks to avert any evil consequences by sacrifice. The good news that follows her prayer seems to her to promise happiness.

In the Aged Servant's report of the supposed death of Orestes, we find a spirited account of a Greek chariot race. Even though the race is entirely imaginary, all the details are mentioned: the number of chariots used, the assignment of places, the conduct of the race, and even the accidents and their results.

Chorus

Note the function and nature of the Chorus. Do not forget that the stasimon at the end of each act calls for choral chanting and solemn dance.

Likeness to Hamlet

Note parallel passages and events. For instance, the queen tries to comfort Hamlet by saying, "Thou know'st 'tis common; all that lives must die." So Clytemnestra cries to Electra, "Hast thou alone to bear a father's loss? Art thou the only mourner?"

As the ghost comes to warn Hamlet, so her dream stirs Clytemnestra.

As Claudius proposes to send Hamlet to England, so Ægisthus plans to have Electra confined in a vault outside the country.

See if you can find more parallels.

STUDY OF CHARACTERS

1. Compare Electra and Chrysothemis,
2. Has Clytemnestra any justification for her terrible deed?
3. Has Ægisthus any redeeming traits?
4. Why do you think Orestes has delayed so long? What finally spurs him to action?
5. Where in the play is Electra most tragic? least likeable? most pleasing?

ORAL OR WRITTEN COMPOSITION TOPICS

1. The Structure of a Greek Play.
2. The Place of the Chorus.
3. A Greek Chariot Race.
4. Greek Burial Customs.

5. Athens in the Time of Sophocles.
6. Electra's Life in the Palace.
7. A Comparison of the Aged Servant's Vivid Account of the Chariot Race with a Modern Broadcast of a Sports Event.

GAME OF QUOTATIONS

Can you locate the following quotations, giving the speaker and the circumstances under which the lines were spoken? (If you have difficulty locating the quotations, consult the Key, page 486.)

1. Time can heal, a gentle god and mild.
2. A little word, men say,
   Hath oftentimes determined good or woe.
3. A man thinks twice with some great work in hand.
4. In the storm 'tis best to reef the sail.
5. When some angry godhead intervenes
   The mightiest man is foiled.
6. Death is the common lot.
7. Success, remember, is the reward of toil.
8. For mortal man there is no gift
   Greater than forethought and sobriety.
9. A life of shame is shame for noble souls.
10. Naught is worse than ill advice.
11. Ah, how hard my lot when I must look to safety for my losses!
12. I praise thy prudence, hate thy cowardice.
13. No, but e'en justice sometimes worketh harm.
14. And thou shouldst side with Justice, wert thou wise.
15. Sound words; 'tis sad they are so misapplied.

GENERAL QUESTIONS

Prologue

1. What is Orestes' plan of action?
2. Why is so much care necessary?
3. What was the message of the oracle?

First Episode

1. Who are the Chorus and what is their advice to Electra?
2. Briefly, what was Electra's cause for grief?
3. Describe Electra's life in the palace.
4. How did it happen she was out of doors?
5. How did Chrysothemis differ from her sister in her attitude toward the king and queen?
6. How did Electra regard her sister's conduct?
7. What part did the Chorus take in the play?
8. What news did Chrysothemis bring to Electra?
9. What did Chrysothemis do with the libations her mother entrusted to her?

Second Episode

1. Comment on Clytemnestra's justification of her acts.
2. Should Clytemnestra have resented Electra's words, having given her permission to speak?
3. Describe the chariot race.
4. With what mingled feelings did Clytemnestra hear of her son's death?
5. Why is the entrance of Chrysothemis dramatic?
6. What is Electra's proposition to Chrysothemis? Why does the latter refuse?

Third Episode

1. Comment upon Electra's lament over the urn of Orestes.
   (It has been criticized on the ground that since the audience knows the urn is empty, the lament loses its effect. What do you think?)
2. Had Orestes realized before how much Electra was suffering?

Fourth Episode

1. How is the audience informed of Clytemnestra's death?
2. What terrible surprise meets Ægisthus?
3. What dramatic reason is there for taking Ægisthus indoors to be murdered?

AIDS FOR
APPRECIATING AND UNDERSTANDING
BEYOND THE HORIZON

Eugene O'Neill

BIOGRAPHICAL NOTES

Eugene Gladstone O'Neill

Eugene O'Neill had only to dip into the experiences of his own life to find material for most of his plays. Of the theater he could truly say,

> "I am native here
> And to the manner born,"

for both his mother and his father were actors. He himself was born on Broadway; and, until he was seven, he "trouped" with his father's company. As able seaman and associate of waterfront characters, he learned the tricks of "dat ol' debil sea." He knew both college and Bohemian life, the inside of a sanitarium, the strange customs of the Far East and South America. Surely no author could wish a richer background for the works of his imagination.

More specifically, Eugene Gladstone O'Neill was born in New York, October 16, 1888. At the age of seven he was sent to preparatory schools, and from 1902 to 1906 he attended Betts Academy. He entered Princeton University but was expelled the first year and never returned.

In 1909 he married Kathleen Jenkins, and a son Eugene was born. After three years the marriage ended in divorce. The next few years were spent prospecting, helping to manage his father's theatrical company, and holding various small jobs in South America and at sea.

In 1912, being threatened with tuberculosis, he entered a sanitarium in Connecticut. His experiences there formed the background for his play *The Straw*. His enforced leisure there had another beneficial result. It gave him ample time for reading and study, so that he began seriously to turn his attention to the writing of one-act plays. To perfect his technique, after leaving the sanitarium, he entered Professor Baker's famous "Workshop" course in playwriting at Harvard. This association greatly helped and encouraged him.

Later he became affiliated with the Provincetown Players, a group of "little theater" enthusiasts, interested especially in new plays that showed promise. He worked with them for about four years (1916-1920), producing first in the crude wharf theater of Provincetown and later in the Greenwich Village section of New York City. In this way almost all his one-act plays and some of the longer ones were placed on the stage.

In 1918 he married Agnes Boulton and two children were born of that marriage. It lasted about ten years. He traveled and worked meanwhile in Shanghai and other parts of the East and lived for a while in France. Here he obtained a divorce and soon after married Carlotta Monteray, an actress.

All this time he had been gaining recognition so that Broadway producers began to seek his plays. Many of them, such as *Desire Under The Elms* and *Strange Interlude,* aroused much criticism because of their subject matter; but their power is undeniable. O'Neill generally ranks as the foremost American playwright, although other writers, notably Maxwell Anderson, are rising to dispute that claim. O'Neill died in 1953, at the age of 65.

It is too early as yet to assign to Eugene O'Neill his exact niche in the Hall of Fame; but that a permanent place of some sort awaits him there, few critics will deny. Indeed the chorus of critics seems almost universally in his favor. John Macy calls him "one of the very few supreme literary men of our time." Stark Young pronounces *Strange Interlude* an "overwhelming milestone in the American Theater." *The Baltimore Sun,* reviewing *Marco Millions,* says, "It gives the final proof that in O'Neill we have a dramatist of the first rank who is also a great poet." *The Sacramento Union* speaks of *Lazarus Laughed* as "a noble and ecstatic tragedy, the most powerful, truest and most beautiful that any dramatist, since Goethe, has given us."

O'Neill received the Pulitzer Prize four times, the medal of the American Academy of Arts and Sciences once, and the Nobel Prize once. His plays have been translated and produced in England, France, Germany, Russia, the Scandinavian countries, and Japan. He has been praised for his sincerity, his versatility, his willingness to try experiments, as well as for his creative imagination and brilliant insight. His later plays, produced after his death, have had long and successful Broadway runs. Eugene O'Neill's place in the list of leading American dramatists seems secure.

His chief plays are:

Bound East for Cardiff	1916	Marco Millions	1927
The Long Voyage Home	1917	Lazarus Laughed	1927
Moon of the Caribbees	1918	Strange Interlude	1928
Beyond the Horizon	1920	Mourning Becomes	
The Emperor Jones	1920	Electra	1931
Anna Christie	1921	Ah, Wilderness	1933
The Straw	1921	Days without End	1934
The Hairy Ape	1922	The Iceman Cometh	1946
All God's Chillun Got		A Moon for the	
Wings	1924	Misbegotten	1952
Desire under the Elms	1925	Long Day's Journey	
The Fountain	1925	into Night	1956
The Great God Brown	1926	A Touch of the Poet	1958

AIDS TO UNDERSTANDING

Sources of the Plot

Who shall say where an author gets the idea for a work which is entirely a matter of creative imagination? Once in a while we may discover some incident or some character which has suggested part of a story; but, in general, authors avoid too close adherence to facts. They prefer rather to blend experiences in their mental crucible and pour out at last a brew of their own mixing, "compounded of many simples, extracted from many objects."

Doubtless O'Neill's seafaring adventures are responsible for the nautical flavor of the play, but, after all, little is told of Andrew's life at sea and in foreign lands. As to what was the genesis of the other characters and the plot, it would be futile and perhaps impertinent to inquire. And why should we care to know? "The play's the thing."

STUDY OF CHARACTERS

1. If Robert had not been so weak physically, could he have succeeded on the farm?
2. Do you blame or pity him more?
3. Is Andrew entirely selfish? weak? Explain.
4. Does Mrs. Atkins contribute at all to the disaster of the play?
5. In what way is Mr. Mayo to blame?
6. Trace Ruth's part in Robert's failure.
7. Who is the sanest and most practical character in the play? Explain.
8. Is Mrs. Mayo a strong character? Explain.
9. What does the child Mary add to the play?
10. Did Andrew succeed or fail?

ORAL OR WRITTEN COMPOSITION TOPICS

1. Farm Life—Is it mere drudgery or a satisfying form of existence?
2. A Trip to the Orient—Compare Andrew's account with what you think you might have seen had you made the voyage.
3. Romance at Home—Andrew said Robert might find at home what he sought. Is that true? What did he want to find?

4. What Constitutes Success in Life?
5. The Mayo Farm as It Might Have Been.
6. Elements of Discord in the Household.
7. A Character Study of Capt. Scott.
8. Dramatic Effects in the Play.

GAME OF QUOTATIONS

How many of the following quotations can you locate?

1. It's just Beauty that's calling me, the beauty of the far off . . . the joy of wandering on and on—in quest of the secret which is hidden just over there, beyond the horizon.
2. You used to be a creator when you loved the farm. You and life were in harmonious partnership.
3. I'm a failure and Ruth's another. . . . But you're the deepest-dyed failure of the three.
4. I'm happy at last. . . . It isn't the end. It's a free beginning —the start of my voyage! I've won to my trip—the right of release—beyond the horizon!

GENERAL QUESTIONS

Act I

1. In the first scene, how and why does the author establish
    a. Robert's weakness and unfitness for farm life;
    b. Andrew's love for the soil;
    c. Robert's dreams;
    d. affection between the brothers?
2. Analyze and explain the temperamental differences between the brothers.
3. What are the prospects for the farm?

4. If Robert had not told Ruth of his love, would
    a. Andrew and Ruth have married and been happy;
    b. the farm have prospered;
    c. Mr. Mayo have died so soon;
    d. Robert have found what he was looking for?
5. Did Robert know that Andrew loved Ruth?
6. Why did Andrew decide to go in Robert's place?
7. What preparations had Capt. Scott made for his nephew's trip?
8. Why was Mayo so angry at Andrew?
9. Was there anything selfish in the conduct of Robert, Ruth, Andrew, Scott, Mayo?
10. What has Act I contributed toward the development of the plot?
    a. What was the situation at the beginning?
    b. What complication changed the situation?
    c. What was the state of things at the end of the act?
    d. How much time is covered by the act?

Act II

1. How much time has elapsed since the last act?
2. What changes have taken place meanwhile—in the family, in the farm, in Ruth and Robert?
3. What significance is there in the appearance of the room?
4. Is Ruth at all to blame for conditions?
5. What has been the cause of Robert's failure?
6. What is each member of the family hoping will result from Andy's return?
7. What does Ruth tell Robert and why?
8. What is the situation at the end of Scene 1?
9. Why does not Robert tell his brother all his troubles?
10. How has Andrew changed?
11. What impression has foreign travel made on him?

12. Why does he not stay at home and help Robert?
13. What does he plan to do before leaving? Why doesn't he do it?
14. What terrible disappointment comes to Ruth?
15. What does Act II contribute to the plot?
    a. How much time is covered?
    b. What momentous happenings have occurred?
    c. Has there been a crisis or turning point in the play? If so, what is it?
    d. What is the exact situation at the end of the act?

Act III

1. How much time has elapsed between Acts II and III?
2. What changes have taken place—in the family, in Ruth, in Robert?
3. What are they waiting for at the rise of the curtain?
4. Is Robert still hopeful? Does this seem natural?
5. How has their "one hope of happiness" gone?
6. Why has Robert not called on Andy for help?
7. How and why has Andy changed?
8. Why is he planning to return to the Argentine?
9. Robert says, "I'm a failure and Ruth's another. But you're the deepest dyed failure of the three, Andy."
    Is this true? Why or why not?
10. May Ruth and Robert "justly lay some of the blame for stumbling on God?"
11. Will Robert's last request to Andy set matters right?
12. Where does Robert want to die? Why?
13. Are you more saddened or relieved by his death? Why?
14. Do you feel more blame or pity for the three chief characters?
15. How has Act III fulfilled the function of a concluding act?

QUESTIONS AND TESTS FOR
COMPARATIVE STUDY

QUESTIONS FOR COMPARATIVE STUDY

Character

1. Show how an element of weakness in Hamlet and Robert Mayo makes the tragedy of each inevitable.
2. Show the difference between Polonius' treatment of his son and daughter, and Mr. Mayo's attitude toward his sons. Which appeals to you more? Why?
3. How are the relations of the older and the younger generations revealed by Hamlet's reproach to his mother and Mr. Mayo's tragic quarrel with Andrew?
4. Hamlet and Robert are both dreamers. In what ways are they alike? Different?
5. Compare a scholar of Hamlet's time with one of Robert's day.
6. Was there the same difference of temperament between Hamlet and Laertes as between Robert and Andrew? Explain.
7. Hamlet gave up his love for his mission; Robert gave up his plans for love. Comment upon the outcome and the wisdom in general.
8. How may Hamlet be said to be a combination of Electra and Orestes?
9. In what ways did Electra's situation resemble Hamlet's?
10. Compare Clytemnestra with Gertrude in regard to guilt, strength of character, punishment.
11. Compare Ægisthus and Claudius.
12. Compare the elements of weakness in Ophelia, Chrysothemis, and Ruth.
13. How did this weakness in each case affect the plot?
14. Name some of the characters in the plays who undergo a

change as a result of circumstances. Explain why. Name some who do not change.

15. List several minor characters in each play. What do they contribute to the plot, to the portrayal of the major characters?

Background and Plot

1. Which plays introduce us to people of high rank and which to those in ordinary circumstances?

2. In which plays are the writers dealing with a background of their own times and in which of a former age? Why is this?

3. Like other Greek tragedies, *Electra* has no comic relief. Find examples of its use in *Hamlet*. Do you find any comic relief in *Beyond the Horizon*?

4. O'Neill's writing is said by some critics to be influenced by Greek tragedy. Can you find traces of this influence in *Beyond the Horizon*? Where in the play does he depart from the Greek tradition?

5. Which of the three plays seems to you most tragic in the outcome? Can you explain why?

Prose and Poetry

1. In the original, *Electra* is written in Greek poetry. Shakespeare also wrote his plays in poetic form. How does poetry add to the intensity and beauty of the plays?

2. Compare the story of *Hamlet* as given in Lamb's *Tales from Shakespeare* with the original play. Which version do you prefer? Why?

3. Modern tragedies are not often written in verse. Can you think of some reasons why modern audiences and modern readers prefer prose?

4. Have you seen or read or heard over the radio any good

modern plays written in poetic form? Discuss these plays in class, telling why you did or did not enjoy them.

Dramatic Devices and Staging

1. Which play has most changes of scene? Why is this?
2. If you were staging a Greek play, a Shakespearean, and a modern, what essential differences would you find?
3. In each of the plays, how does the author acquaint you with the opening situation?
4. Has there been much change in this respect through the centuries? Explain.
5. In which plays are there soliloquies or long speeches? How does the writer of the other play avoid them?

HAMLET

Multiple-Choice Test

Directions: Copy on your paper the number of each question, and after each number write a, b, or c, choosing the one that you think most satisfactorily completes the statement.

1. In Act I soldiers were on guard because
    a. it was the usual custom;
    b. the ghost had been seen;
    c. Fortinbras was preparing an expedition against Denmark.
2. Laertes warned Ophelia against Hamlet because
    a. he thought Hamlet was fickle;

b. he knew a prince could not choose a wife freely;

c. he did not believe Hamlet had paid her any attentions.

3. Rosencrantz and Guildenstern came to Elsinore because
    a. they were sent for;
    b. they wanted to see the coronation;
    c. they liked to travel.

4. Hamlet called Polonius Jephthah because
    a. he was an old man;
    b. he had a daughter;
    c. he was a wise judge.

5. By having the players perform, Hamlet hoped
    a. to entertain his friends;
    b. to prove the king's guilt;
    c. to pay the players for coming so far.

6. Hamlet hesitated to kill his uncle because
    a. he did not want to hurt his mother;
    b. he could find no suitable opportunity;
    c. he was not sure of the king's guilt.

7. Claudius dared not invoke the law against Hamlet because
    a. Hamlet was loved by the people;
    b. Claudius himself might be suspected;
    c. Claudius wanted to protect Hamlet.

8. Hamlet and Horatio make fun of Osric because
    a. he is poor and defenceless;
    b. he is affected in his manners;
    c. they do not like him.

9. The Queen is killed by
    a. Hamlet's sword;
    b. the poisoned cup;
    c. grief.

10. Hamlet says he wishes the next king to be
    a. Horatio;
    b. Laertes;
    c. Fortinbras.

11. The king and queen tried to comfort Hamlet by saying
    a. the death of fathers was common;
    b. Hamlet would profit by his father's death;
    c. he should be happy while he was young.

12. Voltimand reported that Fortinbras
    a. refused to obey his uncle;
    b. promised to give up his expedition against Denmark;
    c. had already dismissed his soldiers.

13. When Hamlet calls one of the players "My young lady," he is talking to
    a. a boy;
    b. the player's wife;
    c. the leading lady.

14. Hamlet was sent to
    a. Germany;
    b. France;
    c. England.

15. Laertes was skilled in
    a. shooting;
    b. fencing;
    c. riding horseback.

16. Ophelia
    a. died of her disease;
    b. was drowned;
    c. took poison.

17. Hamlet went on his voyage
    a. alone;
    b. with Horatio;
    c. with Rosencrantz and Guildenstern.

18. The gravedigger dug up
    a. the skull of Yorick;
    b. a treasure box;
    c. a big stone.

19. Hamlet killed Polonius because
    a. he did not want to be spied upon;
    b. he thought Polonius was the king;
    c. Polonius was a foolish old man.
20. Ophelia in her madness offered her friends
    a. books;
    b. ribbons;
    c. flowers.

True-False Test

Directions: Copy on your paper the number of each question, and beside this number write T, *if you think the statement true;* F, *if you think it false.*

1. At the end of the play no one is left alive to tell Hamlet's story.
2. Hamlet was sorry he had killed Polonius.
3. Hamlet gives good advice to the players.
4. The elder Hamlet killed the elder Fortinbras.
5. Claudius consulted the Danish lords before marrying Gertrude.
6. Polonius had a very high opinion of his own cleverness.
7. Rosencrantz and Guildenstern were true friends to Hamlet.
8. Polonius thought there was method in Hamlet's madness.
9. Hamlet never gave Ophelia anything.
10. The King of Norway helped his nephew prepare an expedition against Denmark.
11. Polonius refused to let Laertes return to France.
12. Horatio told Hamlet he could not see the ghost's face.
13. Polonius' talk may be described by his own words: "Brevity is the soul of wit."
14. Hamlet thought his mother was too old to love again.
15. The king was unmoved by the play *The Mousetrap.*

16. Hamlet trusted his two schoolfellows implicitly.
17. Gertrude saw her husband's ghost.
18. There was no method in Ophelia's madness.
19. Hamlet was sure he would defeat Laertes in the duel.
20. Polonius told Ophelia to encourage Hamlet all she could.

ELECTRA

True-False Test

Directions: Copy on your paper the number of each question, and beside each number write T, *if you think the statement true;* F, *if you think it false.*

1. Chrysothemis was willing to help her sister slay their mother.
2. The Aged Servant was the man to whom Electra had confided Orestes years ago.
3. Pylades is present upon the stage but he has not a speaking part.
4. Orestes was killed by being thrown from his chariot during a race.
5. The Chorus remained on the stage during the entire play.
6. The urn that Electra held contained the ashes of Orestes.

Multiple-Choice Test

Directions: Copy on your paper the number of each question, and beside each number write a, b, *or* c, *choosing the one that best completes the sentence.*

1. The oracle told Orestes to
    a. stay away from Mycenæ;

      b. return and seek vengeance by stealth;

      c. return with an armed force.

2. The Chorus consisted of

      a. Mycenæan women of high birth;

      b. old men;

      c. young girls from Corinth.

3. Clytemnestra blamed Agamemnon for

      a. staying away so long;

      b. helping Menelaus;

      c. sacrificing Iphigenia.

4. Clytemnestra was frightened by a dream in which she

      a. fell from a great height;

      b. saw her dead husband;

      c. was lost in the woods.

5. Chrysothemis warned Electra that Ægisthus was about to have her

      a. killed;

      b. thrown into the sea;

      c. placed in a dungeon.

6. At the end of each episode the Chorus

      a. sang a choral song;

      b. retired from the stage;

      c. went about among the audience.

BEYOND THE HORIZON

Multiple-Choice Test

Directions: Copy on your paper the number of each question, and beside each number write a, b, or c, choosing the one that most accurately completes the sentence.

1. Andrew wanted to leave home because he

      a. was sick of farm work;

      b. couldn't bear to see Ruth and Robert happy together;

      c. wanted to make more money.

2. Mrs. Atkins was

      a. wise and considerate;

      b. selfish and irritable;

      c. jolly and generous.

3. Men disliked to work on Robert's farm because

      a. the work was too hard;

      b. the soil was poor;

      c. Robert was a poor farmer.

4. To Andy the East suggests

      a. smells;

      b. novelty;

      c. beauty and mystery.

5. Of all the foreign places Andy prefers

      a. Singapore;

      b. Sydney;

      c. Buenos Aires.

6. In Buenos Aires, Andrew

      a. made and lost money;

      b. became a multi-millionaire;

      c. married a rich widow.

7. At the beginning of Act III, the appearance of the room indicates

      a. wealth and refinement;

      b. poverty and despair;

      c. happiness.

8. Mary was

      a. a healthy, happy child;

      b. large for her age;

      c. sickly and anemic.

9. Robert annoyed Ruth by
   a. smoking in the house;
   b. being late to his meals;
   c. leaving home frequently.
10. To Robert, "beyond the horizon" meant
    a. a chance to make money;
    b. opportunity to see the world;
    c. fulfillment of his dreams.

True-False Test

Directions: Copy on your paper the number of each question, and beside this number write T, *if you think the statement true;* F, *if you think it false.*

1. Andrew was anxious to travel and see the world.
2. In the First Act the farm was in a prosperous condition.
3. Mrs. Atkins was a valuable member of the household because she gave such good advice.
4. Mr. Mayo was a mild, easy-going man.
5. Andrew found the tropics mystic and alluring.
6. In the course of the play Andrew changed greatly.
7. Andrew would have helped Robert if he had realized his hardships.
8. Andrew's love for Ruth never changed.
9. Each act covers a very short time but years elapse between the acts.
10. Robert looks upon death as a release.

EXAMINATION QUESTIONS

College Entrance Board *

1. Show that the violent deaths in *Hamlet* or in *Macbeth* do not constitute the tragedy of the play.

2. One importance of the novel and the drama consists in the opportunity they afford to meet and appraise significant varieties of character and human experience.

Select from your reading (giving title and author) two novels and two plays. From each of these four works, select and describe at some length an important figure who represents a significant type of human character.

3. "Besides the main characters in a novel or play, there are relatively unimportant persons who contribute to its total effect by serving as instruments in the plot, providing humor, giving local color, or commenting on the action and theme of the story."

Directions: From each of three novels and three plays that you have read, name one minor character such as this quotation describes, and, by using specific illustrations, show in a few sentences what each character contributes to the work in which he appears. This question calls for six brief answers. Follow the model given below.

Model: In Shakespeare's *Macbeth,* the drunken porter is a minor character who provides humor by his delay in answering the knock, and by his foolish suggestions about the identity of

* Reprinted by Special Permission of the College Entrance Examination Board.

the person waiting for admittance. Such actions and words in-tensify, by contrast, the horror of the murder which, as the audi-ence knows, has just been committed.

4. "A plot necessarily implies opposition of some kind be-tween forces. In every novel or play leading characters are op-posed to something. The struggle may be an external one—for the possession of certain papers, for the love of the heroine, for position in society—or it may be an inward one against some overpowering emotion, temptation, or habit—ambition, jealousy, inaction, pride. The struggle may even be against the forces of Nature, cold, or heat, or mountains, or sea. In the best novels or plays, however, the struggle is both inward and outward."

Choose from your reading one novel and one play and explain, with reference to the passage above, the nature of the struggle in each.

5. "It has been said that perhaps the best test of intelligent reading is the capacity for making a good summary."

Directions: Write summaries, of from 75 to 100 words each, of two novels and two plays studied in your classes in English. The model below is intended to suggest the kind of condensation expected in your four answers to this question. After each answer, indicate, as is done in the model, the number of words you have used.

Model: George Eliot's *Silas Marner* is the story of a man's re-generation through love. Silas, a weaver, becomes a lonely miser because of false accusations. Theft of his loved gold in-creases his bitterness toward society. Into his cottage wanders Eppie, unacknowledged child of young Squire Cass. While car-ing for her through her childhood, Silas learns again to love mankind. The recovery of his money affects him less than the revelation of Eppie's parentage and the request of her repentant father that she come to live in the mansion. Eppie chooses to stay with her benefactor, Silas. (95 words.)

6. "The ending of a story should be logical and consistent, and not merely happy or unhappy to satisfy the passing mood of the reader."—Boas and Smith, *Enjoyment of Literature*.

By permission of Harcourt, Brace & Co.

"As to faking a 'sunny' ending, I would see all American magazines and the American editors damned in heaps before lifting my pen for that task."—Joseph Conrad.

Reprinted by permission from Doubleday, Doran & Co., Inc.

"I read for pleasure, mark you. In general I like wedding bells at the end of novels. 'They married and lived happily ever after.'—Why not?"—A. Edward Newton.

By permission of Little, Brown & Co.

Directions: Test the logic and consistency of the endings of two stories (novels, plays, or long narrative poems) by explaining, in about 350 words, the relationship between the main body of each story and its ending.

Your answer to this question will be graded on your ideas, your plan and organization, and your accuracy in writing.

NEW YORK STATE REGENTS EXAMINATIONS

1. In books, as in life, an incident that seems unimportant at the time of happening may lead to momentous results. From the novels and full-length plays you have read, choose any two selections. In each case show by definite references how a seemingly unimportant event led to either a happy or a tragic result. Give titles and authors.

English, Four Years, 1959.

2. In reading, as in life, we may meet some people who are very wise and other people who are very unwise. From your reading of novels and full-length plays, choose a total of two books. For one book, show by definite references why you consider a person in the book to be very wise; for the other book, show by definite references why you consider a person to be very unwise. Give titles and authors.

English, Four Years, 1958.

3. Often a scene in a novel or play is so dramatic that it might be effective if presented on radio or television. The scene may involve an exciting episode, a conflict between two persons, a surprise, or a happy or tragic incident. Choose two such scenes, one from a novel and one from a full-length play, and in each case show by specific references that the scene chosen would be effective on radio or television. Give titles and authors.

English, Four Years, 1957.

4. The possession of moral or spiritual values helps people to face the problems of living. The lack of such values often leads to unhappiness or tragedy. From the novels, full-length plays and full-length biographies you have read, choose two books, and in each case show by definite references how a person in the book was helped or hindered by the possession or lack of such values. Give titles and authors.

English, Four Years, 1956.

5. In literature, the minor characters sometimes interest readers as much as the leading characters. From two or more novels or full-length plays (using at least one book of each type), select four minor characters and show by definite references why each is interesting. Give titles and authors.

English, Four Years, 1954.

6. Some characters in novels and plays are definitely men or women of action; others are more inclined to be thoughtful or imaginative. Show by definite references that an important character in a novel or play belongs to the first group mentioned; in the same way justify placing a character from a different novel or play in the second group. Give titles and authors.

English, Four Years, 1954.

7. A novel or play cannot be regarded as successful unless at its conclusion the main character meets a fate that seems to be the natural result of what he has done or has shown himself to be. Referring to the main character of one novel and the main character of one play, show by definite reference to each book that the above statement is true. Mention authors and titles.

English, Four Years, 1950.

PROJECTS

1. Make models of a Greek, a Shakespearean, and a modern theater.
2. Arrange a scene from one of the plays to be presented before the class.
3. Commit to memory one of the long speeches to recite before the class.
4. Draw a picture, dress a doll, or give a word description to represent the costume of Electra, Ophelia, and Ruth.
5. Make a scrapbook of clippings mentioning any one of the authors, plays, or characters in the play.
6. Arrange a program in which members of the class represent characters in one of the plays. Let the rest of the class guess who is represented.
7. Arrange a program in which Ruth and Ophelia discuss the value and permanence of love.
8. Let Mrs. Atkins and Polonius discuss the value of good advice.
9. Consider how you would put any one of the plays on the screen. Explain to the class.
10. Give a talk to the class on any stage presentation you have seen.

KEY TO QUOTATIONS

Hamlet

	Act	Scene	Line		Act	Scene	Line
1.	V	1	242	20.	III	2	355
2.	IV	5	60	21.	II	2	377
3.	V	2	281	22.	II	2	554
4.	III	4	84	23.	II	2	582
5.	II	2	433	24.	II	2	601
6.	I	2	146	25.	I	4	39
7.	I	4	90	26.	I	3	115
8.	I	1	8	27.	I	2	181
9.	I	2	65	28.	I	2	231
10.	III	1	100	29.	I	5	166
11.	III	2	72	30.	III	4	100
12.	III	4	54	31.	II	2	97
13.	V	2	243	32.	III	1	155
14.	II	2	205	33.	III	3	36
15.	II	2	90	34.	I	4	14
16.	III	1	56	35.	I	2	72
17.	II	2	247	36.	I	5	108
18.	V	2	219	37.	I	3	75
19.	IV	4	53				

Electra

1. P. 231	5. P. 252	9. P. 263	13. P. 265
2. P. 239	6. P. 258	10. P. 265	14. P. 244
3. P. 235	7. P. 261	11. P. 254	15. P. 265
4. P. 236	8. P. 264	12. P 264	

Beyond the Horizon

1. P. 295	2. P. 403	3. P. 403	4. P. 411